P9-DNP-366

# UP YOUR SCORE
# ACT
## THE UNDERGROUND GUIDE

**Chris Arp and Veritas Tutors and Test Prep**

with Ava Chen, Jon Fish, and Zack Swafford

VERITAS NYC
VERITASTUTORS.COM

Illustrations by Julian Callos

WORKMAN PUBLISHING, NEW YORK

Library of Congress Cataloging-in-Publication Data is available.

ISBN 978-0-7611-7439-4

Design by Orlando Adiao
Cover art by John Ritter

ACT is a registered tradmark of ACT, Inc., which does not sponsor or
endorse this product.

Workman books are available at special discounts when purchased in bulk
for premiums and sales promotions as well as for fund-raising or educational
use. Special editions or book excerpts can also be created to specification.
For details, contact the Special Sales Director at the address below, or send
an email to specialmarkets@workman.com.

Workman Publishing Co., Inc.
225 Varick Street
New York, NY 10014-4381
workman.com

WORKMAN is a registered trademark of Workman Publishing Co., Inc.

Printed in the United States of America
First printing July 2013

10 9 8 7 6 5 4 3

# Acknowledgments

This book would never have happened without the initiative and continued support of Matt Bardin, who built Veritas Tutors and Test Prep with true vision, and Margot Herrera at Workman Publishing, for whom the title of senior editor does not begin to suffice. Everyone at Workman has been fantastic, but special thanks are due to Orlando Adiao for his design brilliance, Jessica Rozler and Marta Jaremko for their incredible attention to detail, and Heather Schwedel for, among many other things, her encyclopedic knowledge of popular culture. Ava, Zack, and Jon, you are battle-tested troopers, terrific editors and writers, great mathematicians, and true comedians.

The book also owes a great deal to the experience and wisdom of everyone at Veritas, but mason jars of gratitude are especially due to Teddy Martin and Sam Levin for their overflowing math brains, and to Will Chancellor for his overflowing everything brain. Many shukrans to Steve Reiss for his math magic, and to Gail Ross for her legal magic. Buckets of appreciation to Larry, Manek, Paul, Michael, and everyone who helped create the *Up Your Score* series. Forty-ounce Big Gulps of envy and respect to Julian Callos for his superb illustrations. A German stein of appreciation to my sister, Rachel Ramstad, both for her design advice and her unflagging emotional support. And, as always, rooftop water towers of love to Helene Miller, Bill Arp, Lila Gault, and all my lovely and handsome friends.

—CA

Thanks to Yi-Yi Tsai for being the foundation and support behind all my endeavors. And to Bill McKenzie for introducing me to *Up Your Score: ACT* and teaching me (nearly) everything I know.

—AC

Many thanks to Tim and Angela Fish for being the most supportive parents a kid could ask for, and to Jake and David Fish for being pretty good, as far as older brothers go. Also to Jed Hilbert of Saint Xavier High School for his advice and encouragement as my standardized test guru.

—JF

Thanks to Matt Swafford, Lisa Fitzpatrick, and Xander Swafford for doing the things families do, only better. To Alan Hermanns for irrefutably making my sense of humor what it is today. And to Annabeth, Linus, and Greg, along with Misters E and D. P. et al., for teaching me what I know and therefore was able to apply to the ACT.

—ZS

# Contents

# A Brief History of This Book

## Let's Begin at the Beginning

Two hundred million years ago, the planet Earth was awesome. Gigantic monsters ruled the land. Stegosauruses bellowed primal war cries as they trampled squadrons of utahraptors. Pterodactyls wheeled through the sky, iguanodons nibbled on Jurassic mangoes, and volcanoes exploded nonstop.

Then an asteroid smushed everything, and Earth became as dull as all the other incredibly boring planets in the Milky Way.

But soon, things got better! *Homo habilis* evolved into humans, who created "civilization." There were many different civilizations, and all of them were uniquely interesting—but the best was certainly the Mongolian Empire, because Mongolians put butter in their tea.*

Civilization started off simple. You put some seeds in the ground, slaughtered a few animals, murdered a few enemies, went to sleep, then woke up and did it again. It was a straightforward cycle of farming, slaughter, murder, and sleep.

But, as time went on, things got more complicated. Now you had to do things like write *Beowulf,* invent the cotton gin, and file quarterly tax returns. Different people took different jobs and had to learn about such highfalutin ideas as "medicine" and "the economy." So instead of simply grabbing a rake and a sword at age five, kids now had to go to school. As civilization increased in complexity, kids had to stay in school for longer and longer. Eventually, civilization created college.

But were kids supposed to just *stroll in* to whatever college they wanted? Not in the United States! In 1926, the College Board administered the first Scholastic Aptitude Test, or SAT, which was created to help schools decide which students to admit. The test was designed to judge a student's ability to *reason* and posed questions that required a certain amount of puzzling to understand. But in 1959, a man in Iowa named Everett Franklin Lindquist decided that the SAT was not an accurate gauge of college readiness, so he created the American College Test, or

*They would later be surpassed by the people of the United States, who put butter in everything.

ACT. "Reasoning? I don't care about *reasoning!*" Lindquist said. "I want to know if these stinkin' kids know their stinkin' *facts and stuff!*"* His new test was designed to determine a student's knowledge of the basic high school curriculum.

Regardless of whether kids decided to take the ACT (which was, at first, favored by the cowboys and cowgirls of the Midwestern states) or the SAT (which was favored by the latte-sipping preppies of the coastal states), they had to study. There were a number of popular methods for preparing for the test:

- Reading every book ever written and doing every math problem ever created—at least twice
- Paying a professor of applied aeronautics $5 to take the test for you
- Weeping
- Picking "C" for every answer choice, arguing that "C" could also stand for "Correct"
- Digging a hole in the ground and sitting in it

*He almost definitely did not say this.

But by far the most popular study method was buying an enormous test-prep book and working through it. These books were not only heavy, but they also had the magic power of making you fall asleep after reading three words. As students moved through these books, they pined for the good old days of the volcanoes and the iguanodons and the utahraptors, before stupid college had ever been invented by stupid civilization.

## But Then Something Great Happened . . .

One fateful day in the late 1980s, three high schoolers from Ithaca, New York, named Larry, Manek, and Paul were sitting around the cafeteria studying for the SAT. They were using a phone book–sized study guide and decided that it sucked.

"It's decided: This book sucks," Paul said. "It's incredibly boring, the instructions are confusing, and the sample questions are filled with errors."

"For sure," agreed Manek. "It is as dull as the SAT itself."

"We should write our own test-prep book, but make it useful and funny and clear," said Larry.

"And it should be filled with sex and violence," Paul added. "I generally prefer books with sex and violence."

So they wrote *Up Your Score: The Underground Guide to the SAT,* which turned out to be the best study guide ever written, even though they couldn't put in as much sex or violence as Paul wanted. While they couldn't know it at the time, that book would finally set Earth back on course to being the coolest planet in the Milky Way.

The *UYS* troop did a lot of smart things with their book. They made it interesting and funny. They filled the margins with cartoons. And they were wise enough to keep the book as brief as possible, while still covering all of the information and strategies necessary to ace the SAT. Plus, it was current. Every other year, one or two high schoolers who had earned a perfect score on the SAT were brought in as guest editors, so that they could share their knowledge and experience with readers and keep the book up-to-date.

## Years Later

**B**ut Larry, Manek, and Paul did one not-so-smart thing. They ignored the ACT. In 2013, they realized their mistake and decided that students needed an *Up Your Score* for the ACT. But they had a problem: None of the original *UYS* troops had taken the ACT, plus they were so old that most of their jokes were about dial-up modems, Myspace, and the original *90210*. They had to find an author who had abundant ACT experience and was still in the flower of youth. Luckily, they discovered Chris Arp, a teacher and writer, who, along with his colleagues at Veritas Tutors and Test Prep in New York City, had ushered many students to ACT glory.

### MEET YOUR GUIDES

Chris knew he needed a crack team to help him write the book. So he went on a whirlwind tour of our great nation, searching for perfect-scoring high schoolers who had wisdom and strategies to share. Starting in New York City, he rented a dirigible from Brooklyn Bob's Discount Dirigibles, and floated slowly westward.

His first stop was Portland, Oregon, where he set his ship down among the small-batch coffee shops and fixed-gear

### Veritas What?

Veritas is a global tutoring and test-prep company based in New York City that helps students radically improve their scores. How? We use test prep to make you a better thinker and reader. Instead of just tricks and shortcuts, test prep at Veritas is like cross-training for your brain. (Check out our website for free tools to help you up your score and your learning: Veritastutors.com.)

*Chris*

HELLO.

*Zack*

WELCOME TO THE BOOK.

*Ava*

bicycle stores of that fair northwestern city. He pulled out his bullhorn and screamed, "Hey! Are there any high school juniors here who've scored 36 on the ACT and also have wisdom and strategies to share?" All of Portland looked at Chris like he was crazy. Saddened, he went for a stroll-and-cry down a deserted alleyway. There, he was held up at gunpoint by a thief! Chris thought the end was near, when all of a sudden Zack Swafford jumped from the shadows and took the thief out with a swift kick to the groin.

"Holy smoke!" Chris said. "Was that a *kenpo* groin kick, from the famed Hawaiian mixed martial art *kajukenbo?*"

"Duh," said Zack Swafford.

"Have you, by any chance, taken the ACT?"

"I have," said Zack.

"And did you score a perfect score?"

"You could say that," said Zack. "If you were the kind of person who said the literal truth."

"And is there any chance," Chris asked, trying to hide his excitement, "that you have tons of wisdom and strategies to share?"

"Buddy," Zack said, "I have so much wisdom and so many strategies that I don't know where to put them."

So Chris added Zack to his team, and the two traded in the dirigible for a tandem fixed-gear bicycle, which they rode all the way to Kentucky. It took them two days, because they stopped off in Utah to see *The Expendables 2*, which had just come out. They were underwhelmed.

In Kentucky, Chris looked high and low for successful ACT-crushers. He met plenty of smart kids, but nobody quite fit the bill. He searched through schools, libraries, museums. Then he tried grain silos, truck stops, and highway underpasses to no avail. Finally, as a last-ditch effort he found himself trekking through the sewers, where an alligator bit off his foot. "All things considered, this has been a crazy trip," Chris thought. Then he thought: "AAAAAAAAAAHHH OH MY GOD, MY BEAUTIFUL FOOT!!"

He hopped to Norton Hospital. There, a doctor told him about a promising young prosthetics designer named Ava Chen, who was a junior in high school. After she built Chris an amazing new foot (it could play MP3s and was painted a tasteful shade of lilac), he asked her a question:

"Ava, you are a ludicrously impressive young person. Have you taken the ACT and scored a perfect score on each and every section?"

"Indeed I have," she said.

"And strategies and wisdom? You got those things?"

"Oh," she said. "I've got those things."

The group, now grown to three, was about to leave Kentucky, when a young man ran up to the group and tugged on Chris's sleeve.

"Quitcher tuggin'!" Chris said. "Can't you see that we're a team of extremely qualified test takers on a mission to bring our wisdom to the world?"

"I'm Jon Fish," said Jon Fish. "And I also got a perfect ACT score. Plus, I'm a Governor's Scholar and a National Merit Finalist."

"*Snort,*" said Chris's nose. "Sure, those are impressive achievements, but do you have any special skills? Zack is a purple belt in kajukenbo, and Ava designs prosthetics. What can you do?"

A sneaky smile sneaked across Jon's face. "Watch this."

He popped his shoulder out of place. Then he popped it back.

Chris dropped his milk shake. (He'd been drinking a milk shake.) Ava and Zack gasped.

"Get. On. Our. Team. Now," Chris said. "And buy me another milk shake."

So the *Up Your Score: ACT* team was completed. They took a submarine to the underwater *Up Your Score* base, and sat down to write the Sacred Tome of Test-Taking Truths that you now hold in your hands.*

WHAT'S UP?

*Jon*

*If this is the 2024 edition, not only will this be an e-tome, but that "hands" reference is probably out-of-date, as you have doubtless replaced your hands with sleek, multiplatform, data-processing 5G iHands.

# CHAPTER 1

# Everything You Always Wanted to Know About the ACT

## (But Were Afraid to Ask)

*For one thing, it's three hours and 25 minutes of test-taking deliciousness.*

## Before We Dive In, Any Questions?

**Yeah. First off, do I really have to read this book?**

Excellent question. The answer, of course, is no. You can skip reading this book and go take the test without preparation. You will, however, get a lower score and likely be rejected by the college of your choice, attending instead the prestigious Uncle Bert's Institute of Shrugging, where you will have the opportunity to major in Nothing and minor in Angry Birds Studies. *Or,* you can congratulate yourself on picking a book that will carry you to ACT greatness without reducing you to sobs of boredom or dry heaves of despair. After reading this book, you will get a higher score and be accepted to Super Harvard (it's located within Harvard University, but it's *much* harder to get into), before moving on to a life of unlimited excitement. The choice is yours.

**What are standardized tests and why do colleges love them so much?**

The whole point of standardized tests is to provide colleges with an "objective" assessment of your academic ability. Think about it: Your grades are only as impressive as the school that gives the grades, and your recommendations are only as worthwhile as the teachers giving those recommendations. A standardized test score is important because it is *standardized,* meaning that everyone takes the same test.

We know that makes the standardized tests sound *super important* and, thus, *super terrifying.* But this also means that standardized tests are a great opportunity to improve your college application. The standardized test is just *one* test (unlike your grades, which reflect all of your classes), and you can improve your score by studying and preparing. In other words, the standardized test pays back *huge returns* on your investment of time and energy.

**What exactly is on the ACT?**

The ACT is three hours and 25 minutes of test-taking deliciousness. It begins with an enticing appetizer of an

English Test, which covers grammar and style. The English Test asks 75 questions in 45 minutes and is kissed with a delicate foie-gras foam. Then, to cleanse the palate, we get the Math Test, which ranges from pre-algebra to basic trigonometry. This asks 60 questions in 60 minutes and comes with a refreshing arugula salad. We're then served a rich and creamy Reading Test, which includes one passage each from Fiction, Humanities, Social Science, and Natural Science and is drizzled with a bacon-and-prune reduction. It asks 40 questions in 35 minutes. And I hope you saved some room, because we still have the Science Reasoning Test, which can include passages and graphs about Biology, Chemistry, Physics, and Earth Science experiments. This section asks 40 questions in 35 minutes and is crammed full of tender duck meat. In 2005, the ACT added a dessert: an optional Writing Test, in which students are given 30 minutes to write an essay in response to a prompt. This always comes at the end of the test, and it is always made of chocolate.

The "optional" Writing Test is a little confusing. We will go into greater detail in the chapter about the Writing section, but we'll give you a little teaser: Unless you're applying to an engineering program,* the Writing section is not really optional. *You must eat dessert!*

Each section of the test includes questions from multiple "subsections." For example, the English Test has 40 usage/mechanics questions and 35 rhetorical skills questions, with the questions all mixed together. Sometimes you won't be able to tell whether you are answering a usage question or a rhetorical skills question. Does it matter which is which? Of course not! You just have to get it right! We will discuss the different subsections in much greater detail when we get into the relevant chapters for each section. For now, here is a handy chart of the subsections within each section, which you can print out and show to your friends to become the most popular kid in school:

*Many engineering programs, including MIT's, require the Writing section. So you're still not off the hook.

—Ava

## ACT QUESTIONS

| | | |
|---|---|---|
| **ENGLISH** | Usage/Mechanics | 40 questions |
| | Rhetorical Skills | 35 questions |
| **MATHEMATICS** | Pre-Algebra/Elementary Algebra | 24 questions |
| | Intermediate Algebra/ Coordinate Geometry | 18 questions |
| | Plane Geometry/Trigonometry | 18 questions |
| **READING** | Prose Fiction | 10 questions |
| | Social Science | 10 questions |
| | Humanities | 10 questions |
| | Natural Science | 10 questions |
| **SCIENCE** | Data Representation | 15 questions |
| | Research Summaries | 18 questions |
| | Conflicting Viewpoints | 7 questions |

## SAT or ACT?

**So what's the big difference between the SAT and the ACT?**
As we mentioned, the ACT was created as a correction to the older SAT. While the SAT is intended as a reasoning test, one that determines a student's ability to work through confusing or tricky questions, the ACT is designed to test whether a student knows the content of a standard high school curriculum. In other words, while the SAT tries to test a student's ability to wrestle with a problem, the ACT is designed to test what a student *knows*.

At least, that is the difference in theory. In truth, both the ACT and the SAT require reasoning *and* knowledge. But they are still very different tests. So . . . *how* are they different?

There are quite a few differences between the tests, but the one that needs to be mentioned front and center is that the ACT is *noticeably faster* than the SAT. If you average out the number of questions over the total time of the test, the SAT gives you 62 seconds per problem. The ACT gives you 49. "Big whoop,"

## Quick and Easy Ways to Improve Your College Application

I. Create an app that generates healthy quinoa-and-kale salads using wind energy, and distributes the salads via Facebook to the hungry.
2. Never stop succeeding. Not for one second.
3. Staple a $10 bill to your list of extracurricular activities.
4. Promise to donate a new state-of-the-art science or performing arts center designed by a Pritzker Prize–winning architect. Ask your mom to pay for this. Don't forget to say please.

you might say, "that's only 13 seconds difference." Think about it this way: The SAT is giving you almost 25 percent more time *on every question*. That is a difference that you can feel.

The other big difference between the tests is that they are created with different *philosophies*. This might seem strange, because they are both trying to do the same thing: determine a student's preparedness for college. But the SAT is all about testing your ability to reason and wrestle through a problem. So the test writers are more likely to create questions that feel "tricky," or, to some students, seem needlessly complex.

Here's a typical scene of your head wrestling with a tough SAT problem:

EYES: Reading, reading. Done.
BRAIN: I don't get it.
EYES: Okay, let me try again. Reading, reading. Done.
BRAIN: Oh, okay. Now I think I get it, let me try this. *(Does some stuff.)* Didn't work. I want to climb out of this skull and move to Azerbaijan.
MOUTH: I'm hungry.
BRAIN: Not now, Mouth. Eyes, try reading it again.
EYES: Reading, reading. Done.
BRAIN: Oh! I missed that it said "EXCEPT." Eyes, you suck.
EYES: That's needlessly aggressive.
BRAIN: Okay, let me try . . . this! *(Does stuff.)* Yes! It worked!
MOUTH: I'm hungry.
BRAIN: Enough, Mouth.
*(Curtain)*

The ACT, on the other hand, is all about testing your *knowledge*, so the test writers are more likely to create questions that are straightforward, *as long as you know the material being tested*. Most ACT questions look like the ones you've been doing for homework since freshman year.

Here's a typical scene of your head wrestling with a tough ACT problem:

**Eyes:** Reading, reading. Done.

**Brain:** Got it. Shoot! I don't remember this. Memory!

**Memory:** 'Sup?

**Brain:** Do you flip the numerator and denominator when you add fractions?

**Mouth:** I'm hungry.

**Brain:** Can it, Mouth. Memory, we only have 42 seconds left.

**Memory:** Ummmm . . .

**Brain:** Hurry! Just 35 seconds left.

**Memory:** Remember Ms. Peerendonk's fifth-grade math class? You gotta find the least common denominator.

**Brain:** Oh, yeah! Thanks.

**Memory:** Ms. Peerendonk was the one who smelled like red wine.

**Brain:** That's enough, Memory, we have to keep moving.

(*Curtain*)

In other words, the ACT is more about remembering how to solve problems and less about figuring out what the problems are asking you to do.

A difficult question on the SAT is more likely to make you

If you can't decide which test to take, you can always take both. It can't hurt (except for the potential loss of sanity . . . ).

—Jon

*Actual ACT tests can be found in the book *The Real ACT Prep Guide,* while actual SAT tests can be found in *The Official SAT Study Guide.* Together, these two books weigh four thousand pounds and are the basis of the home workout guide *Getting Ripped by Pumping Books You Don't Want to Read.*

pull out your hair and say, "I don't understand what this question is even *asking.*" And while most of the questions on the ACT require only common knowledge, a more difficult question is more likely to make you pull out your hair and say, "Gosh, I used to *know* this; how could I forget?" Some people find the SAT too tricky, or even unfair. Some people find the ACT boring, or think that it requires that you review too much content.

Now let's get specific: The ACT has a Science Test, while the SAT does not. The Science section tests a student's ability to read and compare graphs, charts, and data tables as well as their sense of logic. The SAT explicitly tests vocabulary, while the ACT does not. The ACT tests punctuation far more heavily than the SAT. SAT questions offer five answer choices, whereas the ACT questions offer four, except for math, where they offer five. The SAT includes math questions for which you need to provide the answer, rather than pick among answer choices. The ACT math questions are all multiple choice.

Also, the ACT tests one subject at a time. You take English, then Math, then Reading, then Science, then ("optionally") Writing: five sections total. The SAT, on the other hand, has 10 shorter sections and has you wrestle with Critical Reading, then Math, then Writing, then *back* to Math, then back to Critical Reading, etc. Again, whether you prefer to get all of your math done at once or mix up your sections is a matter of personal preference.

There are a *ton* of opinions out there about the relative advantages of the ACT and the SAT, but the best thing you can do is to take a practice test of both the SAT and the ACT,* timed, in a setting that allows you to concentrate for the three-plus hours required to take either test. If you score much higher on one than the other, then . . . *take that test!* But if the resulting scores are similar (and they probably will be), then what matters is how you *felt* while taking the tests. Which test was more enjoyable? If this question is impossible to answer, try this one: Which test made you want to pull out a smaller percentage of your hair?

## THE ACT VS. THE SAT: A HANDY CHART

| | ACT | SAT |
|---|---|---|
| **MATERIAL TESTED** | Standard high school curriculum; more advanced math knowledge; stronger emphasis on punctuation; Science Reasoning section tests ability to read tables and graphs | General reasoning and problem solving; stronger emphasis on vocabulary; requires that students come up with their own answers for some math problems |
| **LENGTH** | 175 minutes; 205 with essay. Per-question time: 49 seconds | 200 minutes; 225 with essay. Per-question time: 62 seconds |
| **FORMAT** | Multiple-choice questions; optional essay | Multiple-choice questions; grid-in questions; essay prompt |
| **ACCEPTED BY** | All four-year colleges and universities | All four-year colleges and universities |
| **SECTIONS** | English, Mathematics, Reading, Science, and an optional Writing section (total of five sections) | Reading, Writing, and Math (total of 10 sections) |
| **OFFERED** | Six times per year (September, October, December, February, April, and June) | Seven times per year (October, November, December, January, March, May, and June) |
| **HIGHEST POSSIBLE SCORE** | 36 | 2400 |
| **HOW THE TEST IS SCORED** | Each section is scored on a scale of 1 to 36, and the final score is your average; no points are deducted for wrong answers. | Each of the three sections is worth 800 points, and your composite score is the sum; points are deducted for wrong answers. |
| **DO COLLEGES AUTOMATICALLY SEE ALL MY SCORES?** | No. You can take the ACT multiple times and submit only your best test-date score. | Depends. Some colleges require you to submit all your scores. Many allow you to use Score Choice, which lets you choose which test-date score you send. |

On the facing page is a handy chart outlining the differences between the two tests. Remember: Every college in America accepts both ACT and SAT scores. You decide which test you want to take.

### What is a "good score" on the ACT?

Each section of the ACT is scored on a scale from 1 to 36. Then the four sections are averaged to give you a **composite score** between 1 and 36. If you score a 36, then you are thrown a parade and given hugs and maybe even asked to be a guest editor for this book.* If you score a 1, then you're kicked out of the country.

### For real, what score should I shoot for?

Totally depends. If you're aiming for Yale, then you want to score 34 or higher. You want to shoot for a 30 for Bates College, a 28 for Sewanee, or a 26 for Seattle University, to pick some random examples. Schools almost always post the average scores of incoming freshman on their websites. But remember that these numbers only reflect the typical scores of students entering these schools. They are not minimum requirements, nor do they guarantee that you will be accepted.

And remember, your ACT score does not exist in a vacuum. It's considered alongside your grades and curriculum, your essays, your extracurricular activities, and your recommendations. If you are the president of your school's green energy club and you spearheaded the initiative to install solar panels on a third of the homes in your town, then wrote a novel about the experience called *The Girl Who Kissed the Sun*, which won a Pulitzer Prize, then you may still be accepted if you score below a school's average. If, on the other hand, your greatest achievement so far is memorizing the theme song to *Pretty Little Liars* (and sometimes you forget how the end goes), then you might need to score a little above the average to make up for your lackluster résumé.

But, as we said, your ACT score is the hairy, scary number that college admissions officers call "objective." The ACT score

## How High Should I Reach?

＊And if you score a 42, the graders recognize that your test transcended reality and discovered the meaning of life.
　　　　—Zack

(or SAT score, if you go that route) is the one number that compares you, on a level playing field, to every other student who is applying to that school. This means that while the score is far from the *only* factor in deciding whether you will be admitted to your dream school, it is one of the most important factors. Again, this is both an intimidating fact and, should you choose to accept your mission, a gigantic opportunity.

### What about the PLAN?

Some high schools administer the PLAN test, a practice ACT that's designed to give sophomores an idea of their current score range and point out areas where they might need to study. At one hour and 55 minutes long, it's an hour shorter than the ACT. Here are the PLAN section lengths: English (50 questions, 30 minutes), Math (40 questions, 40 minutes), Reading (25 questions, 20 minutes), Science (30 questions, 25 minutes). If your school does not offer you the PLAN, you can order a test at act.org.

### Who writes the ACT?

Well, back on page 2 we told you about Everett Franklin Lindquist creating the ACT. The company he started now employs tons of test writers. They create multiple ACTs every year. The company also writes exams that are used within specific professions (like English language and career readiness tests).

And that's the whole truth.

**The True Story of the ACT-bot**

### Is that really the *whole* truth?

Since you asked, no. But what we are about to tell you is a secret, *so* secret that if anyone found out that we told you, we would be "taken care of." So keep this between us. . . .

The Lindquist story is a cover-up! Here's how it actually went down:

Fifty years ago, in the Jornada del Muerto desert of New Mexico, a group of archaeologists unearthed an interesting fossil. It didn't look like an *Elasmosaurus platyurus*, or even a *Dunkleosteus dinichthyidae*. Peering closely, one archaeologist said that, more than anything, it looked *kind of* like a piece of an enormous killer robot from outer space.

That's when the ground began to quake. The archaeologists slowly backed away. A metal arm the size of a Mack truck burst out of the ground! The archaeologists shrieked and ran as the arm grabbed one of their cars and hurled it toward a gas station, where it exploded. Then the gas station also exploded, sending out fiery shrapnel in glorious, slow-motion 3-D!

A titanic robot pulled itself from the ground, blotting out the very sun with its fearsome head. The archaeologists called the army, which sent its best helicopters and tanks. But the robot grabbed the helicopters and tossed them at the tanks, causing explosion after explosion after explosion.

It was basically the coolest thing ever.

But then things got a lot less cool. The robot introduced itself as the ACT-bot. It told the assembled archaeologists, armed servicemen, and gas station attendants that it did not want to

This fight scene brought to you by Michael Bay.

—Jon

## ACT Scores of Famous Americans

| | |
|---|---|
| 18 | William Faulkner |
| 20 | John Cena |
| 21 | Marilyn Monroe (and Marilyn Manson, coincidentally) |
| 23 | That guy who narrates the trailers for disaster movies |
| 26 | LBJ |
| 30 | Barack Obama |
| 32 | Steve Jobs |
| 34 | Waka Flocka Flame |
| 35 | Supreme Court justice Sonia Sotomayor |
| 36 | John Cena (He took it twice.) |

conquer the world. Rather, it wanted to test everyone on his or her ability to tackle college-level work within a time constraint.

"In-how-many-ways-can-a-group-of-four-fruits-be-selected-from-a-basket-of-ten-apples-and-six-pears-so-as-to-always-include-an-apple?" boomed the robot's staccato voice.

"Huh?" said an archaeologist with a PhD from Yale.

"BZZZZZZZ!!!" A loud buzzer sounded from the robot's chest. "Too-slow!" The archaeologist was vaporized—along with the laminated copy of his PhD that he carried in his pocket.

"Correct-the-following-sentence," the ACT-bot continued. "Marsha-and-Brady-and-Sam-spent-the-afternoon-taking-a-nap."

Private James McCurdy, from Galveston, Texas, answered heroically. "'Naps!' It should be 'naps'!"

A loud "CORRECT!" echoed across the dunes.

The pedagogy-obsessed ACT-bot now resides in an undisclosed location, carrying out its grim machinations on a grand scale by pumping out test after test.

## That is terrifying *and* believable. Do I need any special skills to take the ACT?

If you've been attending high school for the past three or four years, you will not need any special skills. The ACT-bot does, however, demand the mastery of some normal skills. Ask yourself, can you do all of the following?

**1. Can you carry a form of photo identification?** You'll need to bring a passport, driver's license or permit, school or state ID to the test center to prove that you are yourself. If you don't have any of these, you can bring a letter of identification from your school or notarized statement. Slide the card, booklet, or letter into your pocket and you should be fine.

**2. Can you stay awake for three hours and 25 minutes?** We will talk about endurance and focus in the next chapter, but right off the bat you should know that you need to be conscious for the duration of the test.

❋ I only listen to audiobooks read by Taylor Lautner. If you listen closely enough, you can hear his abs contracting.

—Zack

**3. Can you read?** Obviously you can, because you're reading this—unless you're listening to this as an audiobook, hopefully being read in a sultry British whisper by Robert Pattinson.❋

**4. Can you fill in little bubbles?** If not, here's a refresher: Put your pencil over the desired bubble. Lower the pencil until it touches the page. Move the pencil back and forth. Make sure to practice this at home before the real test.

**5. Can you flip pages?** This might be tough. Think of this as clicking a "next page" button on an iPad, but in real life. Don't be too rough! You might rip out the page. Make sure to practice this at home before the real test, too.

**6. Do you remember everything you ever learned about math, reading, science, and grammar?** If you can't immediately recall every detail of everything you've ever learned, don't worry. We are going to cover everything you need to learn (or remember) in the following chapters.

**7. Do you know how to efficiently move through a long standardized test?** Don't worry about this one either. Starting in the next chapter, we're going to talk *a lot* about effective strategies to get the most out of your three hours and 25 minutes.

**8. Do you know what is appropriate test-taking attire? How to snack effectively? How to sit properly?** We'll cover all this in the last chapter of the book.

## A Series of Pep Talks

**I have to admit, this whole "prepping for the ACT thing" is really harshing my mellow. Any advice for how to get psyched to study?**

We've discovered that when it comes to getting pumped to study, one man's pep talk is another man's funeral dirge. So we've enlisted the help of some outsiders to offer a variety of perspectives. Let's begin with some positive-minded advice:

**Pep Talk from a College Professor:** "The knowledge tested on the ACT is, for the most part, the kind of knowledge that will be very useful in college. Preparing for the ACT is, in a way, like

Like all Harvard grads, he majored in Condescension.

—Jon

Excuse me? Majored? At Harvard we call them "concentrations."

—Harvard Grad

preparing for college, and a good score on the ACT will translate to a head start in your first university courses. Also, college professors should be paid more. Just sayin'."

**Pep Talk from a Graduate of Harvard University:** "Getting a high score on the ACT increases your chances of matriculating at my alma mater. You'll be able to cheer on the Crimson Cockatoos against the dreadful Yale Periwinkles (you probably don't understand those words yet, but you will). You'll learn a great deal, place into a terribly prestigious law school, and, of course, take your nightly cognac at the Harvard Club in New York City. Oh, and Harvard graduates don't pay for groceries."

**Pep Talk from a Test-Prep Book Publisher:** "A perfect score on the ACT will open up a world of opportunities for you, including the possibility that you could become a guest editor for *Up Your Score: ACT*, the 2016–2017 edition!"

**Pep Talk from Another High Schooler:** "One night, all of my friends were heading out to a raging party. '*pRty 2nite*,' they tweeted. '*No cn do. :( ACT krammin*,' I twote back. Then the raging party was hit by lightning and my friends all suffered minor burn damage. Now I'm the least-burned kid at school, which has been a major boost to my popularity."

If you are a more pessimistic person, you might find these people more motivating:

**Pep Talk from a Human Resources Director:** "I see résumés all the time from people who didn't study and did poorly on the ACT. They went to not-so-challenging colleges, where they didn't have to do any work. So they spent their time playing Frisbee golf, which they always call 'frolfing.' At the top of their résumés, they write that they are 'Insane Frolfers.' Most of these people end up frolfing alone in the sewers."

**Pep Talk from a High Schooler Who Is Studying Way Harder Than You:** "I'm clocking about three hours of ACT prep per night. My walls are covered in problems that I've gotten wrong. I call them my 'Walls of Shame.' I weep when I look at my Walls of Shame. When I take the test, I am going to get most of the questions correct. Because the test is graded on a curve (which means your raw score is compared with other raw scores before you are given a final score), I am making it much harder for you to get even a decent score. If you don't study harder, your average, standard performance will give you a less-than-average, less-than-standard score. I can't believe I've wasted this much study time talking to you. Now I'll have to punish myself by staring at my Wall of Shame."

**Pep Talk from Your Dad:** "The ACT costs money. My money. If you don't study and prepare adequately you are wasting money. My money. And my money doesn't grow on trees. Kids these days think that money grows on trees, but if they went out and looked at a tree they'd see that trees have leaves, not money. But they're too busy with their iPhones and their PSPs and their eyeliner and their various shows on ABC Family Channel and . . . *(head droops, falls asleep)."*

**Pep Talk from a Fifth-Grade Bully:** "If you don't study for this test and do well, I'm going to punch you with my fist."

**Pep Talk from a Tenth-Grade Bully:** "If you don't study for this test and do well, I'm going to post a video on YouTube of you getting punched by a fifth grader. I'm gonna add background music by mau5trap and some slo-mo visual effects and it's gonna go viral."

**Okay, but what if I study really hard and *still* don't do well?**
The bad news is that you can study your tail off, memorize every mathematical formula and grammar rule, read your entire biology textbook in a night, and *still* mess up on test day. This can happen for a number of reasons:

1. Instead of bringing your admission ticket to the test center, you bring a coupon for six free doughnut holes from the Dungeon of Donutz. After you're rebuffed by the admissions staff, you try to bribe them by offering them the

Who needs college when you have six free doughnut holes?

—Zack

coupon. They consider this for a long time, because c'mon, free doughnut holes. But ultimately they don't let you in.

2. Instead of number-2 pencils, you bring number-3 pencils. The optical scanning devices that score the tests say to themselves, "Well, I *can* read that pencil lead, but it's not up to code, so I won't. Automatic 0."

3. You get so bored during a reading passage that you begin to daydream about being Beyoncé. Then, instead of finishing your test, you mentally spend the next hour dancing with inhuman precision and singing with astonishing power.

4. You misbubble an answer, which throws off all of your answers by one bubble. You realize this at the very second that the proctor calls, "Time's up." You frantically try to erase your bubbles, only to have your test snatched away. You watch your incorrect answer sheet disappear into the pile. You tilt your head back and scream "NOOOOOOOOOO!!!!!!!!!!!!!" to the heavens, but the gods only smirk at your misery.

5. It's hot in the room and there is a sticky spot on your desk, so you get distracted and are thrown off your game.

Some of these difficulties can be remedied. Definitely remember to bring your admission ticket and a valid form of identification. Definitely remember to bring some number-2 pencils and calculator. If you discover that your desk or work space has a noticeable flaw (a wobbly chair, a scarred or sticky desktop, a pile of decomposing animal remains), immediately tell the proctor, who should be able to help you out.

And remember that *you can always retake the ACT*. You are allowed to take the test up to 12 times, and you choose which scores are sent to colleges. You pick the test date, and those scores (and *only* those scores) will be released. This means that you cannot "combine" scores (by picking your English score from one date, for example, and the Mathematics score from another).

That signed picture of you with One Direction does not count as a photo ID and is just embarrassing.

—Jon

But it also means that you can take the test until you get the scores you want, then send just those scores. This is very different from the SAT. With the SAT, there's no guarantee that you can send only your best scores. Some colleges look at your most recent scores, others look at the best section scores across all the times you've taken the test, and still others will consider only scores from your best test date. The point is, with the ACT, you control which test colleges get to see. This is a great advantage, as you can retake the test without fear of colleges judging you for (or even knowing) how many times you took it.

## The Score on Scoring

### What Does "Scaled Score" Mean?

The ACT scales your raw score by comparing it to all of the other raw scores that kids achieved on that test. Let's say you get 57 questions correct on the English Test. If most other kids got fewer right, then your scaled score might be a 27. But if most other kids did better, then that raw score of 57 might become a scaled score of 23. It all depends on how other kids did on the same test. (There is some other math involved in scaling scores, but basically that's how it works.)

### How is the ACT scored?

Here are the basics: First, they add up all of your correct answers to create a raw score for each section. So if Jeremiah gets 62 correct answers in the English Test, 50 in the Mathematics Test, 32 in the Reading Test, and 33 in the Science Test, his raw score would be: 62, 50, 32, 33.

The raw score is then converted to a scaled score between 1 and 36 on each section. So Jeremiah's raw score might be scaled to: 27, 29, 29, 27. The composite score, or overall score, is the average of these four numbers. Jeremiah's composite score would be 28. This is the number that college admissions officers would call his "ACT score."

If you choose to take the Writing Test, you will receive two additional numbers, a writing score and a combined English/Writing score. First, your essay will be read by two readers, who will each give the essay a grade between 1 and 6. If the graders disagree by more than one point, a third reader will step in to settle the dispute. The two scores will be added to create a Writing subscore between 2 and 12. Then you'll receive a combined English/Writing score, which gives the Writing subscore one-third weight and your English composite score two-thirds weight to create a new grade between 1 and 36. Did your head just explode? Well, scoop it back up and check out this example: If Jeremiah scores a 27 on the English section, and an 11 on his essay, his combined English/Writing score might go up to a 29, but if he scores an 8 on his essay, his combined score could go down to a 25. Regardless, your combined English/Writing score does *not* affect your overall, composite score; it is a separate number. We will talk more about the essay and how it is scored in the chapter on the Writing section.

Finally, your score report (the sheet with your scores that you receive online and by mail) will list a national rank, which looks like a percent, next to each section score. This tells you the percentage of students in the nation who scored at or below your score. So, if your score of 32 in English earns you a rank of 92, that means 92 percent of the other test takers in the nation scored a 32 or lower, and you should feel awesome. The ACT claims that these scores are supposed to help you decide which subjects to pursue in college, but we all know these percents exist to make you feel great, mediocre, or crummy, depending on your rank.

One nice thing about the ACT is that it does *not* penalize you for guessing. This means if you're not sure of an answer, you *must* guess and put down an answer for every question. We will discuss this in more detail later, but for now you should go ahead and tattoo PUT DOWN AN ANSWER FOR EVERY QUESTION on your forearm.

### Why is the scoring scale out of 36?
Who knows? We're pretty sure it has to do either with the ancient Mayan calendar or the lost city of Atlantis. Or it might be a Kabbalah thing....

### How many wrong answers can I get in each section and still get a perfect score?
The answer to this question varies, because your score is scaled, so it depends on the performance of everyone else taking the test

Proctors can serve as great alarm clocks. When they announce "five minutes left," finish the question you're on and immediately bubble in the rest of the answer sheet. Then pick up from where you left off, taking comfort in the fact that you have a 20-25 percent chance of scoring points on questions that you haven't even looked at yet.

—Ava

**Classic Rejected ACT Essay Prompts**

1. Is caramel too sweet? Discuss.

2. Should I start watching *How I Met Your Mother*? It just seems like such a commitment.

3. What was the effect of Mikhail Gorbachev's domestic economic policies on contemporary Marxist political philosophy?

4. Are you thirsty?

on that date. But in general, you have to answer every question correctly in order to get a perfect score. More often than not, toward the top end of the score curve, each question you get wrong will take a point off your scaled score. That's why our student authors are so darned impressive!

**What if the ACT makes a mistake and marks one of my answers as "incorrect" when I really got it right?**

We've actually never heard of this happening. But there is always a first time for everything, right? If, after looking at your score report, you think that they have made a mistake, you can send a letter to:

ACT Records
301 ACT Drive
P.O. Box 451
Iowa City, IA 52243-0451

Be sure to include your score report and an explanation.

If they agree with your assessment, they will either send you a corrected score report or sign you up to retake the test (woo-hoo!) free of charge.

**How do I get my scores?**

When you sign up for the test, you will create an ACT Web account at actstudent.org. Your scores should be available on the website within four weeks of your taking the test. Irregularities either on your information sheet or at the test center can delay your score report. If your score is delayed, it is important that you pull all of the hair out of your head and run screaming through the streets. This is the only guaranteed way to speed up getting your score. The ACT says that almost all scores are reported within eight weeks of taking the test. If your score takes longer than eight weeks, call the ACT at 319-337-1313 and let out a loud, prolonged scream into the phone. We can't guarantee any results, but at least you'll have tried. . . .

# Practice, Practice, Practice!

## So how do I study for this test?

Um, read this book?

But then, *after* you read this book, you will need to practice. A lot of test-prep books (Princeton Review, Barrons, Kaplan, etc.) include lots of practice tests, but there is really no substitute for the real thing. We recommend that you purchase *The Real ACT Prep Guide*, 3rd Edition or later, which includes five real ACT tests. By the time you finish *Up Your Score,* you will know how to move through those tests, how to analyze the test after you've finished, and how to learn both from your successes and your mistakes. Other, section-specific study advice will be presented in later chapters.

You should also remember that taking the ACT for real can be a practice opportunity. As we mentioned, you can take the test up to 12 times and choose which test date's scores you want to send to colleges.

## Whoa, hold up. You want me to read this book, and then take tests in *another* book?

Reading about strategies and content is all well and good, but learning about the ACT without practicing on real ACTs is like reading about riding a bike without getting on a bike. Think about test taking as if it were the ancient Aztec sport of Severed-Head Basketball. Sure, a coach can tell you how to pass the bloody head and how to shoot the bloody head up toward the hoop. He can even tell you how to sacrifice the losing team to Quetzalcoatl, the snake god. But until you get out there and toss around a *real* bloody head, take a couple hundred shots at the basket, and sacrifice some *real* losing teams, you're never going to become a champion. And only true champions can earn the glory of also being sacrificed to Quetzalcoatl.

All that said, if for some crazy reason you still don't feel like taking a three-and-a-half-hour practice test, here are a few tried-and-true methods for motivating yourself:

## Introducing Tutor Tips

At Veritas Tutors and Test Prep, we've accumulated a lot of experience helping kids make great gains in their ACT scores. How exactly do we do this? Some of our techniques are obvious (we make kids practice a lot), but some have been crafted over the course of years. Throughout this book, we will unveil some of our trade secrets. Keep an eye out for **What Do Tutors Do?** passages in the margins!

**1. Set a goal.** Every large project feels impossibly long if you cannot see the light at the end of the tunnel. If the schools you are interested in have an average ACT score of 29, write a big "29" on a piece of paper and put it up on your wall. That's your goal. That's your light at the end of the tunnel. Once you get that score a few times on some practice tests, then you've done what you need to do. All that's left is to take the test. This strategy worked for the founding fathers of America. They just wrote "Become the dominant world superpower" on a piece of paper and got to work.✳

✳ This is the less-known, less-exciting first draft of the Constitution.

—Zack

**2. Make a schedule.** We avoid large projects because it feels like there is an infinite amount of work to be done. It is crucial, then, to break the work into chunks. If you have the time, give yourself a week for each content chapter in this book. If you work on only five to ten pages per day, the whole project will feel *much* more manageable. While you're at it, you can schedule in the rest of your life. A typical entry could look like this: "Monday: Wake up. Think about going back to sleep. Go back to sleep. Wake up again. Scratch belly. Brush teeth. Glance at floss. Don't floss. Shower. Drive to school. Park car. Attend all classes. Look attractive in hallways. After school, drive home. Read five to ten pages of ACT book. Do all homework. Turn on television. Look at television. Love television. Eat dinner. Digest dinner. Brush teeth. Glance at floss. Don't floss. Get in bed with book. Sleep." (We will discuss scheduling in more detail in Chapter 3.)

**3. Study with friends.** Misery loves company. If you study along with some friends, then they can go pick up your book after you've thrown it across the room.

**4. Treat practice tests like the real thing.** If you are going to spend three-plus hours on a practice test, you might as well do it right. Don't take the test while lying in bed with *Awkward* playing on your laptop. Go somewhere quiet (there are buildings called libraries, pronounced *lie-brare-eez*, where people used to go before the Internet was invented, that are perfect for this); turn off your phone (there *is* an off button, we swear, usually on the side or top of your phone); and *focus*. The harder you try during practice tests, the more you will increase your test-taking ability. Also, getting psyched up and nervous about a practice test is great preparation for getting psyched up and nervous about the real test.

## The Digital Future

**I read that the ACT might start administering its tests by computer. Is that true?**

Yes. In May of 2013, the ACT announced that in the spring of 2015 it would likely begin giving the test on computers in schools that were equipped to administer it that way. The ACT will *also* continue to offer paper-and-pencil versions. It also said that the content of the test will remain the same—just displayed on a screen instead of printed on a page.

Any more questions? No? Good. Now, we cannot lie: The ACT-bot has created a long test and cooked up some tough problems. This is all a recipe for potential anxiety. So in the next chapter, we're going to talk about some of the ways that stress can secretly (and not so secretly) mess you up, and show you the best ways to crush that stress—just like Spider-Man crushed the Nazi menace in *Spider-Man #43*, then went on to do very well on the ACT in the much-less-popular *Spider-Man #44*.

# CHAPTER 2

# Keeping Your Cool

## Anxiety and the ACT

Here's a practice ACT-style question:

**1.** Are you feeling stressed about taking the ACT?
   **A.** Duh.
   **B.** Nope. I'm always successful in everything I take on, with zero exceptions.
   **C.** Not really. I'm pretty confident that this year all of the answers will be B. Because, why not?
   **D.** No. I'm completely insane.
The correct answer is: A.

The ACT, like any standardized test, is a stressful prospect. It looms in the future like a dark, somewhat hazy, human-consuming beast. You know that it is long, you know that it is relatively important, and you know that some of the questions can get pretty rough. What's *not* stressful about that?

The truth, however, is that preparing for and taking the ACT is totally manageable. There are only so many things you have to learn and only so many strategies you need to practice. But stress can distract you, frighten you, make you a less-effective studier, or simply waste your time.

That's why we need to talk, right up front, about anxiety. Anxiety is actually one of the ACT-bot's most nefarious weapons, because it is so subtle and personal. That's why, around here, we call it "the Darkness."

Pssst! Stress is good. It means you care about the results. But letting stress rule your thoughts? That's bad. Instead, use stress as motivation to prepare for the test—because you *can* beat it. I'll bet you a Rice Krispies treat.

—Ava

## The Darkness: A Maelstrom of Fear

First, we'll talk a little bit about what the Darkness can feel like, and then we'll tell you how to manage the stress—and even make it work to your advantage.

One thing to understand from the get-go is that our minds react to stress in a number of different ways. Think of these as stages that you can move through. In fact, you can experience each of these stress reactions over the course of one day—or even one (particularly brutal) hour! Let's take a look at these stages:

## I. OSTRICHING

The regal ostrich is famous for its stress-management strategy. When freaked out, the ostrich digs a hole with its beak, then sticks its head inside the hole until it feels the danger has passed. While we might laugh at this ridiculous strategy (seriously, how is this animal not extinct?), it turns out that we also do this all the time. *

When faced with something as frightening as the ACT-bot, one of our first impulses is to think about something else—and think about it *really hard*. Maybe we sign up for the interpretive dance team and go to every practice. If that's not enough, we campaign to become captain of the interpretive dance team and demand that the team practice twice a day! In the bookstore, we deliberately avoid the test-prep section (and pester the clerks for interpretive dance books).

This strategy of avoidance is popular because it distracts us from what we fear. And it is effective, because we can react to any intrusion of test stress by signing up for the interpretive dance team in the next town over. **

## 2. "WORKING"

Once we realize that we are ostriching, we may say to ourselves, "Okay, self, it's time to grow up, muster some courage, and face the monster head on." We buy a test-prep book, and then we get to "work."

What is "working," with quotation marks? It's exactly like ostriching, but instead of burying your head in other activities, you bury your head in ACT materials. Sounds good, right? Looks good, too! But here's the thing: Your body is working, but your mind is not. You make a hundred million flash cards but never look at them; you open up the book and read half of one paragraph, then skip forward a few pages and read another half paragraph.

*Why else would every American kid have a personal sandbox?

—Ava

** Before I learned how to cope, I was a member of 17 different interpretive dance teams.

—Zack

Maybe you wrestle with a couple of questions, but you stop if they seem too rough. After about 35 minutes of this, you've done your "work," and you've put off stress for another day or so.

"Working" is one of the most dangerous forms of stress, because it pretends to be productive. When we "work," we are putting on a *performance of effort* in order to satisfy some watching, vengeful god of standardized tests. We are logging hours so that if we fail, we can say, "It's not my fault; I did my best and put in the time."

## 3. BOUNCING

Eventually we might recognize that we are "working" but not really working. We say to ourselves: "Self, snap out of it! We *actually* have to work, like *for real*. Stop being such a coward and Do. Some. Stuff." So we settle into our favorite chair, open to the first page of a practice test, click our mechanical pencil, and jump into it . . . and then realize 10 minutes later that we've been imagining a bare-knuckles sing-off between Adele and Taylor Swift. We refocus, reclick our mechanical pencil, furrow our eyebrows, and dive back in . . . only to resurface, staring at the exact same problem, having spent five minutes imagining a meat-free, earth-friendly, low-carb, low-sodium bacon cheeseburger.

*What's going on?* Well, this is what neurosurgeons and neuroscientists (probably) call "bouncy brain." You are willing to focus and do some serious work, but your brain disobeys and takes every available opportunity to go off on a more attractive thought-path.

This might seem surprising, but a bouncy brain is also caused by stress. Even though you have wrestled with your mind and *told* it to focus, it is still intimidated by the prospect of the ACT. Even though *you* might want to study, your annoying *mind* is still afraid.

## 4. REALIZING THAT YOU ARE, IN FACT, THE STUPIDEST PERSON IN THE HISTORY OF THE PLANET

But let's say we *are* able to face the test. We think, "Okay, ACT, you are quite fearsome, but I'm a competent person, at least

*No! Never flip to the back mid-test! Staple the back of the book shut if that's what it takes!

—Jon

sometimes, and I can handle you." You look at a problem, you wrestle with it for a second, you find an answer, you circle it. Unable to help yourself, you flip to the back and check to see if you got it right. (Don't pretend you don't do this.)* You're correct! Hey, hey! Who's the big scary test now, right? Move over, Watson and Crick, there's a new discoverer-of-the-double-helix-structure-of-DNA in town!

Then you try the next problem. It's a little tougher. You try one strategy, then another. Nothing works. Are you supposed to flip the denominator and the numerator? Let's try it. Nope, your answer is not one of the choices. You're about to close the book and check into the Sad Sack Hotel for a five-day weep, when *BAM!* You have an idea! You try it out. You get an answer. Is it one of the options? It is! You flip to the back. . . . You got it right!!!!

Ticker-tape parade! Mark Zuckerberg tweets about how smart you are, and you tweet back: "Oh, Zuck, c'mon, there's room in the world for two paradigm-changing wunderkinds." But then you pause. That problem *was* kind of hard. Let's try one more. You read it and *immediately* know that it's impossible. You don't recognize a third of the terms. You wouldn't even know where to *look up* the concepts they expect you to have mastered.

There's only one logical conclusion: You are, in fact, the stupidest person in the history of the planet.

Okay, first off: You can't be the stupidest person in the history of the planet. These three people, at least, are far stupider than you:

1. Amunet, born 327 B.C., Egypt; once asked a slave driver why she had to build pyramids all day. The slave driver chuckled and told her to go ask the pharaoh. She did, and was beheaded.
2. Birgis Khan, born A.D. 1234, Mongolia; great-nephew of warlord Genghis Khan; was told to conquer the 3,000 square miles to the west of the empire; instead, he conquered 3,000 square miles to the north. The phrase "as dumb as Birgis" is still used in Mongolia today.

3. Leif Erikson, born A.D. 970, Iceland; landed in America, but instead of creating a world superpower like the Puritans did, he just picked some grapes and brought them back to Iceland. Did you know that October 9 is "Leif Erikson Day" in the U.S.? Didn't think so. (We didn't make that up. We swear.)

But, even though you are not the stupidest person in the history of the planet, it is almost guaranteed that at some point, you will *feel* like that person. This kind of self-criticism is very dangerous, because it can lead you to the false conclusion that you will never be able to do well on the test, so you shouldn't try. *This is the worst thought that can ever pass through your head.* And it probably will, at least once, while you are preparing for the test.

And here's the crazy thing: These four stress reactions manifest themselves *when you take the actual test.*

You "ostrich" every time you read a problem and immediately say, "Oh, I can't do that one." Instead of giving your brain a chance to wrestle with and work through the problem, you look at some of the scarier words and give in to your fear.

You "work" when you write down a series of numbers under a math problem, then try adding them or subtracting them to see if *something* happens, or when you underline every other word in a reading passage, then copy those underlined words in the margin. You're not actually thinking during this work, but, rather, creating the appearance of thinking in the hopes that this will trick the ACT-bot into believing that you're really working, so it'll reward you with a good score.

Your brain "bounces" when your mind wanders away from a science passage before you are done reading it, or when a whole paragraph passes in front of your eyes without your brain absorbing a single word. When you are taking the test, it is very easy to be overwhelmed *without knowing that you are overwhelmed.* A bouncy brain is a good indication that you are feeling the stress.

One of the bad things about these stress reactions is that they waste time, leading to even more stress, even more negative reactions, and even more wasted time. It truly is a vicious cycle.

—Jon

Finally, you think of yourself as "stupid" every time you give in to frustration. You wrestle and struggle with the problem and come to the conclusion that you are just too dumb to ever hope to solve it.

Altogether, the kind of stress that the ACT-bot inspires is a gigantic roadblock between you and your desired score. Luckily, there are ways of handling the Darkness.

## The Light: Studying Without Stress

B efore we begin, let's answer that scariest, worst-possible, despairing question: "Why even try?"

The reason to study and prepare for the ACT is that by doing so you will, of course, improve your score. This will not be the miraculous outcome of some mystical, secret process; it is a simple fact. If you study and practice, your score will improve.

But will it improve *enough*? Will it be worth the effort?

Of course it will! If you take a practice test right now and score an 18, then bringing your score up to a 23 will open the door to a whole new group of colleges and universities. If you score a 26 on your first practice test, and then after months of studying score a 28, you've still pulled yourself above the thousands of applicants who will submit a 26 or 27 as their score. *Any* improvement, no matter how small, is a real improvement that will have real results.

And needless to say, you *are* going to raise your score significantly, because you've had the good luck of purchasing *Up Your Score: ACT.*

So let's talk about managing stress.

There were about 1.65 million ACT takers in the class of 2012. A score of 26 put you in the 84th percentile, whereas a 28 put you in the 91st. You pulled yourself above 115,000 people by gaining two points!

—Zack

## First, Make a Plan

I n 1775, General George Washington was super stressed. All of the colonists, including the most politically powerful men and women, had asked him to throw off the yoke of British tyranny.

Like, now, please. The Brits were equipping their *gigantic navy* to sail to America with their *actually trained army*, and General George could do little else but survey his raggle-taggle group of farmers and say, "Drat."

There was so much to do! He had to turn his posse o' angry farmers into an army, set up fortifications, construct about a zillion boats, produce ammunition and firearms, gain the support of France, invent guerrilla warfare, recruit a zillion more angry farmers, and the list goes on. He was totally overwhelmed.

Every project, be it building a chair or birthing a nation, looks completely daunting at first. And it is the same with preparing for the ACT. You have to read this book, including each chapter on each test section, and practice by taking a number of practice tests. Then you have to take the actual ACT, possibly more than once. The sheer size of the project distracts you from each part. The psychological strain can become so great that you either "ostrich" or "work" or study with a bouncy brain.

What did Washington do? Let's look at the following entry, from John Adams's journal of 1775:

> Spaketh with Gen. Washington this morning. He requested a Weekly Calendar. I enquired as to the purpose of such a Thing. He requested that I enquire less often, and instead shuteth fast my Mouth and doeth as I am told. I complied posthaste. The Calendar in Hand, the Gen. didst marketh upon each Week a separate Goal, all the Goals together contributing to the overall Attainment of Freedom for our Great Nation. I complimented him on his Foresight, to which he did respond by encouraging me to remove my Self from his Presence, as he finds me Distractingly Un-Handsome.

In other words, Washington broke up his many goals into small, easily managed chunks. This greatly decreased his stress

**Other Famous Plans**
- FDR's New Deal
- Hayato Ikeda's Japanese economic miracle
- Ava's plan to buy two cans of Pringles, and eat one in the car on the way home and the other while watching a *Project Runway* marathon

and allowed him to focus on the task at hand. In fact, you could say that good organization is our true Founding Father!

You should do the same thing. Here we've proposed three plans, one for if you have at least three months before the test, one if you have only three weeks, and one if you have really let things slide and have only three days.

## THE THREE PLANS

There are a number of ways to use this book, depending on your circumstances. Let's say, for example, that you are a plan-ahead type and are three months away from the test. We recommend you follow this schedule:

### The Three-Month Plan
**Month One:**
- Read the first six chapters of the book. This includes the Introduction, Strategy, English, and Math chapters.
- Each week, read at least two magazine or newspaper articles to bring up your reading level. (For more on this, see page 243.)
- After two weeks with the book, take your first practice test in *The Real ACT Prep Guide.*
- Go on at least two hikes to clear your mind and commune with nature. This can also be accomplished by downloading the Commune with Nature app, which will show you a flora and fauna slideshow while playing a recording of ambient nature sounds.

**Month Two:**
1. Read the Reading and Science chapters, and the chapter on the Writing Test.
2. Move up to at least three challenging articles per week.
3. Take two more practice tests from *The Real ACT Prep Guide.*
4. If you start to get stressed out, go watch the movie *War of the Worlds* and feel thankful that we are currently not fighting a war of the worlds.

If you have only three hours before the test and you still haven't started preparing, you have our permission to break down and sob uncontrollably.

—Jon

### What Do Tutors Do?

For one thing, we make plans and schedules for our students. Another big part of our job is making sure that our students actually stick to their schedules. We might meet with a student on a weekly basis, but we also send regular emails to ensure that a student is getting his or her work done. This is why our students hate us so much!

When you do your studying for the week, you should think *only* about the designated material for *that* week. When your brain starts to wander toward *all* of the work you still have to do, recognize that your brain is being disobedient and correct it. Try the following speech:

"You are my brain. If you do not stop wandering, I will force you to watch *Air Bud: Seventh Inning Fetch* four times in a row."

**Month Three:**

1. Review Chapters 3 through 8, paying extra attention to the chapters that deal with those sections of the test that are the most difficult for you.

2. Take at least two more practice tests, noting the types of problems that you are getting wrong. Spend time studying those question types.

3. The week before the test, read the last chapter, which deals with the last 24 hours before the test. We also recommend reviewing the chapter on Strategy again.

4. When the test is complete, go buy yourself something nice to reward yourself for being so prepared. We recommend buying a Pillow Pet, because it is both a pillow and a stuffed animal, which is an incredible value.

### The Three-Week Plan

If, on the other hand, you only have three weeks, we recommend the following schedule:

**Week One:**

1. Read the Introduction, Strategy, and English chapters of this book.

2. Take one test from *The Real ACT Prep Guide*. Don't worry about your score yet.

3. Look at yourself in the mirror and say: "Don't freak out. I still have more than two weeks to learn everything I need to know for this test."

4. Freak out a little bit. Then calm down.

**Week Two:**

1. Read the Math chapter. It is long. Give yourself at least three days to get through it. Really work through all of the practice problems to burn the concepts into your head. Then read the Reading chapter.

2. Take another practice test. Pay attention to those problems that you answered incorrectly. *The Real ACT Prep Guide*

gives an explanation of every problem, and reading these will help ensure that errors do not repeat themselves.

3. Throw a "Test Is Next Week" party. At a "Test Is Next Week" party, you sit in a chair and bite your lip and tap incessantly on the table. Nobody else is invited.

4. Don't be afraid to take naps and breaks from studying. Just remember to put in at least one hour of test prep every day, including weekends.

**Week Three:**

1. You're doing great! Finish the book.

2. Take a final test in the *Prep Guide*. Read the explanations for any wrong answers.

3. Start to get psyched. Sure, you've felt a bit rushed and stressed out these past few weeks, but you've done a lot more than a lot of people.

4. Go into that test and kick some test butt. Afterward buy yourself something nice for putting in an honest three weeks of work. Get some Jell-O. Have you had Jell-O recently? It's better than you remembered.

## The Three-Day Plan

Finally, if you have three days, here's what we recommend:

**Day One:**

1. Scream and curse. Curse at yourself, curse at the world, curse at the ACT.

2. Now that you've gotten that out of your system, read the Introduction and Strategy chapters of this book.

3. Now that you are acquainted with the test, we want you to take *only* a math section from a real ACT in the *Prep Guide*.

4. Use your mistakes to find out which concepts you've forgotten. Find them in the Math chapter and review them.

**Day Two:**

1. Scream as you brush your teeth in the morning.

2. Take an English section from the *Prep Guide*. Find the grammar concepts that you screwed up on the test and read about them in our English chapter.

3. Read the entire Reading and Science chapters. Fortunately, they are not too long.

4. Before bed, read the final chapter of this book. It is very helpful.

**Day Three:**

1. Wake up. Take the test using our strategies.

2. Walk out chuckling at all the knuckleheads who took more than three days to prepare. You are the winner, my friend, you are the winner.

3. Assume you've done a great job.

4. Buy yourself something nice for putting in an honest three days of work.

5. Sign yourself up for the next test date and follow the three-week schedule listed on the previous page. *Just in case.*

## Be Here Now

Once you've created your study plan, you still need to *study*. The secret to successful, stress-free studying is to focus on the present moment, rather than on the past or the future. This is a little trick that we've picked up from the ancient Chinese tradition of Zen Buddhism.

There's a story in Zen Buddhism about a monk who is locked in prison. The various versions of the story don't say *why* he is thrown in prison, so let's just assume that he was jaywalking. Anyway, he's in jail, and he's going to be executed the next day, because the emperor is crazy opposed to jaywalking. Lying on his cot, the monk thinks about the past and weeps over the memory of his mother and father, his little cat Boopsy, his days at the monastery, etc. Then he thinks of tomorrow and weeps at the idea of, you know, getting executed. But *then* he clears his mind of both

the past and the future, and the tears dry on his cheeks. He is able to look at a beautiful sunbeam and reflect on the dancing motes of dust. By eliminating the past and the future and focusing on the present moment, he is able to find a place of peace.

Then he's executed, but that's not the point of the story.

The point is that the present is *almost always* a place of peace, mentally speaking. Unless you have just broken your fibula or were recently dumped by your one true love via group text, it is very rare that you are *currently* feeling misery. Almost all of your stress and sadness and fear comes from dwelling on either the past or the future. Whenever stress rears its ugly head, remind yourself to return to the present moment.

When you are reading the Math chapter of this book, for example, eliminate any idea of the upcoming ACT and any discouraging memories of past math classes or assignments, and let your mind focus on only what you are reading. If your thoughts wander back to the dreaded future or miserable past, don't worry; this is completely natural. Shut your eyes, remind yourself to focus, and start again.

Focusing on the present moment is the kind of skill that monks practice *for their entire lives*, and many never master it. Do not expect to become a focus guru right away. But with practice, your focus will improve. The important thing is to recognize when you are thinking of the future or past, and refocus yourself.

And don't forget: Practicing staying focused on the present moment during study sessions is also practice for the actual test.

*This is a good tip to use during the test as well.

—Ava

# Still Stressed? Good!

## Other Classic Motivational Fears

• Fear of cavities
• Fear of getting expelled
• Fear of getting fired
• Fear of *Gruelspracht*, the German demon that cooks children who do not finish their steins of beer

O f course, none of this will completely relieve test stress. At no point will you sit back in your La-Z-Boy, kick up your feet, and say, "I'm a stone-cold master of the ACT."*

But that's a good thing! If you are able to map out a plan and focus during your study sessions, then you should use the leftover stress as motivational fear.

Motivational fear is like normal fear, except you channel it to do the work you need to do. Just as an engine transforms fuel into a force for movement, so you should transform all that leftover fear into a force for motivation. If you wake up in the middle of the night thinking about a reading passage with long, sharp claws and glistening, gore-covered teeth, *use that* by attacking a reading passage the next day. If you're worried that your speed on the English Test is not up to snuff, then take out a timer and practice speeding up (a strategy that will be covered in the next chapter). In other words, stress, in small doses, can inspire you to work. Let this happen.

And if that stress becomes overwhelming, just glance at your schedule and reaffirm that you do, indeed, have a plan. As time goes by and you start to feel more prepared, your fear will diminish (or, at least, start to feel like the irrational reaction that it really is).

And if that doesn't work, remember, it's just a test. In the grand scheme of problems (including hunger, disease, civil war, Viking invasion, and really deep splinters), this one ain't so bad.

Unfortunately, anxiety is not the *only* obstacle between you and a killer score. Even with a cool head, you might find that the ACT is long, fast-paced, and, at times, pretty tough. In the next chapter, we're going to look at some insanely effective strategies that will help us move through the test like Jason Statham's fist moves through anything that opposes Jason Statham.

*Or maybe you will, but this means that you've gone insane and need to go to the hospital.

# How to Be Smart

## Key Strategies for the ACT

"Accidentally" flash the many books in your backpack.

Meditatively scratch your chin.

Read while walking.

**D**id you know that every year the smartest people in the world get together in a Marriott hotel in Pittsburgh for a top-secret meeting? No, you did *not* know that.

At that top-secret meeting—which is attended by such luminaries as the physicist Stephen Hawking, chancellor of Germany Angela Merkel, and the team who invented, designed, and programmed the Kardashians—all the smart people talk about one thing: how to maintain the illusion of their "natural genius."

You see, the truth is that people who are thought of as "smart" are actually just being really *strategic* in how they think. They know that there are certain *ways of thinking* that are more effective, and they want to keep those ways a secret and hold on to their power. They close this meeting every year by cackling with glee and rubbing their hands together, muttering, "The rest of the world will *never* know." Then they head to the buffet for all-you-can-drink pineapple punch and all-you-can-sing karaoke.

Luckily, we have unearthed some of the secret strategies of "smart" people for taking on the ACT-bot. And it all starts with . . .

## Building Your Endurance

**O**f the many annoying qualities of the ACT, one of the most aggravating is that it is *really freaking long*. Even more irritating, the ACT-bot has decided that nap breaks are not allowed.

This means that you need to work on your endurance.

But how do you do that? Well, allow us to teach you the very old-fashioned way—by telling you one of the lesser-known fables of the ancient Greek teacher Aesop. It's called "The Arrogant Horse and the Butterfly."

One sunny day in the clover field, the Butterfly landed on the Horse's ear. "Hi, Horse," the Butterfly said. "I just came to say good-bye, because I'm migrating south to lay my eggs." "Gross," said the Horse, "but moving on—how far south are you going?" "One hundred million butterfly-miles," said the Butterfly. "I could never fly that far without practicing, so I'm training by flying back and forth over the clover field." "Pshaw," said the Horse, "I can run across this clover field in a nanosecond." Then he went back to munching clover. The next day, the Butterfly landed on the Horse's ear again. "Today, I'm training by flying back and forth over the hill." "Pshaw," said the Horse, "I could run up that hill in my sleep," then went back to nibbling clover. This continued for a month. The Butterfly practiced by flying increasingly long distances, until finally he told the Horse that it was time to leave. "I'll race you," said the arrogant Horse. They both took off. After half a butterfly-mile, the Horse exploded from exhaustion.

And that's why the ancient Greeks rode butterflies.

The lesson here is that you should treat taking the ACT like the butterfly treated flying south: by building toward your goal. Begin by taking one practice section (which, clocking in at between 35 and 60 minutes, is probably all you'll have time for on a school night), but pretty soon you will want to be sitting down for two sections (which you might have to do on a weekend morning, or on a night when you don't have a lot of homework). By the time you are comfortable with two sections in one sitting, you should block out time on a weekend morning to take a *whole test*, with one 10-minute break between the second and third sections. If you have the time, try ramping up over the next five weeks by following this schedule:

If you dive straight into a full-length practice test, then your most-likely-disappointing score will frustrate you. But when you start out by dominating a single English section, you'll feel like the king of the world and be eager to take on those next two sections.

—Jon

**WEEK ONE:** One practice section per day, three days a week.

**WEEK TWO:** On one of those days, try two sections.

**WEEK THREE:** Same deal, but on a weekend day, try three sections in one sitting. On the other two days, just do one section. We don't want you to die of exhaustion.

**WEEK FOUR:** Take the weekdays off (you should still read this book, obviously), but try to take a whole test (including the writing section) in one sitting on the weekend.

**WEEK FIVE AND EVERY WEEK AFTER:** Try alternating. One week, you can practice individual sections on weeknights. The next week, save up and take a whole test on the weekend. If you can stick to this schedule, taking the real test will feel like no big deal, because you've done it before.

## Speed

Even worse than the length of the ACT, however, is the speed. You have to move *fast*. We're not talking zooming-car fast, or even runaway-train fast; we're talking about cheetah-getting-shot-out-of-a-cannon-in-a-movie-that's-being-fast-forwarded fast.

Here's how it feels to take the ACT:

Proctor: "Hi there. Welcome. Okay, please make sure that your pencils are sharpened, your calculator has batteries, and that your phones are all on silent. Okay, then open your test and begin, aaand now close your test because it's over. Please hand in your test booklets and enjoy the rest of your day!"

As with endurance training, the best way to increase your speed is to take gradual steps. You can begin by taking a section with no time constraint at all. Start a timer, and see how long the section takes. If you finish with time left over, check your score. Was it perfect? If it was, *Jeezum Crow! Put this book down and go take the test for real!* But if you did not get a perfect score, then you should take that as a sign that you need to study a bit more and, more important, you probably need to take more time.

If, in the more likely scenario, it took you more time than is officially allotted to finish the section, then you know that, like every other student on earth, you need to work on tightening up your speed. Take another section, but this time do it with a timer next to you, and take only as much time as is allotted for the section. Keep your eye on the clock! As you approach the test date, you're going to want to shorten the time you are allowing yourself to take the section. If you practice with a few minutes *less* time than is allowed, then the real test will feel luxurious, which is a great place to be.

"BUT WAIT!!!" we hope you are screeching. "Your advice for endurance and speed totally sucks! Basically, you're just telling us to *go faster* and *endure more test*, but you're not telling us *how!*"

To which we respond: You're exactly right, screeching student. Which is why we are about to unveil the Grand Strategy, the Emperor of All Techniques, the High Holy Excalibur of Test Destruction. . . .

> If you're not a watch wearer, wear one (or have it on your desk) during practice tests in order to get used to checking one for the real thing.
>
> —Jon

## The Grand Strategy: Skipping and Coming Back

Skipping and coming back? That's it? Kind of underwhelming, right?

We know, it sounds simple, and it *is* simple. But if you can learn to naturally skip and come back when you encounter a difficult problem, it will make a world of difference for your performance on the ACT.

Here's how it works: If you've wrestled with a problem for a few seconds, and you do not yet know how to answer it, skip it. Circle the number of the problem to mark it, tackle two more, then come back and try again.

This basic trick works miracles for two reasons: First, the brain is hardwired to skip and come back. And second, skipping and coming back saves time and frustration. Here's what we mean. . . .

### THE BRAIN IS BUILT TO SKIP AND COME BACK.

Our brains are very efficient machines. When you read, say, a math problem, the first thing your brain does is translate the words into a concept or picture of the problem.

> At a store, dresses usually cost $33.50 each. For their Thanksgiving sale, the store announces that if someone buys 10 dresses, the price of each subsequent dress will be 15 percent off the regular price. If you buy 14 dresses, how much less is the average price per dress than it would be if you were to buy 14 dresses without the sale?

Each word affects the picture: We imagine the 10 dresses, we add four more, though we don't yet know the price of the next four. We know we are going to have to find out the average price of 14 dresses, and the complication is that the last four are getting cheaper. Then we are going to have to compare this average to the regular average price.

Once your brain has created this scenario, it is faced with a number of vague options. It probably does something like this: "Um, we could multiply 14 by the price, and then divide by some number (maybe 15?), or we could multiply the price by 14 and then *subtract* 15 percent of the regular price? And then we have to . . . um . . . do more math stuff?"

Now let's imagine that after going through all of this work (creating the scenario in our brain and running through some initial, hazy strategies), we do not yet have an answer. Our natural inclination would be to *reread* the problem and try again, right?

But here's the thing: The brain is very good at quickly painting the picture of a problem, but it is *very bad* at changing this picture

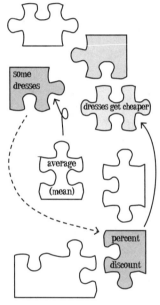

*Our brain's first picture of the problem*

A potential bonus:
If you skip a question,
you may come across
a slightly easier similar
question later in the
section that reminds
you how to do the
one you skipped.

—Jon

once it's created. In other words, it is nearly impossible to go back and wipe the slate of your mind clean of all the work it has done. Even if you try, there will be lingering shadows of your first read, and they will interfere with any attempts to "start over."

So you need to skip and come back. Do two more problems, and then come back and start from the top. Why two problems? Why not one or three? This is because your mind, after it has read a problem, wrestled for a bit, and then moved on, is actually *still processing* information even after you've left. Imagine that your brain has a front office and a back office. After you skip, the skipped problem is moved to the back office, where there is still work going on, even if you are not aware of it.

When you come back to the problem, you will be able to start fresh *and* you will still remember the problem. When you reread the problem, you will already know its elements, and your brain will work something like this:

"Okay, I remember that this problem involves averages, percents, and comparing two different averages. Let's take this step-by-step. What is the average of 14 dresses with no sale to worry about? Well, the price isn't changing, so the average price is $33.50. Now let's find that sale price: The first 10 dresses are at the normal price ($33.50 · 10), which equals $335.00. Here's the hard part: The next four dresses are each going to be 15 percent off that original price. (Take a deep breath; this is going to be a pain in the tush.) Fifteen percent of $33.50 (.15 × $33.50) is roughly $5.03. So the sale price ($33.50 − $5.03) is $28.47. Multiply that by 4 to get $113.88, and add it to our initial 10 dresses ($335.00 + $113.88) to get $448.88. Finally (finally! Almost done!), we get the new average by dividing that total cost by the number of items ($448.88 ÷ 14) to get roughly $32.06. How much lower is our average? $33.50 − $32.06 = $1.44!!!! DONE!"

*Brain's second (or third, or fourth) picture*

### What Do Tutors Do?

Plain and simple: We make our students do a ton of practice test sections. Sometimes it can be very hard to motivate yourself to do *yet another* section, and it's helpful to know that someone is going to shake his or her head in disappointment if you don't.

When we get close to test time, we often have students take a full-length practice test *every weekend,* to build up their endurance for the real thing. This is also useful because it ensures that the student won't be surprised by anything on test day.

Most important, we hold our students' feet to the fire to make sure they're learning and not just reinforcing bad habits. It's one thing to read and appreciate all of the great tips in this book. The real task is to actually do them.

Because you remember the elements of the problem, your second attempt is much more focused. You spend less time figuring out the words and more time thinking about the problem. And if you don't get it right on the second try, skip and come back again! What if you skip a problem, tackle the next, and have trouble with that one as well? Skip it, too! The point here is to wrestle with, not necessarily answer, two problems before you come back.

As you skip and come back to a problem, you might find that, even if you cannot answer the problem, you can eliminate some of the answer choices. Cross them out. We're going to talk about the process of elimination in a second, but for now we can tell you that discarding answer choices is always an advantage. It means you don't have to bother considering them when you come back. And once you've skipped and come back a couple times, and you are confident that you are not going to solve the problem, it is time to guess (which we are also going to cover in a moment).

## SKIPPING AND COMING BACK SAVES TIME AND FRUSTRATION.

Remember, the worst thing about the ACT is that it is *long* and it is *fast*. While skipping and coming back might at first seem like it *takes* time, in fact, it is going to *save* you a ton of time by not allowing you to dwell too long on any one particular problem. This is a gigantic advantage.

Students waste a lot of time staring at a difficult problem, as if staring were the same as thinking. (This is just like "working," which we discussed on page 33.) You might only do this for five extra seconds on one problem, then 10 extra seconds on another, but these "work" sessions add up. When you are consistently skipping and coming back, you will eliminate "work" sessions by moving on after you've wrestled with a problem for five seconds.

The other terrible thing about "work" sessions is that they *increase your frustration*, which negatively affects your endurance. You might not notice it at the time, but when you stare at a tough problem, your Frustrate-o-Meter (which is located

somewhere above your liver) is moving from "middling" to "high." Even if you *do* eventually solve the problem, you've still made yourself more frustrated. This frustration carries into the next problem, where it will interfere with your thinking, thus making you even more frustrated. Many, many smart kids burn themselves out by allowing their frustration levels to get out of hand.

But when you skip and come back, you recognize that a problem is tough *and you leave it*. You don't give the problem enough time to frustrate you with its difficulty. You move along, solve some problems, then come back and either solve the difficult question or skip again and come back later.

If you've ever tried boxing or taken a boxing lesson, you've probably been told to "stay light on your toes," and that "footwork is more important than punching." The idea here is to stay in constant movement, giving your opponents very few opportunities to land a punch. In the same way, skipping and coming back is like staying light on your toes during a test. You are in constant motion, never stopping long enough to let a problem drain your time or contribute to your frustration.*

**A heads-up:** We consider skipping and coming back so important that we are going to talk about it in some of the test-section chapters as well. By the time you are done with this book, you will have a PhD in Skipping and Coming Back, and it will make you a much better test taker.

* Or punch you in the face, depending on the kind of test.

—Jon

## Guessing and Eliminating Wrong Answer Choices

What if you've skipped and come back to a problem a couple of times, and you simply aren't getting it? Well, remember how we said that wrong answers don't lower your score? This means that you should put down a guess. Correction: It means that you *must guess*. There is no downside to guessing, so you only stand to gain.

But there is stupid guessing and intelligent guessing. Stupid guessing is choosing answer choice B because you like Banana Bread and Bears. Intelligent guessing is choosing answer choice B because both C and D are clearly wrong. In other words, you should guess after eliminating clearly wrong answers. Take a look at the following fairly simple problem.

The South Bronx in New York is the birthplace of East Coast hip-hop. In 2011, it produced 60,000 pounds of East Coast hip-hop. If the neighborhood produced 110,000 pounds of East Coast hip-hop in 2012, by roughly what percent did the weight of the South Bronx's East Coast hip-hop increase from 2011 to 2012?

A. 65%
B. 85%
C. 125%
D. 145%
E. 160%

Now, let's say you forget how to deal with percentages mathematically. You skip and come back twice, and nothing's happening. What do you do? Well, take a look at your answer choices. C, D, and E are all above 100 percent. A 100 percent increase would take us from 60,000 to 120,000, which is too high, so we can eliminate C, D, and E. Now, we can guess between A and B and have a 50 percent chance (instead of our original 20 percent chance) of picking the right answer!

You can combine the process of elimination with skipping and coming back to become a truly strategic test taker. On the first pass of a monster problem, try to eliminate *one answer choice*, thereby lopping off one of the monster's mucousy appendages. Skip, do two more problems, come back, and if the problem still isn't crystal clear, see if you can eliminate another answer choice. Now the monster should have only a slimy, limbless torso and a grotesque head full of needlelike teeth. If, on another pass, you can chop away the head and/or zero in on the answer, then that's great. If not, you have now read the problem *three times* and can take a very smart guess.

In other words, you are missing out on a huge advantage if you are only looking for right answers. Strategic thinkers read through a problem and, if it presents *any challenge at all*, they start to carve off obviously wrong answer choices. *Then they leave, rather than waste time and frustrate themselves.* They slay a couple more problems—or perhaps simply chop off a few more limbs—and then come back, either for a killing blow or to make a strategic guess.

A helpful analogy: A she-Viking named Vultra and her idiot cousin Bolti are surrounded by zombies. Vultra whirls back and forth from zombie to zombie, making precise, focused chops, rendering each zombie less and less of a threat, until she has massacred them all. Meanwhile, Bolti is taking gigantic swinging hacks at one zombie, getting his sword stuck, pulling it out, and taking another hack. All the while, five more zombies close in behind him, their gory mouths open, their rotten tongues writhing in anticipation.

Sorry, got a little carried away with our fantastic analogy. The point is, you'd rather be Vultra than Bolti. Now, let's recap the last two chapters.

> This is especially important on the Reading Test, where a tough question might not have an obviously correct answer, but rather an answer that's slightly better than the rest.
> —Jon

## In Summary

In the last chapter, we talked about the various forms of pre-test stress (ostriching, working, bouncing, thinking you're stupid) and recommended you fight them by creating a schedule and practicing staying focused on the present moment in your study sessions.

In this chapter, we've talked about building up your endurance and speed by using the most important strategies of all: skipping and coming back, and guessing intelligently by eliminating wrong answers. If you can handle all of these strategies, then you are going to see real improvements in your ACT score.

So that's it, right? You can shut the book and go play *Frolicking Through the Fields on a Warm Summer's Day* for the PS3? Totally! Nice meeting you!

Oh, wait—there is one more little thing. You have to review a ton of stuff, like grammar rules and scientific reasoning and reading and essay writing and math. Now, you are most likely familiar with a lot of this material, but some of it might be new. So go grab a glass of lemonade (or Lem-N-Ade Flavored Beverage), and let's begin with the first section: the English Test.

# CHAPTER 4

# The English Test

## Like That Annoying Uncle Who Corrects Everything You Say

## The Nutz and Boltz of Proper English

The English Test, you might remember, is the first course of the ACT-bot's nightmare meal. This section is like the uncle at the family reunion who interrupts your hilarious story to correct your grammar. Don't you just *adore* that uncle? Well, this section is like that uncle, multiplied by 75.

At first glance, the English section looks like a reading test. It consists of five passages, ranging in subject matter from *The Four Merry Fops of Bathton Manor* and *An Addendum to the Disquisition on the Migratory Habits of the Yellow-Throated Finch* to *Why Are Rocks Rocks?* and *My Mom's Most Bestest Cake.* In other words, these passages can be about anything, and there is a healthy chance that they will be boring. What makes the English section different from the Reading section is that instead of focusing on comprehension, it emphasizes grammar, punctuation, and organization. Portions of each passage are underlined, and the ACT-bot provides a number of answer choices as possible corrections for the underlined segment.* Here's an example:

> \* Stuff that's not underlined is assumed to be correct, even if it includes the most awkward wording ever.
> —Ava

Before the next <u>raid; Bartholomew</u> the Viking had to practice his pillaging.

A. NO CHANGE
B. raid, Bartholomew
C. raid because Bartholomew
D. raid is the time when Bartholomew

(The answer is B, by the way.)

The section has a whopping 75 questions: 40 mechanics questions and 35 questions about rhetorical skills, in no particular order. The mechanics questions test the nuts and bolts of writing: They might ask you whether a sentence requires a comma rather than a period or a semicolon, or whether the subject of a sentence agrees with the verb. The rhetorical skills questions, on the other hand, look at the big picture: the organization of a paragraph or passage, the transitions between sentences and paragraphs, and the main idea of the passage as a whole. A rhetorical skills question might ask you whether a particular sentence is necessary within the passage or if it can be taken out altogether.

Rhetorical skills questions are tricky for me because each sentence influences the way I read a passage, so asking me whether or not a sentence is unnecessary can rattle my feel for what the passage is about.

—Ava

*I, too, was once a Grammar Hound. Have no fear. We will reform you.

—Jon

Regardless of which type of question you prefer, you have to answer all of them, and there are better and worse ways to move through the section. The worse way is to be what we here at *Up Your Score* call a Grammar Hound. A Grammar Hound focuses *only* on errors; it speed-reads through the passages, stopping at the underlined portion and plugging in each answer choice until it finds one that it likes.* Don't do this.

The better way to move through the section is to read through the passage as if it were a regular piece of writing. Instead of breaking down each sentence into subjects, verbs, etc., just pay attention to what the passage is saying. When you see an underlined portion, correct the mistake on your own *before* looking at the answer choices. The reason to do this is to have your own idea of the correct answer. Think about it: The ACT-bot has created a whole bunch of tempting corrections. If you know what you're looking for, you won't be tempted by other answer choices. It's like shopping. If you don't have a list, then you're going to grab an armful of Double Stuf Oreos and a box of Mountain Dew Code Red, because those things *look* delicious. Then you're going to get home and realize you forgot the eggs and flour.

And why should you pay attention to the substance of what you're reading? Because many of the rhetorical skills questions require that you understand the content of the passage. How are you going to answer a question about the main idea of the passage, for example, if you've been paying attention only to whether each subject agrees with each verb?

Oh, and another thing. You'll notice that most of the grammar questions provide you with a NO CHANGE option. You're going to be nervous about picking NO CHANGE, because there must be *some* mistake, right? I mean, the ACT-bot wouldn't just underline something that's *correct*. Right? RIGHT?!?!

The ACT-bot designed the NO CHANGE answer choice as a form of mental torture to make you doubt yourself. But here's the thing: NO CHANGE is often the correct answer! Some ACT gurus claim that up to a quarter of the grammar questions do not require a correction. So don't feel too nervous about picking NO CHANGE, if none of the other answer choices seems better.

Here's a bonus pro tip: If you're not sure about the error being tested in an underlined section, scan the answer choices for clues. If some of the answer choices contain plural verbs, for example, while others contain singular verbs, that's a good hint that the ACT-bot is testing subject-verb agreement.

Finally, use the most important strategy of all: skipping and coming back. If you are wrestling with a difficult problem, you must skip the question, tackle two more problems, and then come back to the question. There are a few reasons why skipping and coming back will save your life in the English section. For one, the English section is *long* and requires you to work *fast*. You cannot afford to grumble and groan and chew your cuticles while you rack your brain for an answer. That wasted time might keep you from seeing five easy problems at the end of the section. But much more important than maintaining momentum is the fact that *staring at a difficult problem doesn't help, like, at all.* When you first read an underlined portion of an English passage, your brain will go, "Okay, here's a mistake; here's how I would fix it." If you're right, then great—you pick the answer and move on. But if you're wrong, then it's *really* hard to go back and try again. Your brain has already made its decision, and there is no reset button on your brain. As we explained in the Strategy chapter, you should leave the problem and work on two more, then when you come back you can take a fresh look at the problem and give your brain a fresh chance.

Finally, *finally*, a crucial overall strategy for conquering the English section is to read a lot of quality writing. We can (and will) go over all of the rules that will be tested on the English section, but if you read good writing (this does *not* include text messages, tweets,* retweets, blog posts, or bathroom stall graffiti**), then

* I believe it was Shakespeare who wrote: Lolz @ Romeo's relationship status: more than complicated, bruh. #playwrightproblems.
　　　　—Jon

** Unless you're using Jane Austen's bathroom stall.
　　　　—Ava

all of the rules will become second nature. Think of this reading as ear training—the process of developing a sense of what sounds like a proper English gentleman and what sounds like a third-rate Russian spy trying to pass himself off as a proper English gentleman. (For more on this see page 85.)

In this chapter, we're going to teach you the grammar rules for the mechanics questions (six punctuation rules, four grammar and usage rules, and five sentence structure rules) and for the rhetorical skills questions (five rules in all). That is a total of 20 rules. We know what you're thinking: *20 rules? That's, like, a billion rules!!!* We totally get that, but rest assured that you most likely already know many of them. Our goal in this chapter is to *remind* you how the rules work, and then to show you how the ACT-bot tests each of them. So let's begin . . . right . . . NOW!!!

## Six Punctuation Rules

The mechanics questions can be broken down into three categories: punctuation, grammar and usage, and sentence structure. Let's start with punctuation.

### 1. COMMA: THE GREAT SEPARATOR

The ACT-bot loves commas as much as we love salted caramel cupcakes, and we flippin' *love* salted caramel cupcakes. Seriously, almost half of the punctuation questions are comma questions, so let's really lock this down.

**You already know how commas work: They insert pauses to make the sentence sound right.** Read this sentence:

> My mother who is a tremendous chef first introduced me to salted caramel cupcakes which were popularized by the film *Saline Satisfaction* and I have maintained a solid three-cupcake-per-day diet ever since.

## The Great Serial Comma Debate

For years, grammar scholars have argued over whether we should use the serial comma ("salt, potatoes, and fish") or not ("salt, potatoes and fish"). This culminated in a long and brutal war that cost us the lives of many of our best and brightest grammarians but yielded no clear winner. Regardless, the ACT-bot uses the serial comma.

Speaking of food, blueberries are the best snack for late-night studying. They're small, tangy, and come in large handfuls.

—Ava

Sounds like a Chihuahua on speed, right? That's because it doesn't have commas telling us where to pause. Let's fix it with commas:

> My mother, who is a tremendous chef, first introduced me to salted caramel cupcakes, which were popularized by the film *Saline Satisfaction,* and I have maintained a solid three-cupcake-per-day diet ever since.

Now read this sentence:

> Yesterday, my cardiologist, told me, that I had, the least healthy heart, he had ever seen.

Sounds like a Doberman with the hiccups, right? That's because it has too many commas telling us where to pause. Let's fix it by removing some commas:

> Yesterday, my cardiologist told me that I had the least healthy heart he had ever seen.

There's one more comma rule that you already know:

**Commas set off three or more items in a list.**

> Insulted, I explained to my cardiologist that I had limited my consumption to one cupcake, one more cupcake, and one last cupcake per day.

Those three cupcakes are separated by commas because that's the rule.

To become comma experts, let's take a look under the hood to get a sense of *how* commas work.

## Commas separate asides.

**An *aside* is a clause that is related, but not essential, to the sentence.**

**WRONG:** My cardiologist who holds a degree in medicine from Cornell had never heard of the Three-Cupcake Diet.

**RIGHT:** My cardiologist, who holds a degree in medicine from Cornell, had never heard of the Three-Cupcake Diet.

**Term Talk**

Fancy-pants grammarians call asides "nonrestrictive clauses." This will not be tested, but if you want to sound like you wear fancy pants, go ahead and say "nonrestrictive clauses."

If we take the clause "who holds a degree in medicine from Cornell" out of the sentence, will it still make sense? Yes. That means the clause is an aside, so we set it off from the rest of the sentence with commas.

Let's practice inserting commas into the following sentences in order to set off an aside:

1. These dogs all of which are cutie-wootie little sweet potatoes are rabid and dangerous.
   *These dogs, all of which are cutie-wootie little sweet potatoes, are rabid and dangerous.*

2. Much to his wife's displeasure Mary's dad built a homemade shower right next to the bed.
   *Much to his wife's displeasure, Mary's dad built a homemade shower right next to the bed.*

3. Scott whose ideas are unbearably lame proposed that we go to the state fair and make tie-dyed T-shirts to give to our parents.
   *Scott, whose ideas are unbearably lame, proposed that we go to the state fair and make tie-dyed T-shirts to give to our parents.*

Make sense? Try this one:

4. People who are easily nauseated should not try my new curry.

Did you put commas around "who are easily nauseated"? You shouldn't have. If you take that phrase out, the sentence says that *all* people should not try the new curry, which is not what it's saying. That phrase is *necessary*, so the sentence is correct as is.

Here's another example:

5. Children with tall parents often have sore necks from looking up so often.

"With tall parents" is *not* an aside. It is essential to the meaning of the sentence. Don't add any commas!

## Commas separate independent clauses that begin with conjunctions like "and, but, so."

We call a clause *independent* when it can drive a car and see R-rated movies. In other words: **A clause is independent if it can be read on its own.** An independent clause has a subject and a verb and doesn't require any more information to make sense. "I bought a cupcake" is an independent clause. It can go wherever it wants, unaccompanied. "Because I was hungry" is not independent. It needs more info. If that clause went to a party, everybody would be like, "You don't make sense being on your own. Go home to your mama."

This is a wiggly rule in real life, but on the ACT, if we have two independent, grown-up clauses joined by a conjunction (a word like *and, but,* or *so*), we need to separate them with a comma.

**WRONG:** I went back to the cupcake store and I told the baker that lamentably I would no longer be his best customer.

**RIGHT:** I went back to the cupcake store, and I told the baker that lamentably I would no longer be his best customer.

Both clauses in that sentence are independent. They both drive Ford Fusions to *Gore Battalion 6: Back to the Slaughterhouse.* Even though the sentence totally makes sense without it, the ACT-bot wants you to throw in a comma after that conjunction.

Here's how the ACT-bot will test that rule:

**ERROR: Two indie clauses with a comma but no conjunction.**

**WRONG:** The baker cried on my shoulder, he told me to be strong.

**RIGHT:** The baker cried on my shoulder, and he told me to be strong.

GOOD-BYE FOREVER.

Both clauses are independent, so we need the conjunction *and* after that comma. Let's look at another example:

**WRONG:** I didn't want to cry, I broke down and told him that he would always be baking cupcakes in my heart.

**RIGHT:** I didn't want to cry, but I broke down and told him that he would always be baking cupcakes in my heart.

We need the conjunction *but* after that comma!

### Commas link independent clauses and dependent clauses and phrases.

Independent clause: "I had to find a new favorite food." That clause is understood on its own. It will make friends and live a happy life.

Dependent phrase: "Something as delicious as salted caramel cupcakes." That phrase makes no sense on its own. It will wander the earth, misunderstood, unappreciated, alone.

But don't cry for the dependent phrase, because we can attach it to the independent clause! "I had to find a new favorite food, something as delicious as salted caramel cupcakes." The trick here is to **use a comma to link independent clauses and dependent phrases.** Try it out:

**WRONG:** Much to my chagrin.

**RIGHT:** Much to my chagrin, the bakery was no longer an option.

The dependent phrase "Much to my chagrin" is linked to the independent clause "the bakery was no longer an option" with a comma.

Simple? "Not so simple," says the ACT-bot in a bone-chilling monotone. It has three devious schemes to throw you off.

### Devious Scheme I: No comma

**WRONG:** Hoping that I would find the perfect snack I went to the health food store.

**RIGHT:** Hoping that I would find the perfect snack, I went to the health food store.

---

## What's with All the Phrases and Clauses?

You might have noticed that we keep switching back and forth between the words "clause" and "phrase." Have we gone insane? Not this time. There is a difference between a clause and a phrase: A *clause* contains a subject and a verb, while a *phrase* does not. Do you need to know this for the test? Absolutely not. So you can go ahead and delete this fact from your brain now.

We need a comma after *snack* to link the first, dependent clause to the second, independent clause.

### Devious Scheme 2: Semicolon instead of comma

**WRONG:** After looking around for an hour; I decided that the health food store was the worst place in the world.

**RIGHT:** After looking around for an hour, I decided that the health food store was the worst place in the world.

We are going to talk about the semicolon later; all you need to know now is that this sentence needs a comma to connect those dependent and independent clauses.

### Devious Scheme 3: Ridiculous conjunction

**WRONG:**
Overwhelmed with despair, and I sat in the granola aisle and wept.

**RIGHT:**
Overwhelmed with despair, I sat in the granola aisle and wept.

Get that ridiculous *and* out of there, please.

It is much more difficult to identify these errors by how they sound. You just have to pay close attention to punctuation to get these right. Yay.
—Jon

### A Couple More Random Comma Rules

You might know these rules just from having seen them a million times. But they are tested, so let's include them.

**Dates use commas.** I've been eating cupcakes every day since December 5, 1994.

Put the comma after the numbered day and before the year.

**Numbers use commas.** I've eaten well over 45,302 cupcakes in my life.

Put the comma after each third digit, from right to left.

**Quotes sometimes end in commas.** "Any new snack is bound to be a disappointment," I said to myself.

This rule is true only when the quote is followed by "so-and-so said."

Finally, a subtle rule that might be on the test once, if at all: **Multiple adjectives defining one noun use commas, *if you can say "and" between them.***

**WRONG:** The scrumptious supersweet cupcake is beyond divine.

**RIGHT:** The scrumptious, supersweet cupcake is beyond divine.

The scrumptious *and* supersweet cupcake makes sense, so use a comma.

**WRONG:** The expensive, kale chips are less divine.

**RIGHT:** The expensive kale chips are less divine.

The expensive *and* kale chips does not make sense, so don't use a comma.

As we said, the ACT-bot is programmed to test comma usage like crazy, so let's practice with some ACT-style comma questions:

*"Divine" and "kale chips" don't belong in the same sentence.*

*—Ava*

The career path of Selena Gomez, is far
<u>                                    </u>
                1
more interesting and complex than her fans

might initially suspect. Though she was

only a toddler in the 1990s; so Selena was
<u>                                         </u>
                2
involved in the burgeoning L.A. rap scene.

1. **A.** NO CHANGE
   **B.** Selena Gomez; is
   **C.** Selena Gomez, might be
   **D.** Selena Gomez is

2. **A.** NO CHANGE
   **B.** toddler in the 1990s when she
   **C.** toddler in the 1990s, Selena
   **D.** toddler in the 1990s. Selena

Anyone who can remember Warren G's
3
seminal *Regulate . . . G Funk Era* might be
3
surprised to learn that the drum machine
3
was operated by a then-two-year-old

Selena! At age six, Gomez developed an

interest in becoming a mime, a type of

performer who makes no sound during his

or her performance, and moved to France
4
where the art form was born.
4

**3. A.** NO CHANGE
**B.** Anyone, who can remember Warren G's seminal *Regulate . . . G Funk Era* might be surprised
**C.** Anyone, who can remember Warren G's seminal *Regulate . . . G Funk Era* might be surprised,
**D.** Anyone can remember Warren G's seminal *Regulate . . . G Funk Era* and would be surprised

**4. A.** NO CHANGE
**B.** moved to France, where the art form was born.
**C.** moved to France. The art form was born there.
**D.** because the art form was born in France, moved there.

**Answers: 1.** D; **2.** C; **3.** A; **4.** B

✳ Don't get too excited! We don't mean the end of the English section. Just the end of some hypothetical sentence. Sorry.

—Zack

## 2. THE PERIOD: YOU'VE REACHED THE END, MY FRIEND ✳

This rule is super straightforward: **A period goes at the end of the sentence.** If there is no period at the end of the sentence, then *put a period there!*

For example:

**WRONG:** My annoying mom is always telling me to relax and enjoy life

**RIGHT:** My annoying mom is always telling me to relax and enjoy life.

P.A.P.T. (Put a period there!)

Here's a harder example:

**WRONG:** There is something wrong with Mojo he is not eating his kale chips.

**Right:** There is something wrong with Mojo. He is not eating his kale chips.

This is just like a comma problem. There are two independent clauses with no conjunction word (and, as, so), so after "Mojo" you should P.A.P.T.

Get it? Got it? Good. Moving on.

## 3. THE SEMICOLON: THE NOT-SO-GREAT SEPARATOR

Here's what your teacher told you about the semicolon: "The semicolon is stronger than a comma but weaker than a period." Here's what you said: "That's vague and not really a rule. Where did you learn how to teach?"

Well, *we* all learned how to teach at very reputable teaching schools, and we're going to be specific. Ready?

**A semicolon connects two independent clauses when they do *not* have a conjunction word (and, but, so).**

**Wrong:** The gorilla clearly hates me, he just threw a log at me and bellowed in English, "You are a contemptible villain!"

**Right:** The gorilla clearly hates me; he just threw a log at me and bellowed in English, "You are a contemptible villain!"

The two clauses are independent. They could both hang out on their own. They do not have a conjunction word in between them. So . . . semicolon! Let's look at another:

**Wrong:** The bouquet of bananas did the trick, the gorilla and I are now inseparable pals.

**Right:** The bouquet of bananas did the trick; the gorilla and I are now inseparable pals.

Two independent clauses, no conjunction. "But wait," you say. "We could use a period in both of those examples." That is completely correct. **On the ACT, periods and semicolons are interchangeable.** The *actual* rule is that semicolons should be used when the two clauses are *closely connected*. But the ACT will *not* test that rule, because that rule is vague. It will never give you both a semicolon and a period as answer choice options.

But the ACT-bot *will* test semicolons. How? With devious schemes, duh.

### Devious Scheme 1: Two indie clauses with no conjunction connected with a comma

**WRONG:** Grandma doesn't know how to work the remote, she keeps telling it to "make the TV funnier."

**RIGHT:** Grandma doesn't know how to work the remote; she keeps telling it to "make the TV funnier."

Are the two clauses independent? Yes. Do they have a conjunction word in between them? No. So . . . it should be a semicolon (or a period).

### Devious Scheme 2: Two indie clauses with a conjunction connected with a semicolon

**WRONG:** Teenagers have no respect; so I will teach them a course called "Respecting Your Elders 101."

**RIGHT:** Teenagers have no respect, so I will teach them a course called "Respecting Your Elders 101."

Are the two clauses independent? Yes. Do they have a conjunction word in between them? Yes ("so"). There should be a comma.

### Devious Scheme 3: An indie clause and a dependent phrase connected with a semicolon

**WRONG:** Spartacus challenged the aristocracy of Rome; a group notorious for offing upstarts.

**RIGHT:** Spartacus challenged the aristocracy of Rome, a group notorious for offing upstarts.

The phrase "a group notorious for offing upstarts" is dependent. So the sentence needs a comma.

There is one more use of semicolons that *probably* won't be tested: When it separates a list of three or more items when those items themselves contain commas.

An example:

**WRONG:** Kwame's favorite authors are Dr. Szizlak, a hilarious neuroscientist, Maise Timm, who, at age nine, won the National Book Award for *Creepy Things That Might Be, and Probably Are, in My Closet,* and action star Brock Hardgroove, whose autobiography *Brock Doesn't Care If You Read This* has recently become a bestseller.

**RIGHT:** Kwame's favorite authors are Dr. Szizlak, a hilarious neuroscientist; Maise Timm, who, at age nine, won the National Book Award for *Creepy Things That Might Be, and Probably Are, in My Closet;* and action star Brock Hardgroove, whose autobiography *Brock Doesn't Care If You Read This* has recently become a bestseller.

The first sentence had a million commas and got loopy and confusing. We need to separate each distinct element in the list with semicolons, and use commas only within each element of the list.

Got it? Excellent. Let's continue.

## 4. THE COLON: GET PUMPED FOR SOME MORE INFORMATION!

**The colon comes after an independent clause and introduces a list, an explanation, or an explanatory quotation.**

Here's a **list:**

> Bethany is a fan of all things Swiss: Swiss cheese, Swiss Family Robinson, and Swiss Miss Hot Chocolate with extra marshmallows.

Here's an **explanation:**

> Bethany loves these things for one reason: She likes to hiss the word *Swiss.*

Here's an **explanatory quote:**

> She lives by the mantra: "If it doesn't have the word *Swiss* in it, then you shouldn't be hissing it."

The ACT-bot will test this rule with the following Robo-Tricks:

Eat plenty of fiber to maintain a healthy colon.

—Jon

### Robo-Trick 1: Introduce a list with a comma.

**WRONG:** Grimnock the Ogre demands the following foods, goats, oxen, and unsuspecting children.

**RIGHT:** Grimnock the Ogre demands the following foods: goats, oxen, and unsuspecting children.

Should that be a comma after "foods"? Heck no! It introduces a list, so put a colon there.

### Robo-Trick 2: Introduce an explanatory quote with a comma.

**WRONG:** The unsuspecting child had one thing to say when he saw Grimnock, "Oh, how I wish I had been more suspecting!"

**RIGHT:** The unsuspecting child had one thing to say when he saw Grimnock: "Oh, how I wish I had been more suspecting!"

The quote explains the previous phrase, so there should be a colon after "Grimnock."

### Robo-Trick 3: Use a colon after a dependent phrase.

This is the trickiest colon problem. It will probably appear only once:

**WRONG:** Luckily: Grimnock had already eaten and was more in the mood for a game of Monopoly than a brunch of roast child.

**RIGHT:** Luckily, Grimnock had already eaten and was more in the mood for a game of Monopoly than a brunch of roast child.

The phrase before the colon ("Luckily") is **not independent.** That colon should be a comma.

**Hey, guess what!** You've gotten through most of the punctuation rules, you champion of all grammar! Take a break, and do one of the following restful activities:

+ If it is nighttime, gaze up at the stars until you are filled with a sense of wonder at the majesty of the heavens. If it is daytime, gaze up at the sun until your eyes burst into flames. *

* Disclaimer: We don't actually recommend that you let your eyes burst into flames until <u>after</u> the exam.

—Ava

ONWARD! TO COLLEGE!

+ Go to a museum and stare at a painting until you are more cultured.
+ Take a power nap. Power napping is sleeping while you run on a treadmill and lift weights and guzzle wheatgrass juice.
+ Visualize yourself being done with the ACT, a perfect score in your pocket and a college acceptance letter in your hand. Also, you're riding Pegasus. Flying out of a volcano!

And we're back.

## 5. THE APOSTROPHE: SAVING THE WORLD, ONE CONTRACTION AT A TIME

We use apostrophes for two reasons: **to indicate possession and to contract two words into one word.** Let's start by looking at the four ways we use the apostrophe for possession:

1. For singular nouns that do not end in s, just add **'s**.
   **Mom's** car is bigger, but **Dad's** car has flaming skull decals.
2. For singular nouns ending in s, add **'s**.
   **Tess's** car is the sickest, because she had hers painted with glow-in-the-dark paint.
3. For plural nouns ending in s, add **'**.
   Her **parents'** car is a monster truck, so it's easy to see where she gets her kick-butt-itude.
4. For plural nouns with no s, add **'s**.
   Her **children's** toy cars are also very cool: They turn into robots and fire foam missiles.

For contractions, apostrophes usually replace the omitted letters. Let's contract the following phrases:

**You are** the best. — **You're** the best.
**Do not** deny it. — **Don't** deny it.
**They are** not nearly as cool as you. — **They're** not nearly as cool as you.
**Know what I am saying?** — **Kn'ms'in'?**

*Just adding an apostrophe on a singular noun won't cut it, even if it looks right because it ends with "s." If you don't immediately spot the error in the question, you may be able to see it (or its correction) more easily in the answer choices.*

—Jon

*So true. And remember, the ACT-bot loves to combine possession and singular-plural problems.*

—Ava

That last one was a bit too contracted, but you get the point.

Anyway ... Here are some of the more difficult contractions that the ACT-bot will definitely test you on, because, c'mon, it's not called the ACT-friend, now is it?

### Difficult Contraction 1: Its vs. It's

RIGHT: **It's** difficult to negotiate with ravenous bears.

"It's" is a contraction of *it is*.

RIGHT: This is because an on-the-ball bear takes pains to teach **its** cubs to eat all humans, always.

"Its" is the possessive form of *it*.

### Difficult Contraction 2: Their vs. They're

RIGHT: So when it comes to bears, don't try to appeal to **their** sense of reason.

"Their" is the possessive form of *they*.

RIGHT: **They're** just going to listen politely, and then gobble you up.

"They're" is a contraction for *they are*.

### 6. DASHES AND PARENTHESES

Ds and Ps are rarely tested, but it can happen. Read this section only if you want to be a true master of the English section.

**Dashes and parentheses both separate information that is even less relevant than an aside** (which, you'll remember, is separated by a comma). Often, the separated information will be an interesting but unnecessary explanation or an interesting but unnecessary detail. For example:

LESS RIGHT: Chester A. Arthur, America's best-smelling president, was an ardent supporter of civil service reform.

MORE RIGHT: Chester A. Arthur (America's best-smelling president) was an ardent supporter of civil service reform.

That explanatory aside was almost entirely unnecessary, but it still told us more information about Chester A. Arthur.

I remember that the possessive "its" doesn't have an apostrophe by comparing it with other possessive pronouns, like "his" (not "his's") and "hers" (not "hers's").

—Jon

*This means that if both dashed and parenthetical choices are offered, something else must be wrong.

—Ava

**Less Right:** Chester A. Arthur, my dad likes to call him "Ol' Potpourri," because he could make an outhouse smell like a perfume shop, lived in Kansas for three months, but he didn't like it.

**More Right:** Chester A. Arthur—my dad likes to call him "Ol' Potpourri," because he could make an outhouse smell like a perfume shop—lived in Kansas for three months, but he didn't like it.

**Also More Right:** Chester A. Arthur (my dad likes to call him "Ol' Potpourri," because he could make an outhouse smell like a perfume shop) lived in Kansas for three months, but he didn't like it.

Again, the aside is certainly not necessary to the rest of the sentence, so we should separate it with dashes or parentheses.

The ACT-bot does not test the difference between dashes and parentheses.*Instead, it uses two Cyber-Treacheries.

## Cyber-Treachery 1: Using parentheses or a dash in a sentence that needs a comma

**Wrong:** (After finishing almost all of the pie) Grant's grandmother insisted that she did not much care for pie.

**Right:** After finishing almost all of the pie, Grant's grandmother insisted that she did not much care for pie.

The clause inside the parentheses is essential to the sentence. It should be separated by a comma, not parentheses.

## Cyber-Treachery 2: A comma in a sentence that would be better with a dash or parentheses

**Less Right:** *Moby Dick,* which I've read five times and hated more and more with each read, is a classic of Western literature.

**Right:** *Moby Dick*—which I've read five times and hated more and more with each read—is a classic of Western literature.

**ALSO RIGHT:** *Moby Dick* (which I've read five times and hated more and more with each read) is a classic of Western literature.

That aside is hardly necessary to the rest of the sentence. It should be separated by either dashes or parentheses.

Congrats! You have learned all of the punctuation rules that will be tested on the ACT! Take the following punctuation quiz, then go out to a park and do cartwheels. Don't know how to do cartwheels? Then please preorder our forthcoming book: *Up Your Cartwheel: The Underground Guide to Cartwheeling Through the Park.*

There are three things wrong with Jess'
                                       1
approach to dating. First, she doesn't have

1.  A.  NO CHANGE
    B.  Jess's
    C.  Jess
    D.  Jesses

a natural sense of fashion; her favorite
                              2
"date outfit" is gray sweatpants and a gray

hooded "Everyone Poops" sweatshirt.

2.  A.  NO CHANGE
    B.  sense of fashion, her favorite
    C.  sense of fashion but
    D.  sense of fashion; because

Second, her typical conversation

style (when she's out on a first date) is
                    3

3.  A.  NO CHANGE
    B.  style. When she's out on a first date
    C.  style, when she's out on a first date,
    D.  style, when she's out on a first date

either incredibly loud shouting

or total uninterrupted silence.
         4

4.  A.  NO CHANGE
    B.  total but uninterrupted
    C.  total, uninterrupted
    D.  total; uninterrupted

Its distressing to think that such an
—
5

intelligent and perceptive young woman

could fail to realize that she should just

talk as she normally does. Third, her attitude

is all wrong. Regardless of how much fun

she has, she ends every date with the same

comment. "Sir, this has been dreadful."
—————————————————————
6

5. **A.** NO CHANGE
   **B.** It's
   **C.** Its'
   **D.** It isn't

6. **A.** NO CHANGE
   **B.** comment, "Sir, this has been
   **C.** comment; "Sir, this has been
   **D.** comment: "Sir, this has been

Answers: **1.** B; **2.** A; **3.** C; **4.** C; **5.** B; **6.** D

## Can This Sentence Be Gooder? Grammar and Usage

* Op . . . op . . . op . . .
oppan subject and verb
agreement.
—Zack (channeling Psy)

Unfortunately, the ACT-bot is not solely concerned with your mastery of punctuation. It dedicates even more time testing whether words are being used correctly in the sentences of the passage. There are four rules to remember.

### I. SUBJECTS AND VERBS: LET'S AGREE TO AGREE

Most of the usage questions on the ACT are going to be subject-verb problems. Remember how popular Psy's "Gangnam Style" * was in 2012? You literally could not escape that song. Well, subject-verb problems are like that, except less catchy. So let's tackle the biggest beast first.

There's one and only one rule for subject-verb problems: **The subject has to agree with the verb.**

Is that clear? If not, we can say it louder: **The subject has to agree with the verb.**

Take a look at the following sentence.

**WRONG:** The female frog hop to the lily pad of the cute male frog.

**Right:** The female frog hops to the lily pad of the cute male frog.

The subject is "female frog" and the verb is "hop." Does "the female frog hop" make sense? No. It should be "the female frog hops." It is a singular subject, so it needs a singular verb.

That is really and truly the only subject-verb rule the ACT-bot is testing. But it has found some very clever robo-chicanery to make this harder.

### Robo-Chicanery 1: Throwing a lot of modifying phrases between the subject and the verb

**Wrong:** The female frog, who has been having little success with websites like FrogDate and Croaker, hop to the lily pad of the cute male frog.

**Right:** The female frog, who has been having little success with websites like FrogDate and Croaker, hops to the lily pad of the cute male frog.

By inserting a bunch of modifying phrases in between the subject (female frog) and the verb (hop), the ACT-bot hopes that you will forget whether the subject was singular or plural.

This can be even tougher when the modifying phrase is introduced by a preposition:

**Wrong:** These days, the one perfect male frog in a pond full of mediocre male frogs are so hard to find.

**Right:** These days, the one perfect male frog in a pond full of mediocre male frogs is so hard to find.

The subject (the one perfect male frog) is separated from the verb (are) by the prepositional modifying phrase (in a pond full of mediocre male frogs). The ACT-bot wants to trick you into thinking that "mediocre male frogs" are the subject. Don't let this happen.

### Robo-Chicanery 2: Placing the subject after the verb

**Wrong:** What makes a male frog attractive is a bulbous throat sac, moist eyeballs, and a pungent stench.

In complicated subject-verb agreement sentences, I like to cross out all the unnecessary modifiers, leaving just the simple subject (the main noun) and the verb.

—Jon

**Right:** What make a male frog attractive are a bulbous throat sac, moist eyeballs, and a pungent stench.

The subjects (bulbous throat sac, moist eyeballs, and pungent stench) are placed after the verb (is). Rearrange them so that the subjects come first, and you will immediately see that the verb should be "are."

## Robo-Chicanery 3: Using singular words that are often misused as plural words

Tattoo these words on your forehead: *anyone, anything, everything, everyone, everybody, neither/nor, either/or, somebody, nobody, none, each.*

We frequently use these nouns as if they were plural when we speak. Stop doing that! The ACT-bot *loves* to test these words.

**Wrong:** Each of the members of the boy-frog band Swampy Nights are dreamy.

**Right:** Each of the members of the boy-frog band Swampy Nights is dreamy.

"Each" (the subject) is singular, so the verb should be singular as well.

**Wrong:** Neither a long tongue nor a loud croak are as impressive to me as a secure sense of emotional maturity.

**Right:** Neither a long tongue nor a loud croak is as impressive to me as a secure sense of emotional maturity.

Because both "a long tongue" and "a loud croak" are singular, the "neither/nor" makes this a singular subject, and the verb should be "is."

## Robo-Chicanery 4: Trying to confuse you with groups, which are singular, and members of groups, which are plural

Countries, companies, and departments are singular. But the members of those groups are plural. For instance:

**RIGHT:** America is home to the most fashionable and urbane frogs.

**RIGHT:** At least this is what American frogs say.

America is singular. The frogs in America are plural.

Let's practice some subject-verb problems:

Children today, who have been raised

in a world where songs can be freely

downloaded from any number of websites,

doesn't know about the early days of
———————————————
1
Internet piracy.

1.  **A.** NO CHANGE
    **B.** don't know about
    **C.** does know about
    **D.** didn't know about

Each of the first data pirates were famous
—————————————————————
2
for a unique and fearsome battle cry.

2.  **A.** NO CHANGE
    **B.** the first data pirates had been famous
    **C.** the first data pirates being famous
    **D.** the first data pirates was famous

But what truly made them terrifying
————————————
3
was their eye patches, scabbards, and
——

squawking parrots.

3.  **A.** NO CHANGE
    **B.** made them terrify
    **C.** terrified people about them was
    **D.** made them terrifying were

Answers: **1.** B; **2.** D; **3.** D

## 2. PRONOUNS: THESE SHOULD ALSO AGREE WITH THEIR VERBS

**NOT-SO-GOOD:** Shmuel wants to dance, so Shmuel swallows Shmuel's fear, hikes up Shmuel's pants, laces up Shmuel's dancing shoes, and hits the dance floor like Shmuel owns it.

Was that sentence stupid? Yes. We can't just repeat a noun over and over. Well, we can, but we will sound stupid, and sounding stupid is stupid. Instead, we use pronouns and sound really smart. Witness:

**BETTER:** Shmuel wants to dance, so he swallows his fear, hikes up his pants, laces up his dancing shoes, and hits the dance floor like he owns it.

That sentence sounds much smarter. Thanks, pronouns! But if we use a pronoun to refer to a noun, we need to make sure that **the pronoun agrees with the noun to which it refers.** For example:

**RIGHT:** My beleaguered mother told me that she was sick of my excuses.

"She" is a pronoun that refers to "mother." Let's take a look at another example:

**WRONG:** When my father gets mad, they go to a room and yell at the wall.

**RIGHT:** When my father gets mad, he goes to a room and yells at the wall.

"My father" is male and singular, so that plural pronoun "they" should be "he."

Simple, right? Right! But the ACT-bot has found a way to make things more difficult, because the ACT-bot ♥s making things more difficult. How?

The bot likes to combine tricky singular words with nouns to make the pronoun choice more difficult.

Do you remember our list of tricky singular words? No? Well, then look in the mirror and read backward, because they're tattooed on your forehead.* (Perhaps we should have suggested that you tattoo them on your hands.) We'll remind you: *anyone, anything, everything, everyone, everybody, neither/nor, either/or, somebody, nobody, none, each.*

When the ACT-bot combines these words with a noun, it makes choosing the pronoun tricky. For instance:

* Did you not tattoo them? You didn't even memorize them? Seriously, do it.
—Zack

**WRONG:** Somebody, either the Destroyer of Worlds or the AllKrusher, obliterated my civilization, but they aren't confessing to the crime.

**RIGHT:** Somebody, either the Destroyer of Worlds or the AllKrusher, obliterated my civilization, but he or she isn't confessing to the crime.

Because "either" is singular, the pronoun needs to be the singular "he or she." ("He or she" might sound plural, but it's singular.) Let's look at another:

**WRONG:** Any villain worth their reputation would have left a note saying "I destroyed this civilization."

**RIGHT:** Any villain worth his or her reputation would have left a note saying "I destroyed this civilization."

Because "any" is singular, the plural pronoun "their" should be changed to the singular "his or her."

### 3. MODIFYING PHRASES: IT'S ALL ABOUT PROXIMITY

A *modifying phrase* is a word or group of words that tells us more about something in the sentence. **The modifying phrase needs to be next to the thing it modifies.** For example:

**WRONG:** Terrence Winterbean made a soup for his friend Shantel that was made out of melted Cherry Now and Laters.

**RIGHT:** Terrence Winterbean made a soup out of melted Cherry Now and Laters for his friend Shantel.

The phrase "melted Cherry Now and Laters" modifies "soup," so it needs to be placed next to "soup." Otherwise, someone might think that Shantel was made of Cherry Now and Laters, which is so not true. *

Make sense? Well, the ACT-bot is about to set its phasers to "More Difficult" by opening the sentence with an incorrect modifying phrase.

These can be hard to notice, so let's look at a couple of examples:

*I wish my friends were made out of Cherry Now and Laters. . . .

—Jon

I wish I had friends.

—Zack

> ✳ I'd be impressed if my soup just blew away.
> —Ava

**WRONG:** Blown away by the authentic cherry flavor, the soup completely impressed Shantel.

**RIGHT:** Blown away by the authentic cherry flavor, Shantel was completely impressed by the soup.

Whoever is "blown away by the flavor" has to come *immediately* after the comma. Is the soup blown away by the flavor? ✳ No, ma'am! Shantel is the one blown away, so her name must come immediately after the comma. Let's look at another one:

**WRONG:** Realizing that she had finally found the cook she was looking for, a proposal of marriage was the next logical step for Shantel.

**RIGHT:** Realizing that she had finally found the cook she was looking for, Shantel knew that proposing marriage was the next logical step.

It is "Shantel," and not "the proposal of marriage," that is being modified by the opening phrase. Her name needs to come immediately after the comma.

> If an answer choice changes a sentence by eliminating the possessive noun, it may be a clue that you are dealing with this type of error.
>
> —Jon

Here's the hardest type of modifier mistake:

**WRONG:** Though flattered by her proposal, Terrence's answer had to be no. He was already married to his love of cooking soup.

**RIGHT:** Though flattered by her proposal, Terrence had to tell her no. He was already married to his love of cooking soup.

Even veteran error spotters make this mistake. They see the word *Terrence's* and think that the sentence is correct. After all, we totally understand what the sentence is saying, and it doesn't sound terribly awkward. But "Terrence's answer" isn't flattered, "Terrence" is. The ACT-bot loves to turn the correct noun (Terrence) into a modifying word (Terrence's) in order to trick you.

## 4. ADJECTIVES AND ADVERBS: DESCRIBE AND MODIFY

Hey, guess what: **Adjectives modify nouns, and adverbs modify verbs.** Don't confuse adjectives and adverbs. Let's try this out:

🍂 **What Do Tutors Do?**

When our students work on the English Test, we have two ways of assessing their awareness of grammar rules. Like a nasty middle-school teacher, we might spring a pop quiz, asking them to write a treatise on everything they know about commas or to succinctly define a run-on sentence. It's more likely, however, that we will put a couple of practice problems in front of them and ask them to identify the grammatical concept that's being tested in each problem. If they can't tell, we know we need to review that concept.

**WRONG:** Tuvald's *slowly* cat was led *slow* behind the *slowly* old man, who, luckily, also walked *slow.*

**RIGHT:** Tuvald's *slow* cat was led *slowly* behind the *slow* old man, who, luckily, also walked *slowly.*

Neato burrito? You also need to remember that a cat can be *slow,* or it can be *slower* than another cat, or it can be the *slowest* cat in the history of catdom. Same goes for adverbs. The cat can walk *slowly,* or it can walk *more slowly* than that other cat, or it can walk *the most slowly* of all cats in the history of catdom. You already knew that, right? Good, then we're done here. *Oh wait!* We're not done—because there are two ways that the ACT-bot likes to mix things up.

## Mix Things Up 1: Using words like "more" and "most" with "-er" and "-est" adjectives

**WRONG:** Tuvald's cat is slow, sure, but Bryony's cats, Annie-Rose and Alfie, are more slower.

**RIGHT:** Tuvald's cat is slow, sure, but Bryony's cats, Annie-Rose and Alfie, are slower.

You cannot combine "more" with "slower." So don't!

## Mix Things Up 2: Using adverbs the common way, without "-ly," when technically they need an "-ly"

Now, we know all the cool kids talk like this:

**WRONG:** You're sure not going to find cats slower than Bryony's.

But in this case (and *only* in this case) the cool kids are wrong! They should say this:

**RIGHT:** You're surely not going to find cats slower than Bryony's.

No matter how cool it seems, *do not* lop off the "ly" from your adverbs. Next thing you know, you'll be smoking behind the school, and then you'll be a drug-addicted criminal, and then you'll be dead! Got that?

*Of course, some adverbs don't end in "-ly," such as "well," "far," and "always," to name just a few.*

*—Ava*

You just finished another set of mechanics rules! Only five more to go. Let's take another break. This time, let's ramp up the break-time activities. Try one of these:

- Make $2 million day-trading mortgage-backed securities, then buy $1 million worth of pillows and build the most epic pillow fort of all time.
- Train a giraffe to race, then enter your giraffe in a horse race under the name "Normal Horse." When it bursts out of the gate, everybody's minds will be blown to smithereens.
- Buy a motorcycle (use what's left of your day-trading money) and drive it over five school buses that are all on fire. Actually, on second thought, don't do that. Don't do anything like that; it's terribly dangerous.

## Sentence Structure— Use Your Ears

We started this chapter looking at punctuation marks, then expanded our scope to look at individual words and agreement between words. Sentence structure questions ask us to pull back a little farther, to look at how whole parts of sentences, or even whole sentences, work or do not work.

There are five sentence structure rules tested on the English Test. Luckily, these errors are often pretty easy to catch, because they just "sound" wrong.

### I. SENTENCE FRAGMENTS AND RUN-ON SENTENCES

Have you ever worked as a ticket seller at a movie theater? If so, then you may have had this experience: A six-year-old walks in wearing a fake bushy mustache and an oversize hat and tweed jacket, with a bubble pipe sticking out of his mouth, and asks for one ticket for *Sexy Times at the Murderfest*.

A sentence fragment is just like this kid. Remember our discussion of dependent and independent clauses? (If you don't, go back to page 65.) **A sentence fragment is a dependent clause**

ONE TICKET PLEASE, FELLOW ADULT.

**or phrase pretending to be a complete sentence.** And you should treat a sentence fragment the same way you would treat that kid: Call the cops and send him to jail. (What, you wouldn't do that?)

**WRONG:** As you can see, Officer. This little tyke was perpetrating identity theft, which is a felony.

**RIGHT:** As you can see, Officer, this little tyke was perpetrating identity theft, which is a felony.

In the wrong example, the first sentence makes no sense on its own. It is a dependent clause and a sentence fragment, so it needs to be attached to an independent clause to make sense.

The ACT-bot is obsessed with sentence fragments. Fortunately, it has come up with only one nefarious plot to trick you.

### Nefarious Plot: Placing the fragment next to a related independent clause

**WRONG:** If we keep allowing kids to get away with this egregious behavior. Society will fall apart within months.

**RIGHT:** If we keep allowing kids to get away with this egregious behavior, society will fall apart within months.

The ACT-bot is hoping that when you read the wrong version, your brain will swap in a comma for that period and you will read the two sentences as one. *Don't let your brain do this.* Pay attention, and recognize that the period turns that first dependent clause into a sentence fragment. Let's try one more:

**WRONG:** Prepare for an apocalyptic wasteland of roving gangs and mutant dogs. If you don't lock this kid up tight.

**RIGHT:** Prepare for an apocalyptic wasteland of roving gangs and mutant dogs if you don't lock this kid up tight.

The second clause is dependent, so it cannot be its own sentence.

Here's another thing you might have seen in your years working as a ticket seller: Two grown adults who have taped themselves together in order to buy only one ticket. This is despicable behavior, and it is exactly the same as a run-on sentence. **A run-on sentence is two independent clauses pretending to be one sentence.**

**WRONG:** You must think that I am blind, I can see the duct tape wrapped around both of your heads.

**RIGHT:** You must think that I am blind. I can see the duct tape wrapped around both of your heads.

The first sentence was pretending that it wasn't two totally independent clauses. The ACT-bot will test this with two schemes. One is so easy that it is not even nefarious. The other is somewhat nefarious.

### Not-Even-Nefarious Plot: Shoving two independent clauses together with no punctuation

**WRONG:** People who tape themselves together should be ridiculed they look preposterous and are cheating the movie-theater industry of much-needed income.

**RIGHT:** People who tape themselves together should be ridiculed. They look preposterous and are cheating the movie-theater industry of much-needed income.

That first sentence looks *absurd*. It needs a period (or a semicolon, or a comma with a conjunction, or a word like "because") in order to be less absurd.

### Somewhat-Nefarious Plot: Connecting two independent clauses with a comma

**WRONG:** We should also throw "tapers" in jail, they pose just as serious a threat as do six-year-olds who pretend to be adults.

**RIGHT:** We should also throw "tapers" in jail. They pose just as serious a threat as do six-year-olds who pretend to be adults.

In the wrong version, the comma is pretending to be a period, and we frequently read it as correct because it doesn't *sound* wrong. So this requires some attention and vigilance. Let's look at another:

**Term Talk**

If you want to be super-sophisticated, you can call this error a "comma splice." People will hear you say this and ask one another, "Who's that extremely smart young person?"

**Wrong:** We can throw the "tapers" in one wing of the prison, the children can be locked away in a separate wing.

**Right:** We can throw the "tapers" in one wing of the prison. The children can be locked away in a separate wing.

**Also Right:** We can throw the "tapers" in one wing of the prison; the children can be locked away in a separate wing.

**Also Right:** We can throw the "tapers" in one wing of the prison, and the children can be locked away in a separate wing.

Make sense? In general, **when a comma or period is underlined, check the surrounding sentence for run-ons and fragments.**

## 2. PARALLELISM AND COMPARISONS

The ACT-bot is a robot, and robots do *not* like unpredictability, change, or variety. They like everything uniform and tidy. So it shouldn't be surprising that the ACT-bot is very interested in parallel structure, which means that **similar parts of a sentence should be parallel in form.**

**Wrong:** Playwright Numia Kincaid's works explore the difficulty of modern relationships, the erosion of civic responsibility, and that it's so awesome to be a playwright.

**Right:** Playwright Numia Kincaid's works explore the difficulty of modern relationships, the erosion of civic responsibility, and the awesomeness of being a playwright.

"The difficulty" and "the erosion" are both nouns, so they should be followed by "the awesomeness," which is also a noun. Try this:

**Wrong:** Tomorrow, I want to drink a large milk shake, ride a roller coaster, and spending the rest of the day complaining.

**Right:** Tomorrow, I want to drink a large milk shake, ride a roller coaster, and spend the rest of the day complaining.

The three activities need to be in parallel grammatical form—in this case a verb in the present singular form.

The ACT-bot is aware that lists of three or more similar parts

The opposite interior angles of a set of parallel lines formed by the intersection of a nonparallel line are always . . . Oh, wait— wrong section.

—Jon

make these problems easier to spot, so it has one devious scheme up its robo-sleeve.

### Devious Scheme: Using "either/or," "neither/nor," "both/and" or "and" to link two similar parts that aren't parallel

**BAD:** Either the shark tank goes or I'll have left.

**BETTER:** Either the shark tank goes or I go.

**BAD:** After hearing the new FrankenCats album, I both jumped up in excitement and a high-pitched squeal came out of my mouth.

**BETTER:** After hearing the new FrankenCats album, I both jumped up in excitement and emitted a high-pitched squeal.

Make sure that the phrases that follow "either/or" and "both/and" follow the same grammatical structure. Similarly, when we compare two things, **we need to make sure we are comparing the same type of thing.**

**WRONG:** FrankenCats songs are infinitely better than the derivative band ZombieCats.

**RIGHT:** FrankenCats songs are infinitely better than those of the derivative band ZombieCats.

**ALSO RIGHT:** FrankenCats songs are infinitely better than the songs of the derivative band ZombieCats.

In the first sentence, we were comparing songs to a band. Those are two different types of things, right? We need to compare songs to songs.

Let's ratchet up the difficulty a couple of notches:

**WRONG:** The number of FrankenCats songs that are still relevant is greater than ZombieCats songs.

**RIGHT:** The number of FrankenCats songs that are still relevant is greater than the number of ZombieCats songs.

**ALSO TECHNICALLY RIGHT BUT SOUNDS AWKWARD:** The number of FrankenCats songs that are still relevant is greater than that of ZombieCats songs.

This one is tougher. At first, it seems as though we are comparing songs to songs, right? But we are actually comparing *the number* of songs to songs. The way to spot this is to make sure that you are comparing *exactly* the same type of thing. Check for this any time you see the word "than" underlined or near an underline.

## 3. REDUNDANCY

If you repeat yourself, then you are being redundant. Here is a classic redundant sentence:

**Wrong:** I bought 12 horses by ordering a dozen *Equus equidae.*

Buying 12 horses is the same as ordering a dozen *Equus equidae* (because, as we all know, *Equus equidae* is the scientific term for *horse*). That's like saying, "I bought french fries by buying french fries." Unfortunately, the ACT redundancies won't be quite as obvious. They will be more like this:

**Wrong:** Sitha takes a yoga class every Monday and Thursday of each week.

**Right:** Sitha takes a yoga class every Monday and Thursday.

Because "every Monday and Thursday" means "every Monday and Thursday of each week," it is redundant to add "each week." If you're not paying attention, however, this might slip under your radar. Let's look at some even subtler redundancies:

## Subtle Redundancy: Using the phrases "the reason is . . . because" or "both . . . as well as"

**Wrong:** The reason Sitha does so much yoga is because she wants to attain total enlightenment.

**Right:** The reason Sitha does so much yoga is that she wants to attain total enlightenment.

**Also Right:** Sitha does so much yoga because she wants to attain total enlightenment.

"The reason is" and "because" both mean the same thing. So it's not correct to use them both in a sentence.

The *Evil* ACT-bot. Oh, right. Redundancy.

—Jon

For many usage questions, the most concise answer is correct; they tend to eliminate problems like redundancy and passive voice.

—Jon

**WRONG:** Once she attains total enlightenment, Sitha plans to both sell it for $39.99 a dose as well as market it to young people seeking transcendence.

**RIGHT:** Once she attains total enlightenment, Sitha plans to both sell it for $39.99 a dose and market it to young people seeking transcendence.

The phrase "both . . . as well as" is incorrect. It should be "both . . . and."

A big hint here is when the ACT-bot offers OMIT as an answer choice, this often means that the part underlined is a redundancy. Check to make sure it needs to be there.

## 4. CONSISTENT TENSES

At least once or twice in the English section, the ACT-bot is going to mix up the tense of one of the verbs in the sentence. When you read the sentence, your brain is probably going to go, "Huh?!?! Whaaa—What's happening?!?!" Don't panic. Just use the context of the sentence and even the surrounding paragraph to figure out the tense of the underlined portion. Let's try:

**WRONG:** Because the train will be shut down, I hitchhiked to the wedding.

**RIGHT:** Because the train will be shut down, I'm going to hitchhike to the wedding.

In other words, use the nonunderlined portion of the sentence or paragraph in order to determine the tense of the underlined portion. The ACT-bot does not get very fancy with this rule, but it wouldn't be the ACT-bot if it didn't have at least one instance of tense-tomfoolery.

### Tense-Tomfoolery: Using the past perfect tense incorrectly

When we are talking about the past, **we use the past perfect to talk about an event even more past.** You use this in speech all the time:

*OMIT as an answer choice ends up being right so often that you'd do well to look at that first.

—Ava

**Tense About Tense**
We've found that tense questions are a great place to skip and come back. Because a tense error can spin your head around, it is often useful to give yourself a second look to create a timeline of events.

**RIGHT:** My brother was sad that I had ruined his sequined tuxedo by wearing it while riding in the back of a manure truck.

That "had ruined" is the past perfect. The ACT-bot likes to mess this up:

**WRONG:** I told him that <u>I did not intend to mess</u> up his tuxedo but that life interrupted my best laid plans.

**RIGHT:** I told him that <u>I had not intended to mess</u> up his tuxedo but that life interrupted my best laid plans.

At first glance, that first sentence doesn't look so bad, right? But if you create an imaginary timeline in your head, you'll see that the underlined portion is *even more past*, and it should take the past perfect.

## 5. ACTIVE AND PASSIVE VOICE

**The ACT-bot, just like your grammar teacher, prefers the active to the passive voice.** This does not mean that the passive voice is always wrong. It just means that if one of the answer choices changes the voice from passive to active, you should pick it. As in:

**BAD:** The Queen's jewels were stolen by a masked bandito!

**BETTER:** A masked bandito stole the Queen's jewels!

The second version has a subject (a bandito) doing something (stealing), so it is active. The first sentence has a subject (jewels) being acted upon (getting stolen), so it is passive. In general, the ACT-bot (and most people) prefer the active sentence. One of the few instances in which the passive voice is better is *when we do not know who is acting.*

**BAD:** Some person, presumably, or maybe a ghost or an alien or a super-smart animal, stole the Queen's jewels!

**BETTER:** The Queen's jewels were stolen!

Even though that first sentence is active, it is sillier than the second, passive sentence. The ACT-bot is many things, but it is never silly.

> **Holy mackerel, you finished the mechanics section of the grammar rules!** Your brain is bigger, and your skin radiates with that healthy glow of someone who knows proper sentence structure. But let's take a moment to make sure that you are not celebrating prematurely. Try out this quiz.

**From a note, found on the refrigerator door:**

Dear Burt,

Totally exhausted by <u>your behavior, you</u>
1
<u>won't be surprised that your mother and I</u>
1
<u>have packed up the car and left for a week's</u>
1
<u>vacation.</u> The reason for this should be
1

1.  **A.** NO CHANGE
    **B.** your behavior, the car has been packed and we've left for a week's vacation.
    **C.** your behavior, we've packed up the car and left for a week's vacation.
    **D.** your behavior so we've packed up the car and left for a week's vacation.

obvious, but it is mostly <u>because you never</u>
2
brush your teeth when we ask, you refuse

to go to bed on time, and, worst of all, you

barely touched your broccoli last night.

Nobody could tolerate such a child, even

2.  **A.** NO CHANGE
    **B.** that
    **C.** OMIT
    **D.** as

considering the fact that <u>they were only</u>
3
<u>five years old.</u> There are milk and eggs in the
3

3.  **A.** NO CHANGE
    **B.** they are only five years old
    **C.** the people were only five years old
    **D.** he is only five years old

<u>fridge,</u> eat them for breakfast, lunch, and
4
dinner for the week. You cannot jump on the

4.  **A.** NO CHANGE
    **B.** fridge. Eat them
    **C.** fridge, because eating them
    **D.** fridge; for

bed or spending more than half an hour
      _____
       5
watching TV per day. And don't judge us.

We told you that we would leave if you
                 _____
                      6
didn't shape up, but you didn't listen.

**5. A.** NO CHANGE
   **B.** should spend
   **C.** don't spending
   **D.** spend

**6. A.** NO CHANGE
   **B.** will leave
   **C.** have left
   **D.** are going to leave

Answers: **1.** C; **2.** B; **3.** D; **4.** B; **5.** D; **6.** A

Quiz over. Now we can really celebrate! Throw a party for yourself. May we suggest a few party themes?

- *Not-So-Sweet 16.* Set up one table in an empty room, with a Post-it note that reads: "Now You Are 16."
- *Middle-Ages Hoedown.* Just like a normal hoedown, except everyone wears a sackcloth and no shoes. Instead of swinging your partner do-si-do, you work the land from morning to night. One party guest gets to be the liege lord. He doesn't work the land at all; in fact, he has absolute control over everything. Try to be the liege lord.
- *Future Disco.* You're in the future. Disco music is playing. You get the picture.

Once you've celebrated till you can celebrate no more, rejoin us for some rhetorical skills rules.

## The Big Picture: Rhetorical Skills

Alongside the fine points of grammar, the ACT-bot also tests you on big-picture questions. The rhetorical skills questions focus on the organization of sentences within a paragraph, the organization of paragraphs within a passage, transitions between sentences and between paragraphs, and the main idea of the passage.

Rhetorical skills questions are easy to spot. They're the questions that don't refer to an underlined portion of a sentence but crop up at the ends of sentences, paragraphs, or (most often) at the ends of the passages.

These questions are particularly annoying. It's not that they are more difficult but rather that they ask you to think *differently* about the passage. Up until now, we have been looking at each passage for grammatical mistakes. In other words, we have been Grammar Hounds. It can be a shock when a question suddenly asks, "Did the previous paragraph support the main idea of the passage?" Your head will spin, your eyes will cross, your throat will go dry. You'll think to yourself: "Was I supposed to be paying attention to the *main idea?*"

This is a nasty feeling. But remember, the ACT-bot is very pro-nasty feelings. The best way to handle the shock of rhetorical skills questions is to see them coming and prepare yourself before they can surprise you. There are two ways to do this:

1. Glance at the questions along the margins of the passage. You should be able to spot the rhetorical questions because the answer choices have more text. This will give you a good sense of when you need to get your big-picture brain ready.

2. Look for telltale signs like numbered sentences and numbered paragraphs, as these indicate that an organization question is coming.

Luckily, there are only five rhetorical skills rules. Unluckily, they can get a little hairy. So take a deep breath.

Hold it. . . . Hoooooooold it. . . . Let it all out! Let's go.

## I. ORGANIZATION OF SENTENCES WITHIN A PARAGRAPH

If you come across a paragraph with numbers in front of each sentence, **prepare yourself to put those sentences in better order.** Read this:

(1) But most scientists are overlooking the rare Philacteron bat who, after leaving its perch at six months, never calls home or even sends a card. (2) Granted, Bosephius bats demonstrate many traits that are commonly considered impolite. (3) Bosephius bats are known throughout the science community as the rudest bats in the world, but this is a questionable generalization. (4) Surely, this behavior makes the Bosephius bat look positively warm. (5) After all, they emit a loud burp whenever they fly, they only squeak about themselves, and they are notoriously stingy tippers.

Which of the following is the correct order of sentences?
A. 2, 4, 1, 3, 5
B. 3, 4, 1, 5, 2
C. 1, 3, 5, 4, 2
D. 3, 2, 5, 1, 4

Just reading that paragraph is enough to give you a headache. And then the task of rearranging that paragraph in the correct order is like a headache that has its own headache. If only there was some sort of rockin' strategy to solve it, right?

Well, guess what, double-headache-head? There is a rockin' strategy to solve it!

### Rockin' Strategy for Organization Problems

Start by finding the first sentence. Use the openings of sentences, as well as the sense of the paragraph, to help you locate it. Here, Sentences 1, 2, 4, and 5 all start with the kinds of direction terms* —"but, granted, surely, after all"—that we are unlikely to find in an opening sentence. More important, Sentence 3 has that *general, broad statement feel* of an opening line. It is the kind of statement that makes us think there is more to come.

The ACT-bot hates to begin paragraphs with words like "but" or "since" or "and." Knowing this will help you eliminate first-sentence candidates.

—Ava

*Don't worry. Direction terms are fully explained on page 98.

Once we've determined that Sentence 3 is our first sentence, we can eliminate choices A and C. Now we just need to find our second sentence. *But wait!* We can use the strategy again! Look at our remaining answer choices: Only Sentences 4 and 2 could come next. So test them both out. Sentence 4 makes *no sense* as a second sentence, so eliminate B. Sentence 2 makes sense. That gives us our answer! When we look at D, we see that only 5 makes sense as a third choice. So *by elimination*, we've found that answer choice D must be correct.

Whenever you see a sentence organization problem, you should instinctively search for the first sentence, then let the answer choices be your guide. And if your head starts to spin (we call this Test Taker's Vertigo), then *skip and come back*.

## 2. ORGANIZATION OF PARAGRAPHS WITHIN A PASSAGE

These questions are very similar to sentence organization questions, just on a larger scale. If you see numbers in front of every paragraph, expect this type of problem.

I know what you're thinking: "Oh gee, I sure hope that there is a strategy for these questions. I *really* don't want to organize every paragraph of this passage."

*There is a strategy! It's the exact same one as for sentences!*

But this time there is a twist. When you start a passage, as soon as you see numbers in front of every paragraph you should do two things:

1. Write a super-short summary of each paragraph in the margin.
2. Hunt for a likely first, second, and third paragraph.

Because we don't feel like writing an entire passage, here is a paragraph organization question using paragraph summaries:

**"Life on the Sun" Summaries**

Paragraph 1: Solarnauts are all incinerated.
Paragraph 2: The eternal question, "Can mankind live on the sun?"
Paragraph 3: Solarnauts train in Florida under high-heat conditions.
Paragraph 4: NASA invents Solarnaut program.

Which of the following is the correct order of paragraphs?

**A.** 2, 3, 4, 1
**B.** 3, 2, 4, 1
**C.** 4, 2, 3, 1
**D.** 2, 4, 3, 1

**Answer:** D

## 3. TRANSITIONS BETWEEN SENTENCES

Okay, we exaggerated when we said that *all* rhetorical skills questions are easy to spot. Transition questions look just like mechanics questions, but they are testing the logical flow of one sentence to the next, using direction terms. Direction terms can either lead us further into an idea ("thus," "so we see," "therefore," "so") or in a contrary direction ("however," "nevertheless", "but", "regardless"). As in:

> Angad was tired of being the shortest kid on the team, **so** he bought a pair of Extendo-Legs on the black market. The Extendo-Legs fit perfectly, **but** they didn't allow him as much range of movement.

As you might have already guessed, the ACT-bot will mess with your mind by replacing a same-direction term with a contrary-direction term, and vice versa.

**WRONG:** The children were tired from a day of video games, but they decided to take a power nap before firing up *Driving Without Regard for the Rules of the Road 3: Texting on the Turnpike.*

**RIGHT:** The children were tired from a day of video games, so they decided to take a power nap before firing up *Driving Without Regard for the Rules of the Road 3: Texting on the Turnpike.*

Sentence transition questions can be difficult because, unlike other rhetorical skills questions, it can be hard to tell *why* they are wrong. They just make your brain unhappy. The only strategy

**Common Direction Terms and Phrases**

• After all
• But
• Granted
• However
• Moreover
• Regardless
• So
• Therefore
• Thus
• Or so it would seem
• So we see
• That's only part of the story
• This doesn't take into consideration
• Everything I just said is wrong. Here's what's right:

here is to use the sense of the sentence in order to judge whether the direction term is appropriate. Let's try a tougher one:

**WRONG:** I love the smell of bacon in the morning, and it doesn't compare to the smell of bacon all day long.

**RIGHT:** I love the smell of bacon in the morning, but it doesn't compare to the smell of bacon all day long.

If you come across a transition question and cannot use the sense of the sentence as a guide, then *skip and come back*, please.

## 4. TRANSITIONS BETWEEN PARAGRAPHS

These questions use the same logic as transition-between-sentence problems, but they look very different. Often, the ACT-bot will supply you with a number of different sentences as answer choices. You will have to choose which sentence provides the best transition between two paragraphs.

*Paragraph 1:*
Of all the scientific disciplines, neuroscience seems poised to win the popularity contest. In a recent survey of American undergraduates pursuing bachelor degrees in science, 64 percent of students claimed that they "wanted to play with brains."

*Paragraph 2:*
Written records from the seventeenth century cite instances of Flemish peasants using sticks to poke the preserved brains of rabbits. In the following century, the Swedish naturalist Jan de Bloot wrote in his *Tractatus Physiologica Humanus*: "You guys, brains are superweird, obvi, but also kinda spongy and neat! Icky, right? But also kind of icky cool." As far back as 1830, whole gentlemen's clubs had been established with the explicit purpose of prodding, touching, and discussing brains.

Which of the following sentences, if added to the end of the first paragraph, would provide the best transition between the two paragraphs?

A. Twenty percent responded that they wanted to study "the kind of science that will make me rich," while the remaining 16 percent were undecided.

B. The survey was organized by the National Institute for a Better Understanding of Why Stuff Happens the Way It Does.

C. We should probably call these burgeoning neuroscientists "seventeenth-century Flemish peasants."

D. But perhaps the popularity of the discipline should not come as such a surprise.

Again, **we need to use the sense of the two paragraphs to choose the best transition sentence.** Here, the second paragraph gives us a history of neuroscientific enthusiasm in order to provide a context in which we can understand a recent finding.

Notice how answer choices A and B both refer to the first paragraph but have nothing to do with the second. The ACT-bot loves to provide sentences that fit with only one paragraph or the other but do not provide a transition between the two. This also explains why answer choice C is very specifically linked to the second paragraph but provides only an absurd transition.

This leaves answer choice D. You should confirm your answer by reading it as part of the passage and making sure that the sentence helps us understand how the two paragraphs relate to each other.

## 5. SECRET MAIN IDEA QUESTIONS

This is where the ACT-bot gets a little sneaky. It asks two types of rhetoric questions that rely on understanding the main idea of the passage, which is really more of a reading skill than an English language skill. But haven't we come to expect a bit of sneakiness from a cyber warlord whose only goal is to reduce the planet to an ashen husk?

### Secret Main Idea Question Type I: Supporting Material Questions

Take a gander, if you please, at the following paragraph and question:

The meteoric rise of the Internet has completely overshadowed another invention that was created at approximately the same time. Developed by the computer scientist Sheldon Avram at Bell Laboratories in 1975, the "Solonet" took a very different approach to computer connectivity. Instead of creating a system of signaling devices that allowed computers to share information, Dr. Avram created a mechanism of data transference that allowed one computer to talk to itself. After he successfully tested his first Solonet computer, Dr. Avram boldly claimed that it was "the herald of a new era of digital introspection and solitude."

The author wishes to include the following sentence in the previous paragraph: "The uses were limitless: A computer could carry on a conversation with itself, ask itself questions and make up its own answers, or it could simply gaze at its own wiring, marveling at its own complexity and uniqueness." Would this sentence benefit the passage as a whole?

A. Yes, because it would provide a humorous aside that would lighten the overall tone.

B. Yes, because it would provide examples that allow the reader to better understand a new concept.

C. No, because it would focus only on one aspect of a complex problem.

D. No, because it would add an unnecessary detail.

This question can only be answered if you understand the main idea of the passage: The Solonet was a distinct invention that allowed a computer to talk to itself. The added sentence, which provides an example of *how* the computer talks to itself, is thus relevant and beneficial to the passage. We can then get rid of answer choices C and D. It is relevant *not* because it lightens the tone, but because it expands our awareness of how the Solonet works. The correct answer, then, is B.

A good strategy for these questions is to focus less on the "yes" and "no," and more on the explanations that follow. These explanations tend to give more clues about whether the answer choice is right or wrong.

### Secret Main Idea Question Type 2: Last Sentence Questions

Imagine that a passage about the trials and tribulations of the troubled (and made-up) jazz singer Beatrice Lavigne ended in the following paragraphs:

Following the release of "Songbird," Lavigne gained more recognition than she had ever known. So she surprised everyone when she responded by locking herself in her apartment in downtown Cincinnati. She emerged two years later and, much to the dismay of her fans, released a two-disc album of Scandinavian death metal. The album, *Skewered in the Sewers*, sold fewer than 43 copies, placing it among the worst-selling albums of all time.

In a rare interview with the Newark jazz station WBGO, Lavigne spoke about the colossal failure of her album: "I thought people would dig it. I guess they didn't." When a caller asked her to sing a couple bars of "Songbird," Lavigne politely refused. She was never known to sing the tune again.

At the end of her life, Lavigne could be found in any number of second-rate cabarets, singing in front of an ensemble of drowsy instrumentalists. She finally quit singing altogether in 1982. When asked about her past in an interview for *Downbeat* magazine, Lavigne responded: "Darling, the only complaint I have about my jazz career is that I have always, always hated jazz."

Which of the following sentences would best end the passage?

A. The interviewer asked her to explain herself further, but Lavigne refused.

B. After such a life, who can blame her for turning on the art form that once inspired her?

C. In the same issue, *Downbeat* published a 4-page spread of rare photographs of John Coltrane.

D. Copies of *Skewered in the Sewers* are now available on eBay starting at $13.99.

These questions are tough because they seem, at first, like matters of opinion. Who's to say which sentence would end the passage? Isn't that up to the author? The secret here is that the question is *really* asking which sentence best summarizes the main idea of the passage. Because the main idea of this passage is that Lavigne had a tough life, answer choice B says this most clearly. Notice how the ACT-bot loves to include wrong answer choices that refer to elements of individual paragraphs, as in A and C. Remember that the answer should refer to the passage as a whole and not just one paragraph.

Test yourself with the following rhetorical skills questions:

## [1]

Freestyle BMX was born one Thursday morning in 1992, when Brown woke up and reportedly said aloud: "I'd like to do something extreme today." At that time, Brown was a professor of applied neuroscience at MIT, and was known on campus as a nervous teetotaler who enjoyed a quiet, slow game of chess or, in his more spirited moods, a quiet, slow game of Parcheesi. His quest for extremity, then, was highly out of character.

## [2]

For the most part, human beings have logical brains and logical imaginations. When we see a phenomenon, our minds automatically create a logical reason to explain its existence. If we were to see an elephant walking down Main Street, we would assume that it had escaped from the zoo or broken free of its trainer. If we were to show up at school, only to find it empty, we would assume that we had forgotten that it was a holiday or that there was a fire drill in progress.

## [3]

(A) The sport, in which athletes ride bikes up and down large half-pipe ramps, performing tricks to gain points, was first created by McManistair Brown, or "Mac Man." (B) This would be the logical explanation, but logic is not in Mac Man's vocabulary. (C) Freestyle BMX attained international recognition in the late 1990s. (D) Any casual observer of Freestyle BMX would assume that Brown got his inspiration from half-pipe skateboarders. "That looks fun," he might have said. "I wonder if that would be fun on a bike."

## [4]

He tried a few activities in his office. He spun around quickly in his office chair. "Not nearly extreme enough," the queasy professor concluded. He cut his tie in half. "That wasn't extreme at all," he muttered. Moreover, he went outside, took a deep breath, and ran full tilt toward the wall of the particle acceleration laboratory. He smashed into the wall, chipping two teeth, and collapsed on the grass. "That's more like it," he said.

1. Which of the following places the sentences in Paragraph 3 in the best order?
   A. NO CHANGE
   B. B, D, C, A
   C. C, A, D, B
   D. D, C, B, A

2. Which of the following, if placed at the end of Paragraph 2, provides the best transition to the next paragraph?
   A. These explanations can be attributed to the functionality of the mind, which supplies explanations that allow us to operate even in the face of absurdity or surprise.
   B. But life does not follow such logical chains of cause and effect. In no phenomenon is this clearer than in the genesis of the sport of Freestyle BMX.
   C. We know when the sport of Freestyle BMX became famous across the world.
   D. This is a process that we refine as we get older.

3. Which of the following places the paragraphs in the best order?
   A. 2, 3, 1, 4
   B. 2, 3, 4, 1
   C. 4, 2, 3, 1
   D. 3, 1, 4, 2

4. In Paragaph 4, the word "moreover" should be changed to:
   A. NO CHANGE
   B. However,
   C. Next,
   D. Naturally,

5. Which of the following titles would best suit the passage?
   A. "The Explaining Mind"
   B. "Extreme: The Crazy Creation of a Crazy Sport"
   C. "Mac Man: A Life"
   D. "From Skateboards to Bikes"

Answers: **1.** C; **2.** B; **3.** A; **4.** C; **5.** B

## Moving Forward

*Try to read out of your comfort zone. The ACT English section will probably not include passages from People magazine or TV Guide.*

*—Jon*

Congratulations, you are now a fully accredited grammarian. The next step is to **take real ACT English Tests** from *The Real ACT Prep Guide.* Pay extra attention to those problems that you get wrong. Ask yourself: What rule is being tested here? How did they trick me? View each practice test less as an attempt to get a high score and more as an opportunity to uncover weaknesses and correct them.

Also, as we mentioned before, **read challenging articles and books.** (For more on this, see page 243.)

Finally, the best way to refine and retrain your ear for proper grammar is to surround yourself with people who speak with proper grammar. We recommend hanging out at the following places:

+ Any club where polo is played
+ The opera. You don't need to go inside the theater, just stand near the snack stand during the intermission.
+ Your school's teachers' lounge
+ The water cooler at Merriam-Webster's central office
+ England, or barring that, New England

And avoid the following places:
+ The blogosphere

- The Twittersphere
- Facebook
- Really, the entire Internet
- Any of your friends' houses
- Anywhere that teenagers congregate

Next up, the Math chapter!

# The Mathematics Test

## The Easiest Section—
## If You Know Everything
## About Math

*Math is like the board game Mouse Trap—it follows rules and is trying to kill you.*

## Math: Is It Impossible?

Sometimes it seems like there are two kinds of people: those who understand math and those who do not. Unlike string beans, which you can *sorta* like, or like *sometimes*, math has only two responses: You get it, or you don't. Kids either cruise through math problems without breaking a sweat, or they are crushed into a paste of dust and tears.

But this is baloney. While some kids might have more *interest* in math, all human beings are able to understand all math. Let's repeat that, in italic bold caps: ***ALL HUMAN BEINGS ARE ABLE TO UNDERSTAND ALL MATH.***

When people say that they "don't have a math brain," they mean that they have tried some problems and failed. So they say, "I'm not a math person," and waltz off, guilt-free. But this is a big fat cop-out. If someone can't solve a math problem, it is because he or she has either *forgotten* or *never learned* the concepts involved.

Think of math as a board game. If you were to look at, say, Monopoly, without knowing the rules, the game would look enormously complex. Why are there different colors? What does jail have to do with anything? Why is a shoe racing a top hat? ✳ But once the rules are explained, Monopoly becomes simple. After a few times playing, you may even find it too simple. You might want to move on to something more complex, like Hydro-Monopoly Xtreme, which unfortunately doesn't exist.

In this chapter, we're going to think about math concepts as if they were board games. We'll start by reviewing the rules, then we'll play for a bit, and finally, we'll show you how the ACT-bot uses *these same rules* to create Nightmare Problems.

✳ And why do you get money from a free parking space?
—Ava

Math, more than any section of the ACT, <u>follows rules</u>. Once you know the rules, you know everything and can do everything.
—Zack

## What's on the Mathematics Section of the ACT?

This chapter addresses the areas of mathematics most commonly seen on the ACT. First, we'll focus on arithmetic, then we'll take those concepts and look at problems involving algebra, before moving to geometry and coordinate geometry, which are heavily represented on the test. Finally, we will look at the three scariest math concepts: trigonometry, logarithms, and matrices. We'll break some areas down into basic and advanced sections.

Now, that is a lot of math, so this chapter is going to be long. We recommend that you not read it all in one sitting, as all of that information might destroy your brain. So we've gone ahead and noted moments in the chapter where we think it would be wise to take a break. We've also provided suggestions for break-time activities, because we here at *Up Your Score* like to take our breaks in style.

## Some Quick Thoughts on Strategy

We know we *always* say skip and come back. And we've already mentioned that it is especially important for this section. But say it with us: It's especially important to skip and come back in the Math section!

The most important strategy for the Math Test, without a doubt, is to review and learn the math concepts that are being tested. There are also a few tricks and shortcuts, which we'll show you within the appropriate section. But there is a general strategy that you should always follow, which is . . . *skip and come back!*

Some math problems are going to click as soon as you read them, but some are going to make you say, "Oh, frack this, I'm out." On those tough problems, make sure that you skip and come back to allow yourself a second or even a third glance at a problem.

You might come across a problem that *seems* straightforward, but when you do the math, your answer is not among the answer choices. This simply means that you have misread the problem. But don't just try again like a gorilla! Be an evolved human and skip, do two more problems, and *then* give it another try.

The worst aspect of the Mathematics Test is that you have to complete 60 problems in 60 minutes. This might feel like a luxurious pace during the first ten to fifteen problems. But the questions get more difficult as you progress through the section, because the ACT-bot uses more and more complex mathematical concepts. By the end you will need to math faster than you've ever mathed before. There are only two things you can do to prepare for the brutal pace of this section: 1.) Familiarize yourself beforehand with all of the mathematical concepts. You don't want to waste valuable seconds recalling how logarithms work. Learn (or relearn) this stuff now, so that you can jump right into the business of solving each problem. You can also develop your speed by practicing with math sections. Don't look at this work as "learning," but as "training." When you do a practice section, the point is not to learn *how* to solve a problem, but to develop your ability to solve it quickly. 2.) Skip and come back. Aside from the advantages we just mentioned, the time-saving aspect of skipping and coming back is *crucial* on the Mathematics Test.

Skip and come back isn't only for frustrating problems; it's a great tool for when you're stuck between two similar answers.

—Ava

## LET'S DO THIS . . .

As we move through the chapter, remember to take breaks. Even the most enthusiastic mathlete can overheat his or her brain. Feel free to read a chunk of this chapter, then move to a different chapter for a little while, then run out to the nearest mountain and hike up and down it. Or watch an episode of *Dance Moms*. Or carry a TV up a mountain and watch an episode of *Dance Moms* amid the splendor of the surrounding mountaintops. Whatever floats your boat.

## Basic Arithmetic

Before we launch in, let's pause for a little quiz. Match these words to their definition, please.

| | | | |
|---|---|---|---|
| **1.** | Sum | A. | 2, 4, 6, 8, . . . |
| **2.** | Product | B. | What is left over in a division problem |
| **3.** | Difference | C. | Greater than zero |
| **4.** | Quotient | D. | The answer in an addition problem |
| **5.** | Negative | E. | The answer in a subtraction problem |
| **6.** | Positive | F. | 1, 3, 5, 7, . . . |
| **7.** | Remainder | G. | Less than zero |
| **8.** | Even | H. | The answer in a multiplication problem |
| **9.** | Odd | I. | The answer in a division problem |

**Answers: 1.** D; **2.** H; **3.** E; **4.** I; **5.** G; **6.** C; **7.** B; **8.** A; **9.** F

Haven't run for the hills yet, right? Maybe "quotient" is a little icky, but the rest of the words should be familiar.

Okay, now that your math brain is starting to warm up, take a look at these harder, but hopefully still familiar, words.

**Digits:** 0, 1, 2, 3, 4, 5, 6, 7, 8, 9

**Units Digit:** the digit in the one's place (5,32**6**)

**Integer:** any number, including negatives and zero, that is not a decimal or a fraction

**Consecutive:** in order

**Maximum:** most

**Minimum:** least

**Prime:** any number that can be divided only by 1 and itself. But remember, 2 is the first prime number, not 1!

**Factor:** the integers that can be multiplied into a number. For example, the factors of 18 are 1, 2, 3, 6, 9, 18. (Don't forget to include 1 and the number itself.)

**Multiple:** the answers you get when you multiply by a number. For example, the multiples of 6 are 0, 6, 12, 18, 24, 48, etc.

**Numerator:** the number in the top part of a fraction

**Denominator:** the number in the bottom part of a fraction

**Area:** space taken up

**Perimeter:** the distance around the outside of a shape

**Radius:** the distance from the center to the outside of a circle

**Diameter:** all the way across a circle through the center (twice the radius)

**Chord:** any line connecting two points on a circle

**Circumference:** distance around the perimeter of a circle

**Mean:** average

**Median:** the middle number in a set of numbers (3, 4, 4, **5**, 6, 7, 8)

**Mode:** the most frequently occurring number in a set of numbers (3, **4, 4**, 5, 6, 7, 8)

---

If you find yourself saying, "Hey, 1 can be divided only by 1 and itself; why isn't it prime?" then you're like everyone else on the planet. I'm sure mathematicians have a very good, totally-not-confusing reason why 1 is not prime. For now, just remember that 2 is the first prime number.

—Jon

**Helpful Hint**

We highly recommend that you underline any of these words when you see them in a question. They are likely essential to the meaning of the question. If you overlook them, you will probably get the problem wrong.

Math vocab is just as important as reading vocab. Make sure you know what the problem is asking you to do.

—Ava

---

### Calculator to the Rescue

The brutal pace of the Math Test requires nimble calculator use. In these notes, we're going to show you how to reduce a three-line equation to a couple of button punches on a standard TI-83 or TI-84 graphing calculator.

---

*If you are still unclear about these operations, please e-run to your nearest e-book store, and purchase the classic *How to Travel Back in Time and Pay Attention in Second Grade.*

Are all of those terms feeling a bit friendlier? Don't worry if you aren't 100 percent on all of them. Some (like *mean, factor, numerator,* and *denominator*) will be addressed in more detail later on. For now, let's jump into the first concept.

## PEMDAS, OR THE ORDER OF OPERATIONS

Now that you've reminded yourself about addition, subtraction, multiplication, and division, let's talk about how to combine these operations.*

### How to Play

Take a look at this Flavr-Packed™ problem:

$$(6 \cdot 3)^3 - 12 \div (45^2 + 3) = ?$$

This problem's got it all, huh? Multiplication and division? Check! Addition and subtraction and parentheses? Oh, heck, yes! Exponents? Psh, *as if* we wouldn't include exponents!

In order to solve this problem, you have to know the order of operations. This is very difficult to remember if you don't have a helpful mnemonic device. Oh, snap! You *do* have a helpful mnemonic device: Please Excuse My Dear Aunt Sally, or **PEMDAS,** tells you the order of operations.

$$\frac{(\text{Please})^{\text{Excuse}} \cdot \text{My}}{\text{Dear}} + \text{Aunt} - \text{Sally}$$

In other words, perform the operations in this order: parentheses, exponents, multiplication, division, addition, subtraction. If there are multiple operations of the same type (like two addition operations), move from left to right. Also, when you are doing addition and subtraction, *do not* do addition first and then subtraction; rather, move from left to right, solving addition or subtraction problems in the order they arise. Similarly, *do not* do multiplication first and then division; rather, move from left to right, solving either multiplication or division problems in the order they arise.

There is, unfortunately, one addition to the classic PEMDAS mnemonic. Operations under root signs should also be done at the same time as parentheses (move from left to right to decide which to do first). So, let's add an "R" for "roots" and change it to **PREMDAS,** or **P**lease, **R**ock-fan, **E**njoy **M**y **D**ear **A**unt's (face-melting guitar) **S**olo. Cool?

Now that you know the rules . . .

### Let's Play

---

**PREMDAS**

**1.** $((1 + 5)^2 - (12 \div 2 + 1)^2)^2 \div (5 + 7 \cdot 3) =$

A. 7.5

B. 7.2

C. 6.9

D. 6.5

E. 6

---

**PREMDAS**

**2.** $(13 - 5)^2 - (3 - 4 + 2) + 2 =$

A. 14

B. 65

C. 75.8

D. 122

E. 150.3

---

**PREMDAS**

**3.** $(3^2 + 3) - (5 - 2 \cdot 4) =$

A. 17

B. 15

C. 12

D. 5

E. −7

Answers:

**1.** D

**2.** B

**3.** B

The ACT-bot will use a fraction bar to confuse you when you have to divide with PREMDAS. Just imagine the numerator as an expression inside parentheses, the fraction bar as a division symbol, and the denominator as another parenthetical expression.

—Jon

## Nightmare PREMDAS Problems

Those problems weren't so bad, right? To be totally honest, you're almost definitely *not* going to see problems like that on the ACT. We just wanted you to get comfortable with the concept. Now let's crank it up a notch by showing how the ACT-bot uses these same rules to create more evil problems, the kind you might actually see on a test.

The two most common ways that the ACT-bot arranges difficult PREMDAS problems are: 1.) by using multiple sets of parentheses, in which case you need to work from the inside out, or 2.) by dividing an operation by a number or other operation, in which case you need to PREMDAS before dividing.

---

### NIGHTMARE PREMDAS

1. $\dfrac{45 \div (4 - 2.5) + 2}{5 \cdot (14 \div 3) + 2} =$

Solve to the nearest hundredth.

A. .38

B. 1.26

C. 2.41

D. 3.62

E. 4.53

2. $\dfrac{(23 + 4) \div 5}{6 \cdot (3^2 - 2) + 42 - 5} =$

Solve to the nearest hundredth.

A. .068

B. 9.86

C. 16.91

D. 25.83

E. 37.13

---

**Answers: 1.** B; **2.** A

## NEGATIVE AND POSITIVE NUMBERS

Here's a great way to think about negative numbers: They are just positive numbers with a gloomy outlook on life. When a 3 goes out for a stroll through the park, a −3 sits in his basement, eating an entire tub of Nutella, because who cares, it's not like he's going to do anything with his life anyway, right? Actually, this is not a great way to think about negative and positive numbers at all.

### How to Play

A better way to think about negative numbers is to construct a number line in your head, or to actually draw one.

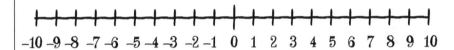

Positive numbers sit to the right of the zero, negative numbers sit to the left. But how do we add, subtract, and multiply with negative and positive numbers?

To add or subtract with negative numbers, put an imaginary finger on your imaginary number line on the first number in the equation.* Then move as many spaces as the second number in the equation. Let the + and − signs direct which way your finger moves.

$$-3 - 5 \text{ (start on } -3, \text{ move 5 spaces to the left)} = -8$$
$$-3 + 7 \text{ (start on the } -3, \text{ move 7 spaces to the right)} = 4$$

In this way, we can see that adding a negative number is the same as subtracting a positive number. Both move your finger to the left. And subtracting a negative number is the same as adding a positive number. Both move your finger to the right.

$$5 + -4 \text{ (start on 5, move 4 to the left)} = 1$$
$$-5 - 3 \text{ (start on } -5, \text{ move 3 to the left)} = -8$$
$$-3 - -3 \text{ (start on } -3, \text{ move 3 to the right)} = 0$$
$$8 + 4 \text{ (start on 8, move 4 to the right)} = 12$$

I love Nutella. I predict that this negative guy will go far.

—Ava

**Little-Known Math Fact**

*Number lines are so named because they were invented by Johannes Ubrecht Numberliner, and not, as many assume, because they are lines with numbers on them.*

* If, as a result of having already taken hours of the ACT, you no longer have an imagination, you can draw a number line in your test booklet, provided you have not also lost your ability to express yourself with a pencil.

—Jon

To multiply and divide with negative numbers, remember that different signs give you negative products, while the same signs give you positive products. Or, as Zack likes to think of it: When you have one negative sign, it likes to stick around; when you have two, one rotates, and they merge and make a plus sign.

$$(+)5 \cdot (+)5 = (+)25 \text{ (two positive signs give us a positive product)}$$
$$-5 \cdot -5 = (+)25 \text{ (two negative signs give us a positive product)}$$
$$-5 \cdot (+)5 = -25 \text{ (one positive and one negative sign give us a negative product)}$$

The same rules apply for division:
$$(-)5 \div (+)5 = -1$$
$$(-)5 \div (-)5 = 1$$

**Let's Play**

| N E G A T I V E | | P O S I T I V E |
|---|---|---|
| **1.** $5 \div -10 - -3 \cdot 4 =$ | **2.** $-15 \cdot -3 - 2 + -26 \div 3 =$ | **3.** $-43 \cdot 22 + -3 \cdot -3 =$ |
| **A.** $-5$ | **A.** $-10$ | **A.** $-937$ |
| **B.** $10$ | **B.** $-6\frac{2}{3}$ | **B.** $-412$ |
| **C.** $11\frac{1}{2}$ | **C.** $12$ | **C.** $0$ |
| **D.** $14$ | **D.** $34\frac{1}{3}$ | **D.** $233$ |
| **E.** $15\frac{1}{2}$ | **E.** $43$ | **E.** $412$ |

Answers: **1.** C; **2.** D; **3.** A

The nice thing here and on the ACT is that both parentheses and brackets are used, which helps organize the order of operations.

—Ava

## Nightmare Neg/Pos Problems

The ACT-bot constructs nightmare problems by making you solve mini-equations within parentheses, all while keeping track of the negativity and positivity of each component. Just tread carefully, remember PREMDAS, and keep a keen eye out for positivity and negativity.

### NEGATIVE POSITIVE
#### Nightmare Edition

**1.** $[(-7 \cdot -2) \cdot -3 + 4] \cdot [(-22 \div -4) \cdot (-10 - 3 + 4 \cdot -5)] =$

**A.** −10,000

**B.** 6,897

**C.** −803

**D.** 412

**E.** 550

**2.** $[((-10 + 3) \cdot -5) \div (-5 - 2)] - [(-21 \cdot 2) + (-6 - 5)] =$

**A.** −48

**B.** −22

**C.** −6

**D.** 20

**E.** 48

**3.** $[(-5 + 3) + (-25) \cdot 2] + -[(32 \cdot -2) - (-13 + 6)] =$

**A.** −10

**B.** −5

**C.** 5

**D.** 10

**E.** 15

Answers: **1.** B; **2.** E; **3.** C

## DIVIDING RULES

Some basic arithmetic problems on the ACT can look very scary. This often means that the bot is testing whether or not you know some of the more common patterns of division.

### How to Play

Knowing these rules can make tough problems a lot easier.

| It's divisible by | If | Example |
|---|---|---|
| | **DIVIDING RULES** | |
| 1 | It is an integer. | Do you really need one? |
| 2 | It's an even number. | Hmm . . . |
| 3 | Its digits add up to a multiple of 3. | 186. $1 + 8 + 6 = 15$ $15 = (3 \cdot 5)$ |
| 4 | Its last two digits form (not "add up to") a number divisible by 4. | 103,424 24 is divisible by 4 $(24 \div 4 = 6)$ |
| 5 | It ends in 5 or 0. | 5,746,893,765 |
| 6 | It is even and divisible by 3. | 522 |
| 7 | There's a rule, but it's complicated; just use your calculator. | |
| 8 | Its last three digits form a multiple of 8. | 10,496,832 $(832 \div 8 = 104)$ |
| 9 | Its digits add up to a multiple of 9. | 34,164. $3 + 4 + 1 + 6 + 4 = 18 = (2 \cdot 9)$ |
| 10 | It ends in 0. | 1,600 |

### Try It Out

Which of the following numbers is divisible by both 8 and 9?

A. 5,470

B. 5,471

C. 5,472

D. 5,473

E. 5,474

This problem could be solved in about 30 seconds with a calculator, or in about six seconds with a brain that knows dividing rules. (Those spare 24 seconds can be used to work on your screenplay about time-traveling dogs who love to rap. Or you could spend them on another math problem, which is probably the better choice.)

Add those numbers up to see which is a multiple of 9. Only answer choice C works. Does it pass the multiple of 8 test? Indeed it does. C is our answer!

**Let's Play**

## DIVISION

1. Which of the following numbers is divisible by both 5 and 6?
   - A. 4,780
   - B. 5,385
   - C. 6,255
   - D. 7,440
   - E. 9,620

## DIVISION

2. Which of the following numbers is divisible by 3 but *not* by 9?
   - A. 47,890
   - B. 48,525
   - C. 58,745
   - D. 59,553
   - E. 63,130

Answers: **1.** D; **2.** B

**Little-Known Math Fact**

*Before the invention of division, the words* numerator *and* denominator *were the names of professional wrestling moves.*

## FRACTIONS

The ACT-bot is a pretty big fan of fractions. This is because fractions look familiar, but many kids fail to grasp them on a deep level. At the bottom, a fraction is a statement of division. What does that mean? Well, read the following story:

The fraction bar is the division sign (÷) with numbers filling in for the dots.

—Ava

## How to Play

One day, a cat, a giraffe, a salesman for a multinational insurance corporation, an alligator, and an ape all sat down to have a delicious cake party. They had 3 cakes to share equally. How should they divide the cakes?

**Step 1:** Cut the first cake into 5 equal pieces. Give 1 to each member of the party.

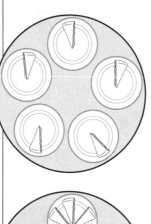

**Step 2:** Repeat the first step for the 2 remaining cakes, until each member has 3 pieces.

Now, as you can see, every member has 3 pieces of cake. Each piece is a fifth of a cake, so everyone has three-fifths $\left(\frac{3}{5}\right)$ of a cake. Get it? The lesson here is that 3 divided by 5 is the same as $\frac{3}{5}$. And *that* is the deep understanding of fractions that you need! (After the distribution of each portion, the alligator ate all of the other animals, then turned on the insurance salesman and ate him, and then wolfed down *all* of the pieces of cake. Let that also be a lesson: Don't put alligators in your examples.)

The easiest way to play with fractions is to multiply them. Just go horizontal, multiplying the numerators of each fraction on the top and the denominators on the bottom.

$$\frac{4}{5} \cdot \frac{6}{3} = \frac{4 \cdot 6}{5 \cdot 3} = \frac{24}{15}$$

To divide fractions, **flip the divisor** (the second fraction in the problem) **and multiply.** We're putting that in big bold letters because everyone forgets to do it.

To add and subtract fractions, we first need to find the

Some test takers—fatigued by the sheer might of the ACT—will start to multiply fractions diagonally, vertically, and northward. Don't let this happen to you.

—Jon

**A Probably Unnecessary Reminder**

The numerator is the top number in a fraction, telling you the number of parts. The denominator is the bottom number, and it tells you the number that makes up the whole. Another way to think about this: A fraction means "top number divided by bottom number," where the horizontal line means "divided by."

**least common denominator** by locating the smallest number for which both denominators are a factor. If that sentence sounded loopy and complex, don't worry. You've done this a million times:

In the problem $\frac{3}{5} + \frac{4}{3}$, we need to find a number that both denominators, 3 and 5, multiply into: 15. Convert each fraction into 15ths:

$$\frac{3}{5} + \frac{4}{3} = \frac{3}{5} \cdot \frac{3}{3} + \frac{4}{3} \cdot \frac{5}{5} = \frac{9}{15} + \frac{20}{15}$$

Then add the numerators:

$$\frac{9}{15} + \frac{20}{15} = \frac{29}{15}$$

To subtract fractions, find the least common denominator again and then subtract the numerators:

$$\frac{5}{8} - \frac{1}{2} = \frac{5}{8} - \frac{4}{8} = \frac{1}{8}$$

There is one more trick that you will need to know: converting improper fractions to mixed numbers and back again. An "improper" fraction has a numerator that is larger than the denominator.*

To convert from improper fractions to mixed numbers, divide the numerator by the denominator. The answer may come out as a whole number with a remainder. That remainder is your new numerator. Check it out:

Look at $\frac{29}{3}$. If we divide 29 by 3, our answer is 9, with a remainder of 2. So we write the mixed number as $9\frac{2}{3}$.

To convert from a mixed number to an improper fraction, you multiply the whole number and the denominator, then add the product to the numerator. Like this:

Look at $5\frac{3}{8}$. Multiply $5 \cdot 8$, and add the product (40) to the numerator (3) to get 43.

*It's also rude at parties and uses the *salad* fork during the *fish* course.

The improper fraction version of the mixed number is $\frac{43}{8}$.

**Let's Play**

**FRACTIONS**

**1.** $\frac{2}{7} + \frac{3}{4} =$

A. $\frac{5}{13}$

B. $\frac{28}{29}$

C. $\frac{29}{28}$

D. $\frac{13}{5}$

E. $\frac{20}{21}$

**FRACTIONS**

**2.** $\frac{7}{12} \cdot \frac{3}{2} =$

A. $\frac{5}{6}$

B. $\frac{18}{7}$

C. $\frac{7}{18}$

D. $\frac{7}{8}$

E. $\frac{8}{7}$

**FRACTIONS**

**3.** $\frac{4}{3} \div \frac{3}{11} =$

A. $\frac{1}{3}$

B. $\frac{9}{11}$

C. $\frac{41}{33}$

D. $\frac{9}{44}$

E. $\frac{44}{9}$

**FRACTIONS**

**4.** $\frac{4}{9} - \frac{2}{5} =$

A. $\frac{-2}{13}$

B. 0

C. $\frac{2}{45}$

D. 1

E. $\frac{11}{2}$

**Calculator to the Rescue**

Your calculator will solve fraction problems for you. Put parentheses around them and use the ( ÷ ) to replace the bar in the fraction. Your calculator will convert the fraction to a decimal, but when you're done, you can change it back by pressing (MATH), choosing ▶FRAC, then (ENTER). Try it!

**Answers: 1.** C; **2.** D; **3.** E; **4.** C

You might have noticed in the above problems that the ACT-bot demands that all fractional answers be reduced to their lowest form. This does not mean shrinking fractions with a shrink-ray, however cool that would be. Here's what it means: Let's say your answer is $\frac{21}{9}$. Can you divide both the numerator and denominator by the same number? Yes, you can divide both by 3. This means we can reduce the fraction to $\dfrac{\left(\frac{21}{3} = 7\right)}{\left(\frac{9}{3} = 3\right)}$. Our reduced answer, then, is $\frac{7}{3}$. If you solve a problem involving fractions, but don't see your answer, always check to see if you can reduce!

Keep in mind that the ACT is trying to test you on more than your calculator button-pushing abilities, so if you find yourself doing ridiculous math . . . stop, skip, and come back later.

—Ava

## NIGHTMARE FRACTION PROBLEMS

The ACT-bot knows that it is a pain in the ear to solve a fraction problem, so to make a more painful problem, it does the logical thing: throws a lot of fractions and operations into one equation. If stubbing your toe sucks, then it must really suck to stub three or four toes, right? The trick here is to find common denominators, and remember PREMDAS! (Also, if you're using your calculator, be careful about entering the correct parentheses.)

## FRACTIONS
### NIGHTMARE PROBLEMS

**1.** $\left(\frac{4}{5} + \frac{2}{6} - \frac{3}{4}\right) + \left(\frac{21}{6} \cdot \frac{15}{3}\right) =$

A. $\dfrac{1073}{60}$

B. $\dfrac{54}{982}$

C. $\dfrac{53}{350}$

D. $\dfrac{64}{203}$

E. $\dfrac{12}{160}$

**2.** $\left(\frac{9}{2} \div \frac{1}{3}\right) + \left(\left(\frac{2}{9} + \frac{15}{3}\right) \cdot \frac{3}{5}\right) =$

A. $\dfrac{-24}{13}$

B. $\dfrac{-12}{21}$

C. $\dfrac{1}{40}$

D. $\dfrac{240}{213}$

E. $\dfrac{499}{30}$

**3.** $\left(\left(\frac{3}{8} \cdot \frac{6}{5}\right) - \frac{7}{9}\right) + \left(\frac{4}{5} + \frac{13}{3}\right) =$

A. $\dfrac{-13}{214}$

B. $\dfrac{-59}{924}$

C. $0$

D. $\dfrac{173}{36}$

E. $\dfrac{21}{4}$

**4.** $\left(\left(\frac{4}{2} \div \frac{2}{4}\right) + \frac{6}{15}\right) - \left(\frac{2}{7} - \frac{2}{14}\right) =$

A. $\dfrac{-32}{3}$

B. $\dfrac{-21}{12}$

C. $\dfrac{73}{78}$

D. $\dfrac{149}{35}$

E. $\dfrac{220}{21}$

**Answers: 1.** A; **2.** E; **3.** D; **4.** D

And remember that the word "of" means multiplication. So $\frac{4}{5}$ of $\frac{2}{3}$ is the same as $\frac{4}{5} \cdot \frac{2}{3}$.

—Zack

Sorry to say, but the ACT-bot is not done messing with you. Even more headache-inducing and *far more common* than the nightmare fraction problem is the nightmare fraction word problem. Just remember to read it twice, remember that fractions are **part over whole,** and cautiously create an equation from the problem.

> After a party, Tayshawn takes home $\frac{2}{3}$ of a pie and splits it evenly between himself and his two little sisters. If the entire pie originally had 1,200 calories, how many calories of pie does his youngest sister, Maggie, eat?

If Tayshawn took home $\frac{2}{3}$ and split the two-thirds with his two sisters, that means he is splitting $\frac{2}{3}$ into three equal pieces (one for him, and one for each of his sisters). We can do this on our calculators in two ways:

$$\frac{\left(\frac{2}{3}\right)}{3}$$

or

$$\left(\frac{2}{3}\right) \cdot \left(\frac{1}{3}\right)$$

Either way, we get the answer that each person gets $\frac{2}{9}$ of the original pie. If the entire pie had 1,200 calories, we just find $\frac{2}{9}$ to get our answer: $1,200 \cdot \frac{2}{9} = 266.67$ calories.

Let's do one more:

> An insurance salesman is walking along a dark alley one night when suddenly he is eaten by the alligator from the cake problem, which has developed a taste for insurance-salesman meat.

**Little-Known Math Fact**

*Until action movies became more popular, audiences flocked to "fraction movies" in which chiseled stars like The Rock and Vin Diesel solved sheet after sheet of math problems, taking no prisoners.*

The alligator leaves $\frac{1}{3}$ of the man in the alley, then goes home and regurgitates $\frac{5}{7}$ of what it's consumed to its children (which is a thing some alligators do). How much of the insurance salesman did the alligator have in its tummy at the end of the night (not including the manflesh from the cake problem)?

If the alligator left $\frac{1}{3}$ of the man in the alley, that means it has $\frac{2}{3}$ of the man in its stomach. So far, so good. If it regurgitates $\frac{5}{7}$ of this to its children, then it only has $\frac{2}{7}$ of the original $\frac{2}{3}$ left in its own stomach. To find out how much this is, we need to take $\frac{2}{7}$ of $\frac{2}{3}$, or $\frac{2}{7} \cdot \frac{2}{3}$, which equals $\frac{4}{21}$, or .19.

**Answer:** $\frac{4}{21}$

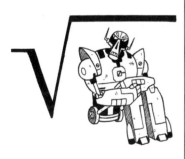

I've always thought of the root sign as a flourished fraction bar, since the number before the root (square root, third root, etc.) is the denominator of the power (½, ⅓, etc.).

—Ava

## ROOTS AND EXPONENTS

A professor once said: "Roots and exponents are like the roots and fruits of a tree." But that's completely ridiculous, and that guy probably isn't even a professor. The lesson: Always check a professor's credentials (a quick Google search should do it) before listening to him or her.

### How to Play

Roots and exponents *are* related. Take a look:

$$4^2 = 16, \sqrt{16} = 4$$
$$5^3 = 125, \sqrt[3]{125} = 5$$

One thing to remember with roots is that (root) 16 can actually be 4 or −4, because (−4)(−4) is also 16. This is true of all even roots, i.e., the fourth root, sixth root, etc.

The cool thing about roots is that, with some practice, you can perform sick root tricks at parties and impress all your friends.

### Three Sick Root Tricks
1. Add roots: $4\sqrt{3} + 20\sqrt{3} = 24\sqrt{3}$
2. Multiply roots: $\sqrt{4} \cdot \sqrt{8} = \sqrt{4 \cdot 8} = \sqrt{32}$ *
3. Factor roots: $\sqrt{18} = \sqrt{9} \cdot \sqrt{2} = 3\sqrt{2}$

**Be Careful!**

$(-2)^4 = 16$

but

$-2^4 = -16$

Remember your PREMDAS!

If a malicious machine programmed only for destruction can be said to be fond of anything, the ACT-bot is fond of playing with that third rule. So let's make sure it's crystal clear. Because $18 = 9 \cdot 2$, then $\sqrt{18} = \sqrt{9} \cdot \sqrt{2}$. But we're not done yet! $\sqrt{9} = 3$. So our final reduced answer is $3\sqrt{2}$. Here are some classic problems that look crazy tough until you realize that you can use root-factoring to make them crazy simple.

### Let's Play with Roots
$$\sqrt{75} \cdot 3 =$$
Reduce that $\sqrt{75}$ to $\sqrt{25} \cdot \sqrt{3}$, which can be reduced further to $5\sqrt{3}$. Multiply this by 3 to get our answer: $15\sqrt{3}$.

Or try this: $\sqrt{243}$.

Because $243 = 81 \cdot 3$, then $\sqrt{243} = \sqrt{81} \cdot \sqrt{3}$. And $\sqrt{81} = 9$. So our answer is $9\sqrt{3}$.

**ROOTS**

1. $2\sqrt{60} =$
   - A. $2\sqrt{15}$
   - B. $4\sqrt{15}$
   - C. $15\sqrt{4}$
   - D. $15\sqrt{2}$
   - E. $15$

**ROOTS**

2. $\sqrt{288}$
   - A. $8\sqrt{3}$
   - B. $12$
   - C. $12\sqrt{2}$
   - D. $14$
   - E. $14\sqrt{2}$

*The ACT would simplify this to $4\sqrt{2}$, but we'll explain that in a second.

**Answers: 1.** B; **2.** C

Even more than testing roots, the ACT-bot loves to test rules about exponents. And just like nightmare fraction problems, nightmare exponent problems are built using simple pieces grouped together to create the appearance of difficulty.

### How to Play with Exponents

In the number $4^3$, the **base** is 4, and the **exponent** is 3. We can play with exponents *only when they have the same base*. There are seven rules to follow when playing with exponents.

1. Multiplying exponents: $4^3 \cdot 4^4 = 4^{(3+4)} = 4^7$
2. Dividing exponents: $5^7 \div 5^3 = 5^{(7-3)} = 5^4$
3. Raising exponents to another exponent:
   $(2^3)^4 = 2^{(3)(4)} = 2^{12}$
4. Raising a base to a fractional exponent: $3^{\frac{3}{4}} = \sqrt[4]{3^3}$
5. Raising a base to a negative exponent: $5^{-3} = \dfrac{1}{5^3} = \dfrac{1}{125}$
6. Raising a base to the exponent 0:
   $7^0 = 1, 9^0 = 1, \text{anything}^0 = 1$
7. Raising a base to the exponent 1: $8^1 = 8, 3^1 = 3$

Got it? Good.

### Let's Play

**EXPONENTS**

1. $\dfrac{3^9}{3^7} =$

   A. 3
   B. $3^2$
   C. $3^4$
   D. $3^{\frac{9}{7}}$
   E. $3^{16}$

**EXPONENTS**

2. $2^3 \cdot 2^{-3} =$

   A. $2^{-9}$
   B. 0
   C. 1
   D. 2
   E. $2^6$

**EXPONENTS**

3. $(4^3)^2 =$

   A. $4^{-1}$
   B. 1
   C. 4
   D. $4^5$
   E. $4^6$

**EXPONENTS**

4. $4^3 \div 4^4 =$

   A. 0
   B. $\dfrac{1}{4}$
   C. 1
   D. 4
   E. $4^7$

**Answers: 1.** B; **2.** C; **3.** E; **4.** B

### Nightmare Exponent Problems

As you might expect, a problem can be made to look harder if a bunch of exponents are grouped together. But the ACT-bot's trickiest trick is to place an exponent in a location that makes it unclear what is being squared, as in: $\frac{4^2}{3}$, which is $\frac{16}{3}$, and should not be confused with $\left(\frac{4}{3}\right)^2$. In the second number we need to square the whole fraction, which gives us $\frac{16}{9}$. Let's try a few:

**NIGHTMARE EXPONENTS**

**1.** $\left(\frac{3}{2}\right)^4 =$

 **A.** $\frac{-2}{11}$

 **B.** $\frac{1}{312}$

 **C.** $\frac{3}{16}$

 **D.** $\frac{81}{16}$

 **E.** $\frac{243}{16}$

**NIGHTMARE EXPONENTS**

**2.** $\left(\frac{4^2}{4^4}\right)^2 =$

 **A.** $\frac{1}{256}$

 **B.** $\frac{1}{8}$

 **C.** 1

 **D.** 64

 **E.** 256

**NIGHTMARE EXPONENTS**

**3.** $\frac{\left(5^3 \cdot 5^{-4}\right)}{5^2} =$

 **A.** $-125$

 **B.** 1

 **C.** $\frac{1}{125}$

 **D.** 25

 **E.** 125

**Answers: 1.** D; **2.** A; **3.** C

Another classic nightmare root scenario is when the bot gives you problems that *appear* to have different bases. Like so:

$$16^2 \cdot 4^3 = 2^x$$

"Wuzzawhaaa?" you say. "Those are different bases! 16 and 4 and 2? Those are different numbers, sister." Well, hold on. You might notice that 16 and 4 are the same as $(2^4)$ and $(2^2)$. So just rewrite the problem:

$$(2^4)^2 \cdot (2^2)^3 = 2^x$$
$$2^8 \cdot 2^6 = 2^{(8+6)} = 2^x$$
$$x = 14$$

Let's try an even tougher problem:

$$\frac{(27^2)}{3^x} = 9$$

Go ahead and change that $27^2$ to an exponent with base 3.

$$27^2 = (3^3)^2 = 3^{(3 \cdot 2)} = 3^6$$

And change that 9 to an exponent with base 3.
$$9 = 3^2$$

So the problem, rewritten, becomes $\dfrac{(3^6)}{3^x} = 3^2$

That's no longer a nightmare. We know that $6 - x = 2$, so $x = 4$.

You try one:

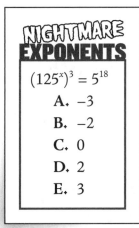

NIGHTMARE
EXPONENTS

$$(125^x)^3 = 5^{18}$$

A. −3
B. −2
C. 0
D. 2
E. 3

**Answer:** D

## SCIENTIFIC NOTATION

Way back in the day, back before the Internet and pizza-crusts-that-are-also-breadsticks-that-come-with-their-own-dipping-sauce, scientists led really difficult lives. If an astronomer discovered Proxima Centauri, she would have to turn to her

## Little-Known Math Fact

*Scientific notation is useful for writing infinitesimal numbers, like the number of points you score in basketball.* Oh! Math burn! Math buuuuuuuurn in your face!

colleague and say: "Oh my gosh, I just found a star that is only thirty-nine trillion, nine hundred and sixty-four billion, five hundred and thirty-two million, six hundred and seventy thousand, two hundred and twelve miles away!" Then her colleague, who had been listening to a Prince cassette on his Walkman, would say: "Oh sorry, I was listening to a sweet Prince cassette on my amazing new Walkman. Could you repeat that?" The astronomer would take a deep breath, then repeat the enormous number. By the time she was done, her colleague would have died from boredom.

Luckily, the heads of several science departments got together and invented scientific notation, which allows us to say gigantic and teeny-weeny numbers without dying from boredom!

## How to Play

Take an enormous number like 9,450,000,000. Actually, YOLO, let's go even bigger: 9,450,000,000,000,000.

There we go. That's a big number.

To write this in scientific notation:

+ Put a decimal point after the first nonzero number: 9.
+ Write each additional nonzero number: 9.45
+ Multiply this by $10^{\text{(number of spaces we need to move the decimal to the right to rewrite the original number)}}$

So the above enormous number then becomes $9.45 \cdot 10^{15}$.

Or take a teeny-weeny number like .000000000327. Again:

+ Put a decimal point after the first nonzero number: 3.
+ Write each nonzero number after the decimal point: 3.27
+ Multiply this by $10^{\text{(\textbf{negative} number of spaces we need to move the decimal to the left to rewrite the original number)}}$

So the teeny-weeny number becomes $3.27 \cdot 10^{-10}$.

### Let's Play

**S$^n$** SCIENTIFIC NOTATION

**1.** Convert 380,000 to scientific notation:

A. $3.8 \cdot 10^{-3}$
B. $3.8 \cdot 10^{2}$
C. $3.8 \cdot 10^{3}$
D. $3.8 \cdot 10^{5}$
E. $3.8 \cdot 10^{1000}$

**S$^n$** SCIENTIFIC NOTATION

**2.** Convert $7.2 \cdot 10^{-5}$ to normal people notation:*

A. .0000072
B. .000072
C. .0072
D. .072
E. .72

**S$^n$** SCIENTIFIC NOTATION

**3.** Convert $1.6 \cdot 10^{5}$ to normal people notation:

A. .00016
B. .16
C. 160
D. 160,000
E. 160,000,000

**S$^n$** SCIENTIFIC NOTATION

**4.** Convert .0000435 to scientific notation:

A. $4.35 \cdot 10^{-5}$
B. $4.35 \cdot 10^{-3}$
C. $4.35 \cdot 10^{2}$
D. $4.35 \cdot 10^{3}$
E. $4.35 \cdot 10^{4}$

*"Normal people notation" is known as "decimal notation" on the ACT.

**Answers: 1.** D; **2.** B; **3.** D; **4.** A

**Nightmare Scientific Notation Problems**

Honestly, scientific notation is so straightforward that the ACT-bot can't do much except include numbers written with scientific notation in more challenging problems. The trick is to convert the numbers from scientific to decimal notation, then solve as usual. If the geometry aspect of these problems makes you weep, go read our geometry section, and then come back and try these again.

**NS$^n$** NIGHTMARE SCIENTIFIC NOTATION

**1.** A flea has a swimming pool that is $4.5 \cdot 10^{-3}$ inches deep, $2.7 \cdot 10^{-3}$ inches wide, and $8 \cdot 10^{-3}$ inches long. How many cubic inches of water does the flea need to fill its pool?

 A. $9.72 \cdot 10^{-8}$
 B. $9.72 \cdot 10^{-5}$
 C. $3.73 \cdot 10^{-4}$
 D. $3.73 \cdot 10^{-2}$
 E. $3.73$

**NS$^n$** NIGHTMARE SCIENTIFIC NOTATION

**2.** A rectangular panel of siding for a skyscraper has a width of $1.9 \cdot 10^{5}$ ft. and length of $2.6 \cdot 10^{6}$ ft. Approximately how many squares with 934 ft. sides will be needed to cover one panel?

 A. $3.3 \cdot 10^{-2}$
 B. $3.3 \cdot 10^{2}$
 C. $5.7 \cdot 10^{2}$
 D. $5.7 \cdot 10^{5}$
 E. $7.8 \cdot 10^{5}$

That itty-bitty swimming pool would be *adorable* if it weren't for the flea.

—Jon

**NS$^n$** NIGHTMARE SC

**3.** $\dfrac{6.2 \cdot 10^{3}}{2 \cdot 10^{9}} = ?$

Try it without a calculator.

(Hint: Use your exponent rules.)

 A. $6.2 \cdot 10^{-7}$
 B. $3.1 \cdot 10^{-6}$
 C. $3.1 \cdot 10^{-3}$
 D. $4.2 \cdot 10^{4}$
 E. $4.2 \cdot 10^{6}$

Answers:
**1.** A
**2.** D
**3.** B

## Advanced Arithmetic

How did you feel about that last section? A lot of it was review, we know, but it also gave us the building blocks for most of the arithmetic problems on the test. You see, the ACT-bot is more interested in testing how you *apply* your knowledge of basic arithmetic in more complex problems. So, let's do that. Again, think of each problem type as a game: Learn the rules, play for a bit, and then we'll show you the more difficult versions of the game.

### PERCENT

Want to know the secret to becoming a successful business tycoon? It's a simple two-step process: 1.) Always be smoking a fat cigar, and 2.) Learn how to use percents. That's right, *percent manipulation is the key to all business.*

### How to Play

Here's what we mean: Let's say you want to become a real-estate tycoon, like Donald Trump. First, build a deluxe apartment complex. Call it something classy, like the Diamond-Encrusted Triple-Platinum Tower.

If everyone wants to buy your apartments, then you want to mark up the price by a certain percent and need to know how to do a percent increase. If there is less demand, then you need to know how to lower the price with a percent decrease. But before all that, you need to know how to find the percent of a number.

### Finding the Percent of a Number

It is very simple to deal with percents using decimals on a calculator. But it is easier to *understand* percents by treating them as fractions. So we'll start by talking about percents as fractions, to make sure you understand them backward and forward. (In the margins we will show you how to solve percents super quick using decimals on a calculator.)

So let's think of a percent as a fraction. (*Percent* literally means "for every 100" in Romanspeak, so if we have 3% of the world's

Writing a percent as a fraction instead of as a decimal will help you avoid careless mistakes, like thinking .9 is equal to 9%.

—Jon

---

**Calculator to the Rescue**

To find 12% of 35, type:

to get 4.2.

---

In any percent problem, keep what _percent_ means clear in your mind: You have a certain number of things out of a set of a certain size, and the percent is the relative number if that set were exactly 100 in size.

—Zack

Skittles, we have 3 out of every 100 Skittles.) 70% is the same as $\frac{70}{100}$, 42% is $\frac{42}{100}$, etc. Once you know this, then you are ready to use the Business Tycoon's Weapon: the part-whole equation.

Here's how this works. Say you need to find 12% of 35. We set up a part-whole equation by plugging the numbers into the following: $\frac{\text{Part}}{\text{Whole}} = \frac{\text{Percent}}{100}$. The $\frac{\text{Part}}{\text{Whole}}$ section of the equation is where we put in our actual numbers, the $\frac{\text{Percent}}{100}$ section is where we put in our percent:

$$\frac{x}{35} = \frac{12}{100}$$

Then we cross multiply:

$$100x = (35)(12)$$

$$100x = 420$$

$$x = 4.2$$

So: 4.2 is 12% of 35.

This also works if you only know the part, rather than the whole. 25 is 40% of what number? Plug the numbers into the equation:

$$\frac{25}{x} = \frac{40}{100}$$

Cross multiply to find that $x = 62.5$ (25 is 40% of 62.5).

Finally, we can use part-whole to find the percent, if we know the part and whole. 30 is what percent of 200?

$$\frac{30}{200} = \frac{x}{100}$$

Cross multiply to find that $x = 15$ (30 is 15% of 200).

Neat trick, huh? Now let's look at how to use the part-whole equation for some real-world problems.

## Percent Increase

Everyone has read about your amazing apartments and demand is high. So you want to mark up the price, because, um, you want more money.

So: You raise the price on your $5,400,250 apartment by 15%. How much does someone now have to pay to live in your apartment?

To solve this, we're going to use the part-whole equation, but we have to modify it a little bit:

$$\frac{\text{New Price}}{\text{Original Price}} = \frac{100 + \text{percent increase}}{100}$$

So:

$$\frac{x}{5,400,250} = \frac{115 \left[\text{which is 100 plus the increase of 15\%}\right]}{100}$$

Cross multiply to find that the new price is $6,210,287.50.

If you know the dollar amount of the increase, you can use the exact same equation to find the percent.

You raise the price of a parking space in your building from $4,600 to $6,250. What percent increase is this?

$$\frac{6,250}{4,600} = \frac{x}{100}$$

Cross multiply to find that $x = 135.9$. But be careful—the "percent increase" refers only to the amount you've added to the original amount. So the percent increase here is 35.9%.

## Percent Decrease

Unfortunately, some residents are finding life at Diamond-Encrusted Triple-Platinum Tower a little less luxurious than they thought it would be. Not enough caviar in their bathroom caviar dispenser, they say. They are moving out. In order to make your apartments more attractive, you lower the price.

---

**Calculator to the Rescue**

To find 115% of $5,400,250, type:

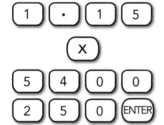

to get $6,210,287.50.

---

Pay attention to the question. Sometimes it'll ask for the new percent (don't subtract 100), and sometimes it'll ask for the percent change (do subtract 100).

—Ava

**Calculator to the Rescue**

To find 85% of
$4,350,000, type:

to get $3,697,500.

**Calculator to the Rescue**

To take 5% off
$2,000 twice, type:

to get $1,900, then type

to get $1,805.

---

You lower the price of an apartment from $4,350,000 by 15%. What is the new price?

We need to modify our part-whole machine slightly:

$$\frac{\text{New Price}}{\text{Original Price}} = \frac{100-\text{percent decrease}}{100}$$

$$\frac{x}{4,350,000} = \frac{85\,[\text{because } 100 - 15 = 85]}{100}$$

Cross multiply to find that the new price is $3,697,500.

If we know both the original and the new price, then we can find the percent by using the same equation.

You lower the price of a parking space from $3,250 to $2,700. What is the percent decrease?

$$\frac{2,700}{3,250} = \frac{x}{100}$$

Cross multiply to find that $x$ = about 83%. But be careful—the "percent decrease" refers only to the amount you've taken away from the original amount. So the percent decrease here is about 17%.

One last thing before you graduate from Tycoon School: If we decrease or increase a percent multiple times, then we need to build a new part-whole equation for each decrease or increase.

Your friendly neighborhood tycoon has promised to decrease the rents by 5% per month for the next two months. If you are currently paying $2,000 per month, what will you be paying two months from now?

*Do not be tempted to add the two percents, and take 10% off $2,000.* Instead, you need to make two part-whole equations.

$$\frac{x}{2,000} = \frac{95}{100} \qquad x = \$1,900$$

Then, use the *new* total for the second equation.

$$\frac{x}{1,900} = \frac{95}{100} \qquad x = \$1,805$$

So after two months, your rent will be $1,805.

Okay, young tycoon! You're ready to go out and buy a seersucker suit and a box of cigars. Then throw those cigars away because they make you smell awful and literally kill you.

**Let's Play**

**1.** 30 is 82% of approximately what number?
  A. 26.62
  B. 28.73
  C. 33
  D. 36.59
  E. 42.21

**2.** What is 5% of 375 rounded to the nearest hundredth?
  A. 16.74
  B. 17.23
  C. 18.75
  D. 19.11
  E. 21.22

**3.** For approximately what number is 60% of the number equal to 68?
  A. 72.56
  B. 88.83
  C. 113.33
  D. 126.54
  E. 154.29

Answers: **1.** D; **2.** C; **3.** C

**4.** The price of a toy is lowered by 35%. The new price is $5. What was the original price to the nearest cent?
  A. $6.23
  B. $7.69
  C. $9.52
  D. $11.28
  E. $13.47

**5.** A car costs $35,000. The price is increased by 15%. What is the new price?
  A. $37,460
  B. $38,220
  C. $39,550
  D. $40,250
  E. $42,340

**6.** A ring's price was decreased by $4 from its original price of $28. What is the approximate percent decrease of the ring's price?
  A. 14%
  B. 19%
  C. 24%
  D. 28%
  E. 32%

Answers: **4.** B; **5.** D; **6.** A

## Nightmare Percent Problems

The ACT-bot's favorite trick is to link two percent increase and decrease problems into one really annoying problem. Just remember to think of the problem as two percent problems and solve the first percent problem, then use that answer to solve the second percent problem. Let's try one:

> The Cooter-Pewter Computer Company releases a new version of its famous laptop, the Ocelot. The price of the new laptop is 20% more than the older version. Nobody buys the new, expensive computer, so the company lowers the price 5%, to $950. What was the price of the old model of the Ocelot?

This problem requires that we move *backward* from a price ($950) that is the result of an increase *and then* a decrease, to the older model's price. So if $950, the discounted price, is what we get after reducing the increased price by 5%, we can go backward by saying that:

> $950 = 95% of the increased price.
>
> $950 = .95 \cdot x$
>
> $\dfrac{950}{.95} = 1000 = x$

$1,000 is our *increased price*, which is 20% over the old model's price. So:

> $1000 = 120%$ of the old model's price
>
> $1000 = 1.2 \cdot x$
>
> $\dfrac{1000}{1.2} = 833.33 = x$

Our original price, then, is $833.33. Try two yourself:

## NIGHT % MARE

**1.** Bert is trying to sell his grandpa's tractor, but nobody is in the market for a $140 vintage Rustbucket-brand tractor. So Bert lowers the price 20%. A few people take a look at the tractor, but still nobody wants it. So Bert lowers the discounted price another 15%. Shirley P. Kibbletiff buys it for her Museum of Agricultural Antiques. How much did Shirley pay?

- **A.** $88.00
- **B.** $90.35
- **C.** $95.20
- **D.** $99.75
- **E.** $103.40

## NIGHT % MARE

**2.** The population of Tumbleweed, Arkansas, in 1990 was 60,400 people. In 1991, when oil was discovered, the population increased by 40%. But in 1992 a massive tornado scattered the oil into neighboring counties, and the population decreased by 20%. At the end of 1992, what was the population of Tumbleweed?

- **A.** 53,539
- **B.** 67,648
- **C.** 75,923
- **D.** 89,622
- **E.** 95,362

Answers: **1.** C; **2.** B

### Little-Known Math Fact

*Ratios are often seen in recipes. For example: 3 parts bacon:1 part all the other stuff (like the tomatoes or flour or whatever).*

## RATIOS

Remember how fractions represent part/whole? **Ratios represent the comparison of two quantities, and on the ACT it's usually part/part.**

### How to Play

Let start with an example:

> At the Bosworth Modeling Agency, the ratio of male models to female models is 3:5. If there are 48 models at the agency, how many women are employed at Bosworth?

Okay, so we know that the agency is three parts male to five parts female. But how do we figure out the actual number of guys and the actual number of girls that work at the agency? To find this out, follow three steps.

Ratio problems are very easy to check after you do them. Just make sure your numbers add up to the total and divide to give you the correct ratio.

—Jon

1. Add your parts to find the ratio total: $3 + 5 = 8$.
2. How many times larger is the real total (48) than the ratio total (8)? It is 6 times bigger.
3. So multiply each part by 6 to convert the ratio numbers to the real numbers of guys and girls. Males: $3 \cdot 6 = 18$; females: $5 \cdot 6 = 30$.

However, if we know only the part size and the total but not the ratio, we have to do things differently:

> At the Beesweerth Modeling Agency, there are 56 models, 35 of whom are women. What is the ratio of men to women at the agency?

This problem is actually easier than the first. Follow these steps:

1. Subtract the known part (women) from the total to find out the unknown part (men): $56 - 35 = 21$.
2. Set up a ratio using the real numbers of men and women: (21 men:35 women)—just like you would with a fraction.
3. Reduce the ratio to get the answer: 3:5.

The last type of ratio problem will give you a ratio and the size of one part, and ask you to find the total number:

> At the Buswurth Modeling Agency, the ratio of male models to female models is 6:2. If there are 12 female models, how many models work at the company?

Follow these steps:

1. Remember the part-whole equation? Let's do the same thing, with a part-part equation! Plug the numbers into the formula: $\frac{\text{part}}{\text{part}} = \frac{\text{real number}}{\text{real number}}$, so $\left( \frac{6}{2} = \frac{x}{12} \right)$
2. Cross multiply to find the number of male models: ($x = 36$).
3. Add the number of male models and female models to find the total number of models: $36 + 12 = 48$.

**Let's Play**

## R A T I O S

**1.** In a certain classroom of 45 students, 15 of the students are awake. What is the ratio of conscious to unconscious students in the classroom?

  **A.** 1:1
  **B.** 1:2
  **C.** 1:3
  **D.** 2:3
  **E.** 4:7

## R A T I O S

**2.** In the land of Bluzrx, the ratio of people who speak Romanian to people who speak Czech is approximately 4:3. No other languages are spoken, and no one speaks both languages. If 3,300 people speak Czech, how many people live in Bluzrx?

  **A.** 7,700
  **B.** 8,528
  **C.** 9,132
  **D.** 10,823
  **E.** 12,830

## R A T I O S

**3.** In Professor Dorris's Enzyme Beauty experiment, the ratio of pretty enzymes to uggo enzymes is 6:5. There are no other types of enzymes. If there are 36 pretty enzymes, how many total enzymes are there?

  **A.** 35
  **B.** 48
  **C.** 53
  **D.** 66
  **E.** 72

Answers:
**1.** B; **2.** A; **3.** D

### Nightmare Ratio Problems
The ACT-bot's laser cannon, when set to "Ratio," shoots out a three-part ratio problem.

> At the Biswirth Modeling Agency, the ratio of men to women to ducks is 1:3:2. If there are 36 models in all, how many are ducks? ✳

You can solve this the same way as you did the first ratio problem. Add up your parts, find out how much larger the real total

✳ Finally, my kind of modeling agency.
　　　　　—Zack

is than the ratio total, then multiply each part by the same number.

1. Add up the parts: $(1 + 3 + 2 = 6)$

2. How much larger is the real total than the ratio total? $\left(\frac{36}{6} = 6\right)$ It is 6 times bigger.

3. So multiply each part by 6:

   $(1 \cdot 6 = 6 \text{ men}, 3 \cdot 6 = 18 \text{ women}, 2 \cdot 6 = 12 \text{ ducks})$

But the ACT-bot can make this even more nightmarish by setting two different ratios for the three elements:

> At the Byswyrth Modeling Agency, the ratio of men to women is 3:5, and the ratio of women to bobcats is 4:3. If there are 94 models, how many are bobcats?

To solve this, we need to first create a three-part ratio by finding the least common multiple of the shared element. Here's how: First off, what is the shared element of the two ratios? Women. In one ratio, the number assigned to women is 5, and in the other it is 4. The least common multiple is 20, so change both ratios so that the number of women is 20. The first ratio becomes 12 men:20 women, and the second ratio becomes 20 women:15 bobcats. Now we can write the three-part ratio as 12 men:20 women:15 bobcats. Then we solve it as we would the previous problem.

Like the common denominator, least common multiple is another similarity between fraction and ratio problems.

—Jon

1. Add up the parts: $(12 + 20 + 15 = 47)$

2. How much larger is the real total than the ratio total?
$\left(\frac{94}{47} = 2\right)$ It is 2 times bigger.

3. Multiply each part by 2:

$(12 \cdot 2 = 24 \text{ men}, 20 \cdot 2 = 40 \text{ women}, 15 \cdot 2 = 30 \text{ bobcats})$

**Let's Play**

## NIGHTMARE RATIOS

1. On Mac's farm, the ratio of camels to dogs to slugs is 4:3:1. There are no other types of animals. If the total number of animals is 16, how many dogs are there?

A. 2
B. 3
C. 4
D. 5
E. 6

## NIGHTMARE RATIOS

2. In a three-color painting, the ratio of red to green square inches is 4:3 and the ratio of red to yellow square inches is 5:2. If the painting is 129 square inches, how many square inches of yellow are there?

A. 24
B. 25
C. 27
D. 29
E. 31

## NIGHTMARE RATIOS

3. In a factory that makes shoes, gloves, and watches, the ratio of shoes to watches to gloves produced is 4:7:3. If there are 70 items made each day, how many gloves are made each day?

A. 11
B. 12
C. 13
D. 14
E. 15

Answers:
1. E
2. A
3. E

## PROBABILITY

So maybe you don't want to become a real-estate tycoon. Maybe, instead, you want to make your millions as a professional gambler? Well, if you learn how to use probabilities, *we guarantee that you will never lose, no matter what any stupid lawyer says.**

*Lawyer's note: *Up Your Score* does not guarantee that you will never lose. Also, lawyers aren't stupid; test-prep book writers are stupid.

Probability says you'd be better off not trying to make millions gambling and instead get a real job. May I suggest the Byswyrth Modeling Agency?

—Ava

## How to Play

Let's say I go to a casino and want to play the classic and super-fun "Guess the Number I'm Going to Roll with This Six-Sided Die." The formula for finding the probability of any event is:

$\dfrac{\text{the number of desired events}}{\text{the number of all possible events}}$. So the probability of rolling a

5 is: $\dfrac{1\,(\text{rolling a }5)}{6\,(\text{rolling a }1{-}6)}$, or $\dfrac{1}{6}$.

If I want better odds, I could, instead of guessing a 5, guess that the number will be even. The odds of this are:

$\dfrac{3\,(\text{rolling a }2,4,6)}{6\,(\text{rolling a }1{-}6)}$, or $\dfrac{1}{2}$.

For even better odds, I can guess that the number will be 1, 2, 3, 4, 5, or 6. In this case the odds are $\dfrac{6\,(\text{rolling a }1{-}6)}{6\,(\text{rolling a }1{-}6)}$, or 1. If the probability is 1, this means it is definitely going to happen. As in: "The probability that I am going to buy a jumbo box of Choco Tacos on the way home tonight is 1."

Probability problems get interesting when we start talking about the odds of more than one event occurring. In general, the way to handle these problems is to multiply the probability of the first event and the probability of the second event.

Why do we do this? Imagine you've got a six-sided die and a four-sided die. You want to know how likely it is to roll two 1s in a row. For the six-sided die, the odds are $\dfrac{1}{6}$ that you will roll a 1. But once you do that successfully, you've got a problem: You still need to roll the four-sided die, and that's not going to come up a 1 every time! So only $\dfrac{1}{4}$ of the time that you roll a 1 on the six-sided die will you *also* get a 1 on the four-sided die. So your probability is $\left(\frac{1}{6}\right) \cdot \left(\frac{1}{4}\right) = \left(\frac{1}{24}\right)$.

Let's try this out:

Dominic has an eight-sided die. What are the odds that he will roll two even numbers in a row?

The odds of the first even roll are $\dfrac{4\,(\text{rolling a } 2,4,6,8)}{8\,(\text{rolling a } 1{-}8)}$, and the odds of rolling the second even roll are $\dfrac{4}{8}$ as well. The probability of rolling both is $\dfrac{4}{8} \cdot \dfrac{4}{8} = \dfrac{16}{64} = \dfrac{1}{4}$.

**Let's Play**

---

**PROBABILITY**

1. With one six-sided die, what is the probability of rolling two multiples of 2 in a row?

   A. $\dfrac{1}{64}$

   B. $\dfrac{1}{4}$

   C. $\dfrac{2}{16}$

   D. $\dfrac{3}{16}$

   E. $\dfrac{5}{8}$

---

**PROBABILITY**

2. With one six-sided die, what is the probability of rolling a 4 twice?

   A. $\dfrac{1}{14}$

   B. $\dfrac{1}{7}$

   C. $\dfrac{2}{7}$

   D. $\dfrac{1}{36}$

   E. $\dfrac{2}{36}$

---

**PROBABILITY**

3. You only like odd numbers. On a spinner with sectors numbered 1–11, what is the probability of spinning a number you like?

   A. $\dfrac{2}{5}$

   B. $\dfrac{3}{11}$

   C. $\dfrac{6}{11}$

   D. $\dfrac{7}{11}$

   E. 1

---

**Answers: 1.** B; **2.** D; **3.** C

## Gift to Grandpa

If you are a wastrel who spends extravagantly, is likely to be duped by con men, and often enjoys bobblehead dolls, then you are a *prodigal, probable robbable pro-bobble.* (Chris's grandpa wrote that joke and guilted us into putting it in the book. "I'm old and I'm tired and you never call," he said. "It would mean so much to me if you would use my little joke that I worked so hard on." Fine, Grandpa, sheesh. "I fought in North Korea," he continued, "but how many times did I get thanked? Not once ever, that's how many times." Thank you for fighting in North Korea, Pop Pop. Your stupid joke is now in the book.)

## Nightmare Probability Problems

There are two ways the ACT-bot creates nightmare probability problems. It might provide a probability and leave out information. Or it might create a situation in which one event affects the following events.

> In a jelly-bean combo pack, there are 12 banana-flavored jelly beans, and the rest are piña colada–flavored jelly beans and Cherry Coke–flavored jelly beans. If there are 60 jelly beans, and the probability of picking a Cherry Coke jelly bean is $\frac{5}{12}$, how many piña colada jelly beans are there?

Set up a part-whole equation (using the probability, instead of the percent, as before) to find out the number of Cherry Cokes: $\frac{5}{12} = \frac{x}{60}$. Cross multiply to find that there are 25 Cherry Cokes. Add your bananas and Cherry Cokes, and subtract this sum from the total to find the number of piña coladas:

25 Cherry Cokes + 12 bananas = 37

60 – 37 = 23 piña colada jelly beans

> In my hatbox, I have 3 berets and 4 top hats. What are the odds of picking out a top hat and then a beret if I do not replace a hat after picking one?

Here, we have to remember that the first event affects the second. The odds of picking out a top hat are $\frac{4}{7}$, but once I've removed that top hat, the odds of picking out a beret are $\frac{3}{6}$, because there are only 6 hats left. Multiply the two odds together:

$$\frac{4}{7} \times \frac{3}{6} = \frac{12}{42} = \frac{2}{7}$$

## NIGHTMARE PROBABILITY

1. Sam, a real butterfingers, drops one card from a pack of 52. While he is searching for that card, he loses another one. Which expression will tell me the probability that both lost cards are hearts?

A. $\frac{1}{52} + \frac{1}{51}$

B. $\frac{1}{52} \cdot \frac{1}{52}$

C. $\frac{13}{52} \cdot \frac{12}{52}$

D. $\frac{13}{52} \cdot \frac{12}{51}$

E. $\frac{13}{52} \cdot \frac{13}{52}$

## NIGHTMARE PROBABILITY

2. In a pack of 64 Jolly Ranchers, there are blueberry, green apple, and purple-flavored varieties. If the probability of picking a blueberry Jolly Rancher is twice the probability of picking a purple-flavored one, and there are an equal number of purple-flavored and green apple Jolly Ranchers, how many blueberry Jolly Ranchers are there?

A. 30

B. 32

C. 38

D. 45

E. 64

## NIGHTMARE PROBABILITY

3. A bag of marbles has 8 green and 14 red marbles. If 2 red marbles are added and you do not replace the marbles after drawing them, what is the probability of drawing 2 green marbles in a row?

A. $\frac{4}{81}$

B. $\frac{14}{78}$

C. $\frac{14}{75}$

D. $\frac{7}{72}$

E. $\frac{7}{69}$

**Answers: 1.** D; **2.** B; **3.** E

And with your gambling winnings, we suggest investing your money wisely. For example, if you currently drive a Toyota, you could save money by upgrading to a velvet chair suspended on the backs of two snow leopards. It just makes good business sense.

**Little-Known Math Fact**

*The most average American is Susan DiMattola of Elk Mound, Wisconsin.*

## MEAN (AVERAGE), MEDIAN, AND MODE

We're going to group these three operations. Two of them are simple, and the third is more complex. So let's start with the easy stuff, because easy stuff is the best.

## How to Play

The *median* is the number in the middle of a set of numbers (4, **5**, 6), while the *mode* is the most frequently recurring number (4, **5, 5**, 6).

To make problems involving median and mode easy, the set has to be in order. So it's wise to arrange the numbers from least to greatest *before* determining the median and mode.

What are the median and mode of the set {34, 6, 12, 4, 35.2, 21, 35.2}?

1. Put it in order: {4, 6, 12, 21, 34, 35.2, 35.2}

2. The median is 21, and the mode is 35.2.

If you have an even number of numbers and you want to find the median, then put them in order and take the mean average (if you don't yet know what *take the mean average* means, you will in five sentences) of the two middle numbers.

What is the median of the set {22, 5, 5, 21}?

1. Put it in order: {5, 5, 21, 22}

2. Find the mean of 5 and 21: $\frac{5 + 21}{2} = 13$

(By the way, the mode in that set is 5.)

So we just mentioned the *mean average*, the third operation, which at first seems pretty simple: Add the numbers together, and divide the sum by the number of numbers.

What is the average of the set {21, 13, 45}?

1. Add 'em up: 21 + 13 + 45 = 79

2. Divide the sum by the number of numbers: $\frac{79}{3} = 26.\overline{3}$.

But things get less simple when we're not given all of the numbers in the set:

The average of the set {12, 5, 7, $x$} is 8. What is $x$?

1. $\frac{(12 + 5 + 7 + x)}{4} = 8$

2. $\frac{(24 + x)}{4} = 8$

**3.** $24 + x = 32$

**4.** $x = 8$

But the ACT-bot wouldn't be caught dead asking you such average average questions. It would be the laughingstock of the Nefarious Testbot Facebook Group! * Instead, it will couch the average question within a word problem.

Like this:

> Mr. Ozell is big into toy trains. On his last three trips to Big Bert's Train Place, he spent an average of $450. If on his first two trips he spent $750 combined, how much did he spend on his third trip?

Well, if his average for three trips was $450, then we can go backward to find the total sum. $450 \cdot 3 = \$1,350$. If he spent $750 on the first two trips, then $1,350 - 750 = \$600$ spent on his third.

### Nightmare Average Problems

Without question, the ACT-bot *is* going to drop some nightmare average problems on you. It has two main ways of creating nightmare problems: 1.) creating a two-step average problem with a missing element, and 2.) creating a problem with "weighted means."

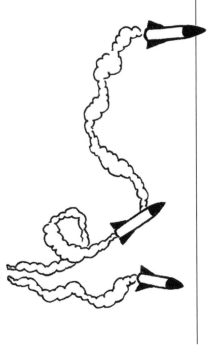

**1. Two-step problems with a missing element.** These problems are almost definitely going to be on your ACT test. Take a look:

> Three students take a test and score an average of 82. What average score do two more students have to achieve to bring the total average up 6 points?

First off, we need to realize that this problem is actually two average problems. In the first, we are talking about three students taking a test, and in the second we are talking about five. Let's solve the first:

1. $\dfrac{\left(\text{Sum of 3 test scores}\right)}{3} = 82$

2. Multiply both sides by 3 to find the sum of the three test scores.

3. Sum of 3 test scores = 246

We can't know which student scored what score, but we *do* know that they all add up to 246. Luckily, that's all we need to know. Now let's do the same thing to the second situation:

1. $\dfrac{(\text{Sum of 5 test scores})}{5} = 88$

2. Multiply both sides by 5 to find the sum of the five scores.

3. Sum of 5 test scores = 440

So the first three students scored a total of 246 and then the five students scored 440. But remember: Those first three scores account for 246 out of the 440 points that the five students scored. This means the remaining 194 points had to come from the two tests those other two students took. So those two students had to score an average of 97.

**2. "Weighted means" problem.** Strap in, because things are about to get a little complex.

> Imagine two teams of bowlers, the Grandpa Gutter-Avoiders and the Strikin' Shirleys (all of whom are named Shirley). There are 8 players on the Grandpa Gutter-Avoiders and 10 players on the Strikin' Shirleys. If the GGAs average 270 in a game, and the SSs average 290, what is the average score of each player?

The trick here is that the ACT-bot *wants* you to take the average of the two averages: $\dfrac{270 + 290}{2} = 280$. It will give you "280" as an answer choice, and you will pick it.

You will be **wrong**.

The trouble here is that *the teams are two different sizes*, so the average for each player is different. What you need to do is find the sum for each group, then take the average of the added sums. Like this:

For the GGAs:

$$\frac{\left(\text{sum of GGA's scores}\right)}{8} = 270$$

1. Multiply both sides by 8 to isolate the sum of the scores.

2. Sum of GGA's scores = 2,160

For the SSs:

$$\frac{\left(\text{sum of SS's scores}\right)}{10} = 290$$

1. Multiply both sides by 10 to isolate the sum of the scores.

2. Sum of SS's scores: 2,900

Add the two sums and divide by the total number of players.

$2,160 + 2,900 = 5,060.$ $\frac{5,060}{18} = 281.11$, which is the actual (weighted) average.

## Nightmare Averages

1. There are 12 students in Ms. Bee's class. The average time spent doodling in Ms. Bee's class is 49 minutes. If two new students join, what does their total time spent doodling have to be to raise the average doodle time to 55 minutes?

   A. 115 minutes
   B. 140 minutes
   C. 182 minutes
   D. 220 minutes
   E. 260 minutes

## Nightmare Averages

2. Class A has 80 students and Class B has 110 students. If the average test score for Class A is 78, and the average test score for Class B is 82, what is the average score for the two classes combined?

   A. 76.8
   B. 80.3
   C. 86.2
   D. 89.1
   E. 94.3

## Nightmare Averages

3. A recent ham hock–eating competition was divided into a men's division and a women's division. The 20 men had an average speed of 9 ham hocks per hour. The 5 women had an average speed of 13 ham hocks per hour. What was the average overall eating speed?

   A. 6.3 hh/hr
   B. 7.2 hh/hr
   C. 9.8 hh/hr
   D. 10.6 hh/hr
   E. 15.3 hh/hr

**Answers: 1.** C; **2.** B; **3.** C

## COMBINATIONS AND PERMUTATIONS

Have you ever had that problem where you're in your closet looking at all your hats and you wonder, "How many ways can I combine a subgroup of these hats to display them on my shelf?" No? Neither have we, but for some reason mathematicians have this problem *all the time.*

### How to Play

So they came up with formulas to solve this problem. 'Cuz mathematicians are always relying on formulas to solve their problems. Check it out:

> Delouise, a mathematician, was in her hat closet. She wasn't happy with the organization of her hats, so she decided to try some new ways of organizing and displaying them. If she has 7 hats in her closet, how many different orders of 5 hats can she create?

Before answering this, we need to ask an existential question: Is "top hat, beanie, cap, stovepipe hat, frog-head hat" different from "beanie, frog-head hat, top hat, stovepipe hat, cap"? Indeed it is! Those are two different ways of organizing the same group of five hats! They look different! Okay, so if order *does* matter, then we are dealing with a **permutation**. Because the order matters, we multiply the number of options for each spot to get the total number of possibilities:

1. There are 7 hats.
2. That gives us 7 options for the first spot. Then, since we will have used one hat already, there are 6 options for the second spot. Then 5 options for the third spot; 4 for the fourth spot; and 3 for the fifth spot. Multiply $7 \cdot 6 \cdot 5 \cdot 4 \cdot 3$ to get 2,520 possible arrangements.

In other words, Delouise is gonna need to take about a week off from her job at the Math-o-drome to go through all those orders!

But what happens when order DOESN'T matter? Check this:

---

*Luckily, order matters only when the problem specifically references the order of something (like hats).*

—Jon

---

### Calculator to the Rescue

To find the number of 5 hat permutations from a total of 7 hats, use the nPr function. Here's how: Press

[ 7 ] [MATH]

Scroll over to PRB, then down to nPr, then press

[ENTER] [ 5 ] [ENTER]

to get 2,520.

Thurmond has a hankerin' for some jelly beans. He has a bowl with exactly 5 jelly beans, each a different flavor (marshmallow, peanut, chocolate, grape, and strawberry). He grabs and eats 3 all at once. How many different groups of 3 jelly beans can he eat?

First off, does order matter? Let's think: Does "marshmallow, chocolate, grape" taste different from "chocolate, grape, marshmallow"? No, both just become choco-grapemallow in your mouth. Because order does not matter, we are dealing with a **combination**. Unlike permutations, which can be figured out by just multiplying the number of available options for each spot, combinations require you to cancel out groups with different arrangements of the same members so that you don't count them twice. That is a total pain in the derriere. So for combinations, we are going to go ahead and insist that you just use a calculator.

Remember how permutations (where order *did* matter) used the calculator's nPr function? Combinations use the nCr function. The *n* stands for the total possible options (in this case, 5 jelly beans). The *r* stands for the number you're going to choose (in this case 3). Punch it in the same way you would nPr, but scroll down one lower to choose nCr. In this case, you should punch in 5 nCr 3, to reveal 10 options.

**Nightmare Combination and Permutation Problems**

It is likely that the ACT-bot will create a nightmare combination problem by having you find multiple combinations from different sets. The trick here is to find the combination of each set, and then multiply them together.

After months spent on VikingMatch.com, Bjorn has a date! Now he has to pick out an outfit: He can pick 2 of his 3 gauntlets, 1 of his 4 hats, and 2 of his 6 boots. How many possible outfits can he create?

In short, with permutations, order *does* matter (think: letters in a word), and with combinations, it *doesn't* matter (think: fruits in a smoothie).

—Ava

Let's do gauntlets first (bronze, silver, and gold; three options that can be picked two at a time); does order matter? No, this is a combination:

3 nCr 2 = 3

Then hats (horn-helmet, talon-helmet, skull-helmet, beret; he can pick one):

4 nCr 1 = 4

Then boots (leather, wool, sharkskin, tiger-skin, emerald, canvas; he can pick two):

6 nCr 2 = 15

Multiply each combination together to get $3 \cdot 4 \cdot 15 = 180$ possible combinations.

Now you try some. Don't freak out—just remember these steps:

1. For each grouping in each problem, decide whether or not the order matters.
2. Use nPr or nCr to get the total number of possibilities for each group.
3. Multiply the numbers you get for each group to get the total possible outcomes for each scenario.

## COMBINATIONS AND PERMUTATIONS

1. At the store Fungeon Dungeon, 2 types of figurines are sold: Gorgorax the Axe, and PuckerLips KissiePoo. There are 4 different varieties of Gorgorax and 5 different varieties of PuckerLips. How many different window displays are possible, if the store owner wants the Gorgoraxes in the front row (which has 4 spots) and the PuckerLips in the back row (which has 3 spots)?

A. 750
B. 900
C. 1,000
D. 1,200
E. 1,440

## COMBINATIONS AND PERMUTATIONS

**2.** For a quiz bowl, there are girls' and boys' teams. A certain classroom wants to send 1 girls' team and 1 boys' team to the championship. If there are 6 boys and 7 girls in the classroom, and a team includes 3 people, how many different combinations of people can go to the championship?

A. 310
B. 520
C. 640
D. 700
E. 750

## COMBINATIONS AND PERMUTATIONS

**3.** A Halloween costume can consist of 1 mask, 1 cloak, 3 accessories, and 4 types of fake blood. If Sally has 3 masks, 4 cloaks, 5 accessories, and 5 types of fake blood, how many different costumes can she put together?

A. 600
B. 650
C. 700
D. 760
E. 820

**Answers: 1.** E; **2.** D; **3.** A

**Stop!**  It's time for a break. You've just consumed many pounds of math, and you need to let your brain settle. For your first break, we'd like to recommend some completely nonmathematical activities:

1. Go to the Math Museum. When they ask if you'd like to buy a ticket, say no.
2. Rent the horror movie *The Number 23* starring Jim Carrey. But don't watch it. It's, like, *full* of numbers. Also, are you seriously still *renting* movies? Get with the times! If it's not streaming on Netflix, it's not worth watching.
3. Go to Pinkberry. Mmmmm . . . Pinkberry.

## Algebra

You know how video game companies have to release new systems every few years? Sony puts out the PlayStation 3, and people line up around the block to buy it. But after playing a few games, those same people start to complain. The graphics are dated. The games are in only two or, at *most*, three dimensions. "Why can't we smell the game?" they ask. "Why are we using controllers when we could be controlling the games with our minds?" Then Sony has to go back to the lab and whip up a PlayStation 4, with trademarked Silky5D visual technology and Smellographic CPU components and Telepath-tronic Controllers.

Well, math is exactly the same. A couple of centuries after arithmetic was created, people started to get bored. So mathematicians decided to release Arithmetic 2: Algebra.* It's just like good old-fashioned arithmetic, but they've hidden some of the numbers by replacing them with letters. You'll have to do mathematical operations in order to decipher those hidden numbers, which we call *variables*.

These mathematical operations are mostly familiar. You'll just be doing arithmetic with variables in order to solve for those variables.

*And, like any new video game system, nerds everywhere immediately complained about it on the Internet.

—Jon

### SOLVING EQUATIONS

In your most basic algebra problem, you will be given at least one equation and asked to solve for at least one variable, or come as close as you can to solving it. The great guiding rule here is to treat the = sign like a mirror, and do the same mathematical operation to both sides.

**Little-Known Math Fact**

*Have you ever noticed that the most common variables are x, y, and z ? That's because mathematics professors frequently use the acronym "XYZ," which means "eXhume Your Zebra corpse elsewhere, we're trying to do math in here."*

### How to Play

Here's what we mean:

$$\frac{x}{2} + 5 = 13$$

Subtract 5 from each side.

$$\frac{x}{2} + 5 - 5 = 13 - 5$$

$$\frac{x}{2} = 8$$

## Little-Known Math Fact

*Variables, once isolated, often report feeling lonely, anxious, and frightened on their side of the equals sign. Mathematicians counter that this is not possible, as variables are nonsentient beings. Variables reply that mathematicians are themselves nonsentient beings. Mathematicians reply that variables are ugly and that they smell like they haven't showered in a week.*

Next, multiply both sides of the equation by 2 to isolate $x$.

$$2 \cdot \frac{x}{2} = 8 \cdot 2$$

$$x = 16$$

This is called isolating the variable, because we have gotten the $x$ alone on one side of the equals sign. We isolate a variable by doing any of the following three operations:

1. Multiply or divide by the same term.
2. Add or subtract by the same term.
3. Raise both sides to an exponent or take the root of both sides.

### Let's Play

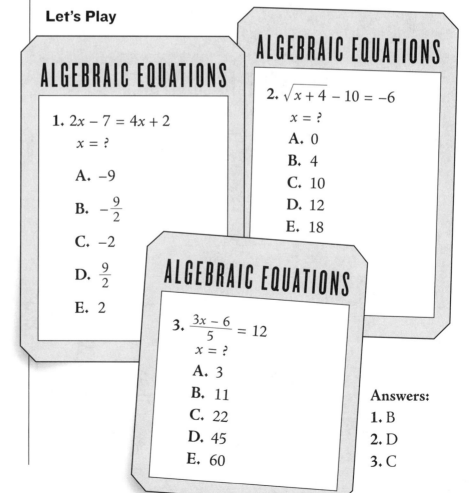

**ALGEBRAIC EQUATIONS**

1. $2x - 7 = 4x + 2$

    $x = ?$

    A. $-9$

    B. $-\frac{9}{2}$

    C. $-2$

    D. $\frac{9}{2}$

    E. $2$

**ALGEBRAIC EQUATIONS**

2. $\sqrt{x + 4} - 10 = -6$

    $x = ?$

    A. $0$

    B. $4$

    C. $10$

    D. $12$

    E. $18$

**ALGEBRAIC EQUATIONS**

3. $\frac{3x - 6}{5} = 12$

    $x = ?$

    A. $3$

    B. $11$

    C. $22$

    D. $45$

    E. $60$

Answers:

1. B

2. D

3. C

**Nightmare Equation Problems**

The ACT-bot's favorite way to create nightmare problems is to create equations with more than one variable, like this:

$$(x + 13)^2 = y - 9$$

Most frequently, the ACT-bot will ask for an answer *in terms of one variable*. In this case, for instance, it might ask for $y$ "in terms of $x$." This means that we need to isolate for $y$, and you don't need to worry about getting rid of $x$:

$$(x + 13)^2 + 9 = y$$
$$x^2 + 26x + 169 + 9 = y$$
$$x^2 + 26x + 178 = y$$

Try a couple yourself:

## ALGEBRAIC EQUATIONS

1. $y^2 + 3 = 4x - 6$

   $y = ?$

   A. $\sqrt{2x - 9}$

   B. $\pm\sqrt{4x - 9}$

   C. $\pm\sqrt{4x + 3}$

   D. $2x + 3$

   E. $4x + 9$

WARNING! **NIGHTMARISH**

## ALGEBRAIC EQUATIONS

2. $\dfrac{\sqrt{x + 2}}{4} = y$

   $x = ?$

   A. $\dfrac{y^2}{2} + 2$

   B. $4y^2 - 2$

   C. $16y^2 - 2$

   D. $y^2 + 4$

   E. $4y^2 - 4$

WARNING! **NIGHTMARISH**

Answers: **1.** B; **2.** C

Don't be afraid to work out the problems in writing. That way, you'll be less likely to forget to modify both sides of the equation. And, if you *do* get lost somewhere in the middle, you won't have to start the whole problem over again.

—Jon

Plus, if you get a chance to check your work, you'll understand how you got your answer.

—Ava

The bot's next trick is to hit you with not only two variables but also two equations. Look at this gnarly little beast:

If $4b - 12y = 12$ and $2b - 9y = 4$, what is $b \cdot y$?

Our best bet here is to **add or subtract the equations to eliminate one variable.** Then we can solve for the remaining variable, and plug it back into one of the equations to find the eliminated variable. "Wait, what?" you probably just said. Don't worry, just follow these steps:

1. Manipulate one equation so that one variable can be eliminated:

In our first equation, we have $4b$, and in the second we have $2b$. Let's multiply that second equation by 2.

$2b - 9y = 4$

$(2)(2b - 9y) = (4)(2)$

$4b - 18y = 8$

2. Subtract the manipulated second equation from the first equation to eliminate the variable $b$.

$$\begin{array}{r} 4b - 12y = 12 \\ - \ 4b - 18y = 8 \\ \hline 6y = 4 \\ y = \dfrac{4}{6} \end{array}$$

3. Now we know that $y$ is equal to $\left(\dfrac{4}{6}\right)$. Plug this back into one of the original equations to find the other variable. Let's plug it back into the first equation:

$4b - 12\left(\dfrac{4}{6}\right) = 12$

$4b - 8 = 12$

$4b = 20$

$b = 5$

Which means that $b \cdot y = (5)\left(\dfrac{4}{6}\right) = 3.\overline{3}$

Of course, this is all easier if they already define one of the variables, which is a typical practice of the ACT-bot:

If $\frac{r+5}{2} = 4q - 8$, and $r = q + 7$, what is $q^2 + r^2$?

Here, we can simply plug the definition of $r$ back into the first equation. Like so:

$$\frac{(q+7)+5}{2} = 4q - 8$$

$$\frac{(q+12)}{2} = 4q - 8$$

$$(q+12) = 8q - 16$$

$$28 = 7q$$

$$4 = q$$

If $q = 4$, plug this into the second equation to solve for $r$.

$r = 4 + 7$

$r = 11$

And if $r = 11$, then $q^2 + r^2 = 4^2 + 11^2 = 16 + 121 = 137$.

Let's try:

## ALGEBRAIC EQUATIONS

**1.** Given $x + 3y = 5$ and $3x - 2y = 4$, what is the value of $x$?

**A.** 1
**B.** 2
**C.** 3
**D.** 4
**E.** 5

**WARNING! NIGHTMARISH**

## ALGEBRAIC EQUATIONS

**2.** If $4(n+3) - 2 = 3 - 2r$ and $n = r - 2$, what is the value of $\frac{n}{r}$?

**A.** −12
**B.** −11.5
**C.** −11.375
**D.** −11
**E.** −10.375

**WARNING! NIGHTMARISH**

## ALGEBRAIC EQUATIONS

**3.** If $p = \frac{2q}{5}$ and $q - 2p = 3p - 2$, what is the value of $3p$?

**A.** −2
**B.** 2.4
**C.** 3.6
**D.** 4
**E.** 5.2

**WARNING! NIGHTMARISH**

**Answers: 1.** B; **2.** D; **3.** B

## ALGEBRA WORD PROBLEMS

Are we feeling more confident about solving for variables? That's great news! But we have some not-so-good news: There aren't that many math problems involving only equations on the ACT. More often, the bot will disguise algebra problems as word problems, because algebra word problems require that you understand *how to set up the equation* to solve the problem.

### How to Play

At the Nutz for More Dough Donut Factory, a large box of doughnuts costs $2 more than a medium box, and a medium box costs $2 more than a small box. If 12 small boxes cost $2x, how much will 5 large and 7 medium boxes cost, in terms of x?

A. $2x + 24$
B. $2x + 34$
C. $2x + 38$
D. $12x + 24$
E. $24x + 34$

So this question, like all algebra word problems, requires that you translate the information from the problem into an equation, which is hard. Or it would be hard, if you didn't know an amazing trick that makes all algebra word problems ridiculously easy.

So if you'd rather do things the hard way, please skip the next step.

### Amazing Trick: Plugging In

This trick was developed by Einstein and Stephen Hawking that one time they had a sleepover party. That's how good it is. Here's how it works:

1. Check to see if there is a variable in the answer choice. If there is, you *must* plug in. (Because this trick rocks so hard that if you don't use it, you are being silly.)

2. **Choose *your own number* to replace the variable in the**

**problem.** It should be a simple number, but not 1 or 0 (2 would be a good choice).

3. Solve the problem using your variable. Circle your answer.
4. Go through the answer choices. Using your variable, see which answer choice yields your answer.

Let's solve the doughnuts problem by plugging in. Read it again. Done? Okay, so the problem said that 12 small boxes cost $2x$. We want to pick an $x$ that will work well with 12. Let's go for 24. So if $x = 24$, then 12 small boxes cost $48. If 12 small boxes cost $48, then each small box costs $4. According to the problem, if a small box costs $4, then a medium costs $6, and a large costs $8. So the answer to the problem, if $x = 24$, is:

$5 \cdot 8$ (for the large boxes) = $40
$7 \cdot 6$ (for the medium boxes) = $42
Total = $82

Then we go through the answer choices, using $x = 24$. The only one that gives us $82 is B. That's the answer!

Plugging in, in other words, **turns an algebra problem into an arithmetic problem by replacing the variable with a number.** Using arithmetic gives you a much better handle on what you're doing, so you should always plug in.$^*$

One final note on plugging in. Always make sure to try *every* answer choice. It is totally possible to pick numbers that work for *two* answer choices. If this happens, just pick new numbers and one of those answer choices will not work, leaving only the correct answer.$^{**}$

Now let's try one with a couple of variables:

The cost of $m$ monocles is $d$ dollars. What is the cost of $t$ monocles at the same rate?

A. $td$

B. $\dfrac{td}{m}$

C. $\dfrac{md}{t}$

D. $mt$

E. $\dfrac{mt}{d}$

$^*$ I like doing this when checking my answers— if you get the same answer using two different methods, it's certain to be the right one!

—Ava

$^{**}$ When you assign numbers to variables, make sure you write them down somewhere (preferably in the scratch work area of your exam booklet, although scratching it into your arm like a Celtic warrior would work, too) so that you don't forget which numbers you've been plugging in for $m$, $d$, $t$, etc.

—Jon

If you have extra time at the end of the section, plugging in numbers is also a great way to check regular algebra problems.

—Jon

So we need to pick three numbers to replace the variables $m$, $d$, and $t$. Let's pick numbers that work nicely with each other: $m = 5$, $d = 10$, $t = 15$. Let's reread the problem with those numbers. Done? Okay, so if 5 monocles cost 10 dollars, then each monocle costs 2 dollars. So 15 monocles would cost . . . $30! That's our answer; circle it so you remember it!

Then plug our variables into the answer choices, and the only one that gives us $30 is B. That's our answer!

### Let's Play

## ALGEBRA WORD PROBLEMS

**1.** Julie wraps bacon around deep-fried shrimp at a rate of $x$ shrimps per hour. Samantha wraps shrimp twice as fast as Julie. In terms of $x$ and $y$, how many more hours will it take Julie to wrap $y$ shrimp?

**A.** $\dfrac{2y}{x}$

**B.** $\dfrac{x}{2y}$

**C.** $\dfrac{y}{2x}$

**D.** $\dfrac{2x - y}{2y}$

**E.** $\dfrac{y - x}{2x}$

## ALGEBRA WORD PROBLEMS

**2.** Matt got scores of $r$ and $n$ on his first two tests of the semester, respectively. If on his next test he scores twice as well as on his first test, by how much did his average increase?

**A.** $\dfrac{3r}{2}$

**B.** $\dfrac{3r - n}{6}$

**C.** $\dfrac{3r + n}{2}$

**D.** $\dfrac{r - n}{2}$

**E.** $\dfrac{2r - n}{6}$

## ALGEBRA WORD PROBLEMS

**3.** Jammer is $x$ years old. Spizzax is twice as old as Jammer, and Liz is 2 years younger than Jammer. In terms of $x$, how much older is Spizzax than Liz?

**A.** $x - 2$

**B.** $x + 2$

**C.** $x + 4$

**D.** $2x + 2$

**E.** $2x - 4$

**Answers: 1.** C; **2.** B; **3.** B

**Nightmare Algebra Word Problems**

Really, *all* algebra word problems are nightmares if you do not plug in. But the ACT-bot can make them particularly complex by adding steps. Take a look at this straightforward problem:

> Myrtle bought a Big Gulp of Mountain Dew: Code Red. If a Big Gulp contains *g* gallons of soda, and Myrtle has already consumed *m* gallons, what percent of the drink has been drunk?

To make this easy, let's plug in 10 for *g* and 7 for *m*. Hmmm . . . 7 out of 10, that's 70%! The right answer will say $100m/g$. But let's make the problem more nightmarish by adding some steps.

> Myrtle and her brother, Pugnacious Bo, bought a Big Gulp of Mountain Dew: Code Red to share. The Big Gulp contains *g* gallons. Myrtle drinks *m* of them and Pugnacious Bo drinks *b*. If *m* > *b* and *m* + *b* = *g*, what is the difference between the percentage of the Big Gulp that Myrtle drinks and the percentage that Bo drinks?

Ruh-roh! Can this be done? Indeed it can! If you plug in numbers, it's just as easy as the first example—you just need to go through a couple more steps:

Let's have *g* = 10 again, and let's keep *m* at 7. So, given that *m* + *b* = *g*, *b* has to equal 3. That means Myrtle drank 4 more gallons than Pugnacious Bo, but what percent would that be? 7 out of 10, again, is 70%. 3 out of 10 means Bo drank 30%. The difference between their two percentages is 40%. The right answer will say: $100m/g - 100b/g$.

The guy's name is Pugnacious Bo. . . . Do you really think he knows how to do algebra?

—Jon

## INEQUALITIES AND THE NUMBER LINE

It is likely that you will also see variables in equations that propose inequalities. When you see these (<, >, ≤, ≥), don't raise your hand to complain that the equal sign looks like a sideways wedge. This will only confuse the proctor. ✳ Instead, read the equation as an inequality.

✳ In the wild, proctors are easily startled by their natural enemies: questions.

—Jon

### How to Play

When reading the inequality 23 < 37, most students will say, "23 is less than 37." They will be correct. But when they read $2x - 7 < 12y + 2$, they are more likely to forget whether the sign means "greater than" or "less than." This is because they have forgotten one of the most important rules of mathematics: **The Hungry Dinosaur Always Eats the Bigger Number.***

Always remember to draw sharp dino teeth on the inequality sign so that it looks like a scary mouth.✳✳ This way, you will instantly know which side of the inequality is bigger. And your test booklet will look boss.

✳✳ More power to you if you can do this and still complete the test on time.

—Ava

In general, we can treat algebraic inequalities the same way we would treat any equation. We just isolate for the variable. For example:

$x - 5 < 37$ is the same as $x < 37 (+ 5)$, which is the same as $x < 42$.

But, of course, the ACT-bot is not content with this. It will often require that you draw this inequality on the number line. Just remember that a dark circle means that $x$ includes that number, while an open circle means that $x$ does not.

*Euclid derived this rule by placing numbers of different sizes in front of a hungry plesiosaurus and recording which number was consumed.

**Let's Play**

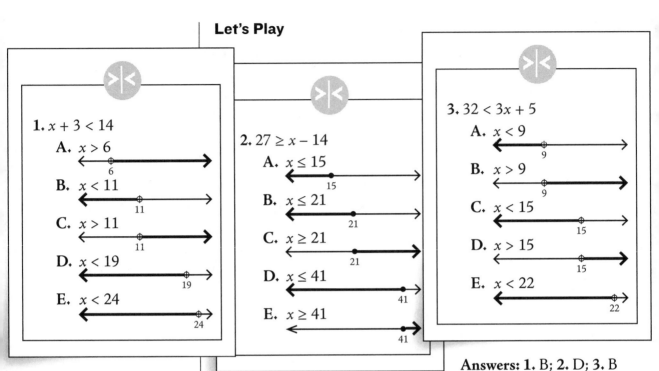

1. $x + 3 < 14$
   A. $x > 6$
   B. $x < 11$
   C. $x > 11$
   D. $x < 19$
   E. $x < 24$

2. $27 \geq x - 14$
   A. $x \leq 15$
   B. $x \leq 21$
   C. $x \geq 21$
   D. $x \leq 41$
   E. $x \geq 41$

3. $32 < 3x + 5$
   A. $x < 9$
   B. $x > 9$
   C. $x < 15$
   D. $x > 15$
   E. $x < 22$

**Answers: 1.** B; **2.** D; **3.** B

### Nightmare Inequality Problems

The nightmare inequality problems trade on a rule about inequalities that many people forget. If, when isolating for your variable, you have to multiply or divide both sides by a negative number, **you have to flip the greater-than/less-than sign.** We've written that in bold letters so that it gets stuck in your brain.

Check this out:

$-5x - 12 < 13$

$-5x < 25$

$x > -5$

In that last step, we divided both sides by $-5$, and so we had to flip the less-than sign to a greater-than sign.

Why is this the case? Well, consider the simple equation $50 > 25$. Makes sense, right? Because 50 is like *totally* bigger than 25, like *all the time.* Let's multiply both sides by $-1$ and we get $-50 > -25$. Hold on, hold on, that doesn't make sense anymore. $-50$ isn't

**Little-Known Math Fact**

*Greater-than and less-than signs were briefly banned from elementary schools in the 1970s in response to complaints that their sharp edges could harm young children. Justice Department lawyers had to prove the difference between symbols on a page and real objects to get the law repealed.*

greater than –25, it's 25 *less*. That's why we have to flip the sign when we multiply by a negative: –50 < –25.

Nightmare problems are created in the hope that you forget to flip the sign. *So don't, you know, forget to flip it.* Also, the bot might make you graph the results on a number line.

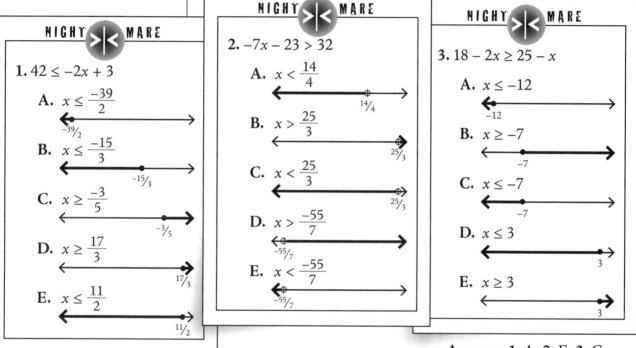

**Answers: 1.** A; **2.** E; **3.** C

## FACTORING EQUATIONS

After a couple hundred years of tinkering with algebra, mathematicians began to see patterns: Certain equations always behaved certain ways. Using these patterns, mathematicians were able to skip a lot of steps and handle complex-looking equations very quickly. * The ACT-bot expects you to know some of these shortcuts, and one of the most popular shortcuts is factoring complex equations into simpler, smaller pieces.

* Thank heavens for lazy mathematicians.

—Jon

## Little-Known Math Fact

*Before you factor, it is considered polite to introduce yourself, and develop a relationship of mutual trust and respect with that equation.*

## How to Play

Have you ever seen one of these?

$$2x^2 + 3x + 12$$

We call that a quadratic, and it is typically in the form $ax^2 + bx + c$, where $a$, $b$, and $c$ are coefficients (or regular numbers) and $x$ is a variable. Now, there are a couple of fun ways to play with quadratic equations (if factoring equations is your idea of fun), but first we need to realize that equations are not always presented in the correct form.

Here's what we want you to do: Whenever you see an algebraic equation with $x^2$ in it, convert it to $ax^2 + bx + c$ form. Like this:

$$3x = -7x^2 + 2 \text{ should become } 7x^2 + 3x - 2 = 0$$
$$2 - x^2 = -12x \text{ should become } x^2 - 12x - 2 = 0$$

Now that we've converted our equation into the right form, we can start factoring the equation. To do this, we first need to remember that a quadratic equation is the product of two simpler, smaller pieces, called *factors*.

A factor is something like $(x + 4)$ or $(x - 2)$. If we multiply two of these together, we will get a quadratic equation. So let's multiply two factors together:

$$(x + 3)(x + 4)$$

We multiply them using FOIL. What this means is that we wrap them up in foil, put them in the toaster oven, come back in five minutes, allow time to cool, then eat them like a delicious Hot Pocket. Ha ha! We're just making a hilarious math joke! FOIL really means that we multiply the *First* terms of each factor $(x \cdot x)$, then the *Outside* terms $(x \cdot 4)$, then the *Inside* terms $(3 \cdot x)$, and finally the *Last* terms $(3 \cdot 4)$. Finally, we add the products together:

$$x^2 + 4x + 3x + 12 = x^2 + 7x + 12$$

Which looks like a perfect quadratic equation, right?

Practice FOILing a couple of times, just to lock this down:

**FOIL**

1. $(x - 5)(x + 5) = ?$
   A. $x^2 + 10x - 25$
   B. $x^2 + 10x + 25$
   C. $x^2 - 10x + 25$
   D. $x^2 - 25$
   E. $x^2 + 25$

**FOIL**

2. $(2x - 4)(3x + 6) = ?$
   A. $2x^2 + 3x - 24$
   B. $6x^2 + 6x - 18$
   C. $6x^2 + 6x - 12$
   D. $6x^2 + 12x - 24$
   E. $6x^2 - 24$

**FOIL**

3. $(x - 10)(2x - 4) = ?$
   A. $x^2 - 20x + 10$
   B. $x^2 - 24x - 40$
   C. $2x^2 - 24x + 40$
   D. $2x^2 + 24x + 40$
   E. $2x^2 - 24x - 40$

**Answers: 1.** D; **2.** E; **3.** C

Unfortunately, it is more difficult to de-FOIL, or factor from a quadratic equation to the two factors. Luckily, there are some helpful tricks.

$$x^2 - 2x - 8$$

First off, do you see how that equation has three pieces: $x^2$, $-2x$, and $-8$? We're going to call those the first, middle, and last terms.

We can see that the first term is $x^2$, so we can construct a piece of our factors, leaving out the integers:

$$(x \quad ) (x \quad )$$

Our two helpful hints are that the last term of the equation is the product of the two integers and that the middle coefficient of the equation is the sum of the two integers. So experiment with integers until you find a pair whose product is the third term ($-8$) and whose sum is the middle coefficient ($-2$). We call this de-FOILing.

$$(x + 2) (x - 4)$$

Again, it's helpful to practice a couple of de-FOILING problems:

(**Hint:** On these problems, it can be easier to work backward. FOIL an answer choice to see if it creates the equation.)

*You won't be expected to factor equations with bizarre, unguessable coefficients, like $\frac{5}{72}$ or the square root of 41.*

—Jon

**de-FOIL**

1. $x^2 - 12x + 20 = ?$
   A. $(x - 6)(x - 2)$
   B. $(x - 10)(x - 2)$
   C. $(x - 4)(x - 5)$
   D. $(x + 4)(x - 16)$
   E. $(x + 4)(x - 8)$

**de-FOIL**

2. $x^2 + 3x - 40 = ?$
   A. $(x - 10)(x + 4)$
   B. $(x - 10)(x - 4)$
   C. $(x - 5)(x + 8)$
   D. $(x + 5)(x - 8)$
   E. $(x + 5)(x - 2)$

**de-FOIL**

3. $2x^2 - 12x - 14 = ?$
   A. $(2x + 2)(x - 7)$
   B. $(2x - 2)(x + 7)$
   C. $(x - 2)(x - 10)$
   D. $(x - 6)(x - 4)$
   E. $(x - 7)(x + 4)$

**Answers: 1.** B; **2.** C; **3.** A

Your standard factoring problem will give itself away because it will involve a quadratic equation and one factor. If you ever see these two components palling around together, know that finding the other factor will unlock the whole problem.

What is $\dfrac{x^2 + 9x + 20}{x + 4}$?

Looks pretty complex, right? That's exactly what the ACT-bot *wants* you to think. But look, there's a quadratic equation (in the numerator) and a factor (in the denominator). That's a Big Fat Hint:

$x^2 + 9x + 20 = (x + 4)(x + 5)$

So we can rewrite the problem and cancel:

$\dfrac{\cancel{(x + 4)}(x + 5)}{\cancel{x + 4}} = x + 5$

Neat, right? These problems look monstrous, but always be on the lookout for the quadratic equation–factor pair and you will be fine. Let's try some:

✳ When you are factoring a numerator like this, you are almost guaranteed that the first factor of the numerator will be the denominator.

—Jon

**1.** Which of the following is equal to $\dfrac{2}{x + 7}$ ?

A. $\dfrac{2x - 14}{x^2 + 14x + 49}$

B. $\dfrac{2x - 10}{x^2 + 2x - 35}$

C. $\dfrac{2x^2 - 4}{x^2 + 5x - 35}$

D. $\dfrac{2x - 7}{x^2 + 49}$

E. $\dfrac{2x}{x^2 - 49}$

**2.** If $y = \dfrac{x^2 - 16}{x + 4} - 5$,

which of the following expressions is equal to

$y - 5$?

A. $x^2 - 14$

B. $x^2 - 9$

C. $x^2 - 5$

D. $x - 9$

E. $x - 14$

**3.** $\dfrac{x^2 + 4x - 12}{x - 2} = ?$

A. $x - 4$

B. $x - 2$

C. $x - 6$

D. $x + 2$

E. $x + 6$

Answers: **1.** B; **2.** E; **3.** E

### Nightmare Factoring Problems

Truly terrifying factoring problems are created by taking out the integers and instead dealing with two variables, $x$ and $y$. To solve these problems, it is wise to commit three quadratic equations to memory:

$$(x + y)(x - y) = x^2 - y^2 \text{ (a.k.a. Dr. PlusMinus)}$$
$$(x + y)(x + y) = x^2 + 2xy + y^2 \text{ (a.k.a. Frau PlusPlus)}$$
$$(x - y)(x - y) = x^2 - 2xy + y^2 \text{ (a.k.a. Mugsy MinusMinus)}$$

Whenever you see one of those three quadratic equations, it is *guaranteed* that de-FOILing the quadratic equation into its two factors will make the problem much easier.

If $(x - y) = 4$, and $x^2 - y^2 = 48$, what is $(x + y)$?

Again, this looks tough, but if you recognize that $x^2 - y^2 = (x - y)(x + y)$, then you can rewrite the problem as $48 = (4)(x + y)$, so $(x + y) = 12$.

Let's try an even tougher one:

If $2x^2 + 4xy + 2y^2 = 18$, $x > 0$, and $y = 2$, what is the value of $x$?

First, we should recognize that every element of that equation can be divided by 2, and rewrite it as $x^2 + 2xy + y^2 = 9$. Recognize that equation? That's right, folks, it's our good friend, Frau PlusPlus! That means it can be rewritten as $(x + y)(x + y) = 9$. And if $x + y = 3$, and we already know $y = 2$, then our answer is $x = 1$!

Try these two:

## X-Treme Factoring

**1.** If $4 + x = y$, what is the value of $x^2 - 2xy + y^2$?

A. 0

B. 4

C. 8

D. 16

E. 64

## X-Treme Factoring

**2.** If $x + y = 5$, what is the value of $5x^2 + 10xy + 5y^2$?

A. 25

B. 50

C. 75

D. 100

E. 125

**Answers: 1.** D; **2.** E

## Advanced Algebra

Now that we've gone through the meat and potatoes of isolating for variables and turning scary equations into less-scary factors, it's time to get serious. You see, it turns out that algebra was not *just* a game of "solve for the variable." The real, secret purpose of algebra is to *understand how equations behave*.

Whaaaaaaaaat?!?! How can math, you are probably asking, behave in one way or another? Well, the answer is actually kind of cool.

Imagine you just invented a new vehicle, called the GoBubble. It's basically a bubble made out of a high-impact, transparent plastic, and it can achieve speeds above 75 mph. Everyone is

**Little-Known Math Fact**

*When an equation behaves badly, it is sent to Equation Reform School, where it is forced to wake up early, do many push-ups, and scrub latrines.*

\* Then you go through it five more times. And go back next year. I never learn.

—Zack

super psyched to buy your GoBubble, but first you have to test it. You run the GoBubble through fog, and it works fine. You drive it into the ocean and discover that it functions perfectly as a submarine! You drive it in lightning and find out that the ion-charged atmosphere slows down your GoBubble. You take it on a dive into hot lava and find that the GoBubble has adequate visibility but tends to melt and instantly kill the passenger. In other words, different conditions cause your GoBubble to behave differently.

In the same way, equations behave differently if you put different kinds of numbers into them. If my equation is $y = x + 3$, then when $x = -15$, $y$ is going to be negative, but when $x = 15$, $y$ is going to be positive. Different kinds of numbers *put into* the equation cause different numbers to *come out*. If we were to write down all of the different inputs and outcomes, we would get something like a *picture of the behavior of the equation*. This is the idea behind **functions.**

## FUNCTIONS

Have you ever been to a county fair? You know how they have those haunted house rides? You go in all excited, get jostled around and yelled at by a middle-aged man in a ghost costume, then come out the other end with the conviction that you never want to ride another haunted house ride for the rest of your life. \* Know those rides? Good, because that's basically how functions work.

### How to Play

Here's what we mean: Numbers go into functions, some stuff happens, and they come out changed. Let's say that I build a machine that adds 3 to every number that goes into it. An 8 goes in, and it comes out an 11. −3.5 goes in, and comes out −0.5. Get it? Well, here's how a mathematician would write that:

$$f(x) = x + 3$$

In a function, $x$ is a placeholder for whatever you put in, be it a number, letter, or result of another function.

—Ava

**Little-Known Math Fact**

*Some numbers are entered into functions and never come out. But we don't talk about those numbers.*

Which is to say: Any number ($x$) that goes in comes out with 3 added on to it. Mathematicians like to make tables that record the domain (numbers that go in) and range (numbers that come out) of their functions. Mathematicians then take these tables of data out to math parties where people dance and show off their latest data tables.

| in | out |
|----|-----|
| -3 | 0 |
| -1 | 2 |
| 0 | 3 |
| 1 | 4 |
| 2.5 | 5.5 |
| 4 | 7 |

There are actually two other ways that mathematicians might write the exact same thing:

| $x$ | $y$ |
|-----|-----|
| -3 | 0 |
| -1 | 2 |
| 0 | 3 |
| 1 | 4 |
| 2.5 | 5.5 |
| 4 | 7 |

| $x$ | $f(x)$ |
|-----|--------|
| -3 | 0 |
| -1 | 2 |
| 0 | 3 |
| 1 | 4 |
| 2.5 | 5.5 |
| 4 | 7 |

As you can see in these charts, $f(x)$ is the same as $y$. They both refer to the output. $x$ always refers to the input.

We'll talk more about ways to use those charts in a bit. First, let's create another, more-challenging number machine.

$f(x) = 2x + 7$

So if we put in 5, we get $2(5) + 7$, or 17. Cool? We can also make things more challenging by plugging in a more complex value:

If $f(x) = 2x + 7$, what is $f(2b + 3)$?

The trick here is to remember to write the input $(2b + 3)$ in every spot that you see an $x$ in the original function. So: $2(2b + 3) + 7$, or $4b + 13$.

Still with us? Darn, you're tenacious! Try this one on for size, hotshot. We can make functions *even more* complex by **placing functions within functions.** As in:

Here are two functions:

$$f(x) = 2x^2$$
$$g(x) = x + 12$$

What is $g(f(4))$?

The strategy here is to *first* run the input (4) through the inner function, *then* run the answer through the outer function. So $f(4) = 2(4)^2 = 32$. Then take $g(32) = 32 + 12 = 44$.

*Still* with us? Oh, c'mon! How complex do we have to make this?!? Well, you asked for it; we're going to ratchet the difficulty up to ten by placing functions within equations.

If $f(x) = 12x - 5$, what is $2f(x) + 10$?

For these problems, just replace the symbol "$f(x)$" with its equation. So that equation will now read $2(12x - 5) + 10$. Then we proceed as usual. ✳ ✳

$$24x - 10 + 10 = 24x$$

Let's crank this up a notch:

If $f(x) = \dfrac{x^2}{2x}$, and $g(f(5)) = 15$, which of the following could be the function $g$?

**A.** $g(x) = 3x - 5$

**B.** $g(x) = 10 + 2x$

**C.** $g(x) = \dfrac{x^2}{2x}$

**D.** $g(x) = x$

**E.** $g(x) = 12 + 3x$

First things first: Run that 5 through the function $f$.

$\dfrac{5^2}{2 \cdot 5} = \dfrac{25}{10} = 2.5$. So if $f(5) = 2.5$, then we need to run

---

✳ I like to think of this as  another version of PREMDAS and substitution. You work from the inside of the parenthetical statements to the outside, substituting as you go. First you put 4 through the $f$ function, then, when you have an answer, you run that through the $g$ function.
　　　　　　—Zack

✳✳ If you find problems with the $f(x)$ notation confusing, just think of it as a $y$, as it is really just another variable to be manipulated.

　　　　　　—Jon

2.5 through function $g$. But we don't know what function $g$ is! Well, we do know that $g(2.5)=15$. So we should run 2.5 through each of the answer choices, to see which one gives us 15. The correct function is B: $10 + 2(2.5) = 10 + 5 = 15$.

Try two more on your own:

### FUNCTIONS

**1.** In the function $z(x) = \dfrac{2x + b}{4}$, and $z(5) = 5$, what is $b$?

A. −2

B. 0

C. 7.6

D. 10

E. 12.3

### FUNCTIONS

**2.** If $r(x) = 3x + 5$, what is $\dfrac{2r(6)}{r(3)}$ to the nearest 100th?

A. 3.29

B. 4.45

C. 6.32

D. 7.93

E. 8.49

**Answers: 1.** D; **2.** A

## Nightmare Function Problems

The best way to take a standard function problem and crank up the fear is to couch the function problem within a complex-sounding word problem.

The rate of release, in gallons per second, for a 10-gauge valve under 30 megatons of subaquatic pressure is given by the function $r(x) = \dfrac{2,400x}{12b} - 45$, where $x$ is the amount of liquid, in gallons, to be converted into steam. If $b$ is a constant, what is $b$ if 35 gallons of liquid has a rate of release of 305 gallons per second?

YIKES! Let us say it again: YIIIIIIIIIIKES!!!!!!

*Thirty megatons on a 10-gauge valve? I say "yikes!" but for a completely different reason.*

*—Ava*

But relax. This problem is actually a standard function problem, even if it is surrounded by complex-sounding words. Do we know our $x$? Yes, $x$ is the amount of liquid, and because there are 35 gallons of liquid, $x = 35$. Do we know what the equation has to equal? Yes, it is all a function for "rate of release," and our rate of release is 305 gallons per second. So plug in our $x$, and set it all equal to our rate of release:

$$\frac{2,400 \cdot 35}{12b} - 45 = 305$$

Then we use algebra to solve for $b$ and find that $b = 20$. Let's try a couple:

> ✳ My favorite part about ordering the Churro Mucho Loco is that you can specify the caloric value you want. You just give them a number and they shove oil and fat into it until it has that many calories.
>
> —Zack
>
> Coincidentally, the number of people who would eat such a churro is inversely proportional to my faith in humanity.
>
> —Jon

## NIGHTMARE FUNCTIONS

**1.** The odds of throwing up after consuming a Churro Mucho Loco ✳ are given by the formula $c(x) = \frac{25x + 30}{b + 25}$ where $x$ is caloric value of the churro and $b$ is the number of years the eater has been eating churros. If $c(x) > 220$, the person will vomit. If Enoch has been eating churros for 15 years, what is the highest caloric churro he can eat without throwing up?

A. 349
B. 350
C. 351
D. 352
E. 353

**2.** Murphy makes money by selling shoes online. He buys shoes at a discounted price and sells them at a profit. He buys the shoes from ShoeSaleTown, which determines its discounted price with the formula discount price = .7(original price) + 5. Then Murphy sells the shoes at a 40% markup. If he sells a pair of Air Force Ones for $124.60, what was the "original price" before ShoeSaleTown's discounted price?

A. 110
B. 115
C. 120
D. 125
E. 130

Answers:
1. B
2. C

**Little-Known Math Fact**

*In the nineteenth century, mathematicians used to decorate their graphs with flying skulls and monkeys in corsets to keep things interesting. Unfortunately, that practice has fallen out of favor.*

What's fallen *in* favor is the practice of using graphing software to make cool pictures, like heart curves on Valentine's Day. (If that's not geeky enough for you, I don't know what is.)

—Ava

## GRAPHING FUNCTIONS

Now, working with functions is fun and all, but things get a bit more interesting once we can *see* the function. By graphing functions, we can create pictures of the functions.

We learned about inputs and outputs in the last section. But if we want to create an *overall picture of an equation's behavior*, then we want to be able to *see*, at a glance, how the outputs change as the inputs change. We do this by *graphing* all of the inputs and outputs on one graph.

### How to Play

Remember those input/output T-charts? Let's make another one for a function:

$$f(x) = 2x + 3$$

| x | y |
|----|----|
| −3 | −3 |
| −2 | −1 |
| −1 | 1 |
| 0 | 3 |
| 1 | 5 |
| 2 | 7 |
| 3 | 9 |

If we use the input as the *x* value and the output as the *y* value, we can chart a point on an *xy*-plane for every number we input into the function. Let's plot the points in our chart:

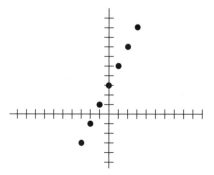

Next, let's draw a line to connect our points. That line is the representation, in graph form, of our function. Neat, right?

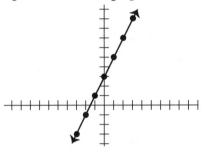

So here's the thing: The ACT-bot is very interested in testing whether or not you understand that the points on a graph represent inputs and outputs, even when you don't know the equation for that graph.

Let's say I have a graph but no function:

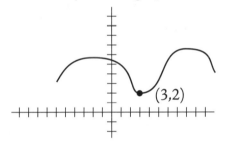

The graph of $f(x)$ is shown above. If $f(w) = 2$, what is $3w + 2$?

The key thing to understand here is that if $f(w) = 2$, that means that our output, or $y$ value, is 2. So find the place on our graph where $y = 2$, and put your finger on it. The corresponding $x$ value for that point is 3. This point tells us that $f(3) = 2$, even though we don't know the equation of the function!

Which means that $3w + 2 = 3(3) + 2 = 11$.

Let's try another.

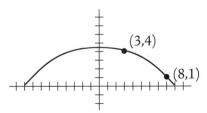

The graph of $g(x)$ is shown at the bottom of page 179. What is $g(3) + g(8)$?

Again, the number inside the parentheses is our input, or $x$ value. Locate it, then find the corresponding $y$ value in order to find out the $g(x)$. Here $g(3) = 4$, and $g(8) = 1$. Add them together to get the answer: 5.

Let's try this out:

## GRAPHING FUNCTIONS

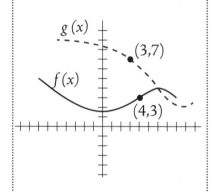

1. The graph above shows the functions $g(x)$ and $f(x)$. What is $g(f(4))$?

    A. 5

    B. 6

    C. 7

    D. 8

    E. 9

## GRAPHING FUNCTIONS

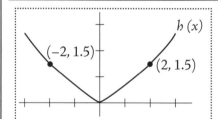

2. Which of the following could be the formula for $h(x)$?

    A. $h(x) = \dfrac{1 + x}{x}$

    B. $h(x) = x - \dfrac{1}{2}$

    C. $h(x) = \dfrac{x}{x + 2}$

    D. $h(x) = (x + 3)^2$

    E. $h(x) = \dfrac{x^2 + 2}{4}$

**Answers 1.** C; **2.** E

## Break Time!

S TOP! Stop doing math! We only have geometry and a few random concepts left. But it's time to take another break. This time, we're going to recommend some activities that will truly relax your mind:

1. Go to Bermuda. Take a photo of a sandy beach, with waves lapping at the shore. Look at the photo. Pretty relaxing photo, huh?

2. Buy a full drum set. Don't play it. There's nothing as peaceful as a drum set that's not being played.

3. Go home. Light some votive candles. Put some Frank Ocean on the speakers. Light some more votive candles. A couple more. Well, now that's too many. When it comes to votive candles, it's all about balance. You'll get the hang of it.

4. Irritate a witch. Hope that she casts a sleep spell on you. Ain't no sleep like sleep-spell sleep.

## Geometry

*The ACT-bot only provides to-scale drawings because of a malfunction in its cruelty processor— mercy is not within its standard programming.
—Jon

If they don't specifically tell you an image is not to scale, it is to scale. Always.

—Ava

W elcome back! We've passed through the rocky mountain pass of some pretty frightening math, shrieking in fear at quadratics, function graphs, and weighted averages. But we've emerged into the greener pastures of geometry.

Many people prefer geometry to all other fields of mathematics, for the simple reason that geometry is far more visual. You can actually *see* the way angles connect, the way circles expand or divide into separate areas when cut by a chord. In other words, geometry makes immediate *sense* in a way that other branches of math do not.

Thankfully, the ACT-bot puts more geometry questions on the test than any other type of math question. Doubly thankfully, most of the pictures are drawn to scale, which means that the pictures are more-or-less accurate depictions of the situation described in the problem.* This is not true of the SAT, so be happy that you chose the right test!

## A Cute Tip

How can you remember that "acute" angles are less than 90 degrees, while "obtuse" angles are more than 90 degrees? Just do what all serious mathematicians do: Draw a little bitty-witty puppy in every angle that is less than 90 degrees. Then you'll say, "Aaawww . . . cute!"

## ANGLES

A long, long time ago, people traveled in parallel lines. They never encountered one another, but trudged along in their loneliness. Then, around 3500 B.C., one young woman left her line to go chat about crop rotation with another young woman. With this revolutionary decision, she created the first **angle.**

## How to Play

**Angles** are formed at the intersection of two lines. Here is a basic angle.

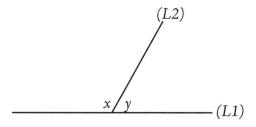

Open your eyes real wide, because you're about to read some big math words. Angles $x$ and $y$ are **adjacent,** because they are located on the same line ($L1$). This means they are also **supplementary;** they must add up to 180 degrees. So if $x = 100$, then $y = 80$. Let's kick this up a notch.

When two lines intersect, the opposite angles are equal. In the image at right, $x = x$ and $y = y$. You eagle eyes out there might also have noticed that $x$ and $y$ are supplementary, so they must add up to 180 degrees. All four angles ($x + x + y + y$) add up to 360 degrees. We can use this understanding of intersections to help us with the most common problems involving degrees.

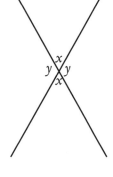

On the top of the next page, two parallel lines ($L1$ and $L2$) are crossed by a third line ($L3$), creating two intersections. The two intersections are exact copies of each other. This allows us to draw conclusions from very limited information.

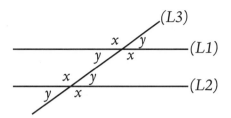

At first glance, angle z (below) may seem unrelated to the 125-degree angle beneath it. But if we recall that both intersections are copies of each other, then all we need to do is find the angle above 125. The two angles are supplementary, so the angle adjacent to the 125-degree angle must be 55 degrees (180 − 125 = 55). This means that z = 55 degrees, as well, since the top intersection is a copy of the bottom intersection.

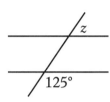

**Let's Play**

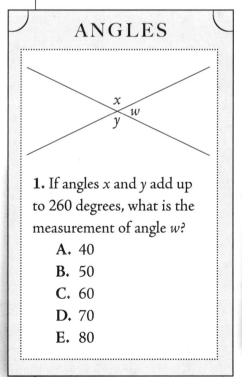

**1.** If angles x and y add up to 260 degrees, what is the measurement of angle w?

   **A.** 40

   **B.** 50

   **C.** 60

   **D.** 70

   **E.** 80

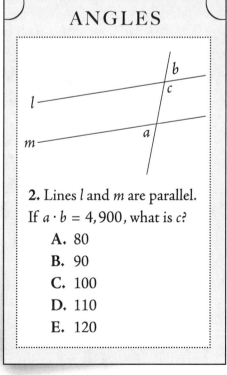

**2.** Lines l and m are parallel. If a · b = 4,900, what is c?

   **A.** 80

   **B.** 90

   **C.** 100

   **D.** 110

   **E.** 120

**Answers: 1.** B; **2.** D

### Nightmare Angle Problems

Nestled comfortably in its workshop of mind-melting horrors, the ACT-bot likes to hide angle relationships within a larger, more complex diagram. Once you can find the intersections, you should be fine.

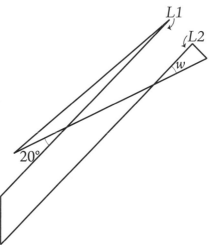

**1.** If lines *L1* and *L2* are parallel, what is the measure of angle *w*?

Look for the line crossing our two parallel lines, and you should be able to locate your two identical intersections. Angle *w* is "across" from the 20-degree angle, which means that it is 20 degrees as well.

### TRIANGLES

You know how movies have love triangles? Like how in *Twilight: The Movie Version*, the girl loves the vampire who loves the werewolf who loves the girl? (Is this what happens? We haven't seen it yet.) Well, movies like *Twilight* would not have been possible if triangles had not been invented. So all y'all Twihards better be thankful.

## How to Play

Here's a triangle:

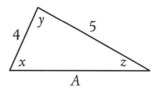

That's a plain, happy triangle, right? Well, here are three important facts about that triangle:

1. $x + y + z = 180$
2. The longest side is opposite the largest angle, the mediumest side is opposite the mediumest angle, and the shortest side is opposite the smallest angle.
3. This last fact is a bit more complex: One side of a triangle cannot be greater than the sum of the two other sides, nor can it be smaller than the difference between the two other sides. So in the above triangle, side $A$ cannot be larger than 9 or shorter than 1. Another way of writing the same thing: The difference between the two other sides < third side < sum of the two other sides.

The bot likes to test three types of triangles:

**EQUILATERAL**
+ all sides equal
+ all angles equal

**ISOSCELES**
+ two equal sides
+ two equal angles opposite the equal sides

**SCALENE**
+ all different sides
+ all different angles

But, to be honest, you are going to spend most of your time dealing with **right triangles,** which come in many shapes and sizes, but always have one right (90-degree) angle.

## Triangle Alter Egos

In addition to equilateral, isosceles, and scalene, a triangle can also be called:

ACUTE

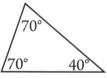

*(All angles are less than 90°.)*

OBTUSE

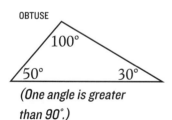

*(One angle is greater than 90°.)*

AND RIGHT

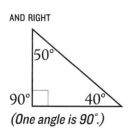

*(One angle is 90°.)*

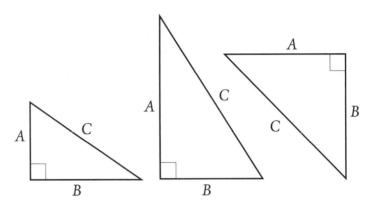

What are you going to be doing with all of these right triangles? Simple: You're going to be using the **Pythagorean theorem** a zillion times. Really? A *zillion* times? Yes, the ACT-bot *loves* the PT—it has literally hundreds of "Pythagorean theorem" posters above its bed.

The Pythagorean theorem involves the two sides, $A$ and $B$, and the **hypotenuse** $C$ (the hypotenuse is the longest side, which is always opposite the right angle): $a^2 + b^2 = c^2$.

### Let's Play

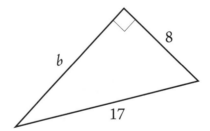

What is the length of side $b$?

Once you've located the hypotenuse (opposite the right angle), you can fill in the formula: $8^2 + b^2 = 17^2$, and then use algebra to solve for $b = 15$.

### Nightmare Pythagorean Theorem Problems

Much like with angles, the ACT-bot's go-to strategy here is to hide right triangles. Just remember that once you have found your right triangle, you can use the Pythagorean theorem. As in:

Careful—
the PT
only works
on right triangles.

—Ava

If the diameter of the circle is $6\sqrt{2}$, what is the perimeter of the inscribed square?

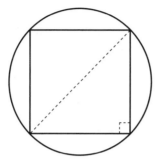

We're cheating a bit here, because we haven't yet told you about circles. But (spoiler alert!) the diameter of a circle is the line that crosses from one point to its opposite point, crossing through the middle. If you draw a line from one corner of the square to its opposite corner, then you've drawn the diameter. More important, you've just drawn a right triangle!

But hold the phone—we only have the hypotenuse. Is that enough information? Well, we know that the other two sides are equal, because they are the sides of a square, so we can write:

$$x^2 + x^2 = (6\sqrt{2})^2$$
$$2(x^2) = 72$$
$$x^2 = 36$$
$$x = 6$$

If the sides of the square are each 6, then the perimeter is 24. (Okay, we haven't told you that the perimeter of a square is 4 times the length of the sides. This problem is *full* of spoilers!)

While you should always keep your eyes open for right triangles in any geometry problem, there are two specific triangles that you should memorize:

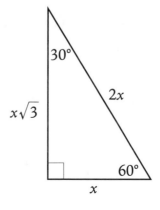
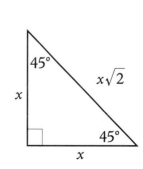

Once you have implanted these two triangles deep inside your brain, a light should go off any time you see a right triangle with a 60-degree or a 45-degree angle. What's important here is the relationship among the three sides. If you don't know, for example, that the length of the hypotenuse of a 30-60-90 triangle is double that of the smallest side, then the following problem would be impossible:*

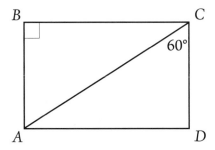

If $AC = 6$, what is the length of $AB$?

Did you locate the hidden 30-60-90 triangle? If the hypotenuse is 6, then the smaller side, $AB$, has to be 3.

## SIMILAR TRIANGLES

The ACT-bot also has a cyber-passion for problems involving similar triangles. Similar triangles are triangles that share a lot of the same interests, like French literature, vegan cuisine, and parasailing—they'd probably work for each other romantically, but no guarantees because love is so complex. JK-ing. We call two triangles "similar" if the ratio of the lengths of their sides is the same. Like this:

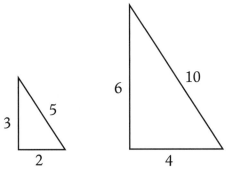

**Little-Known Math Fact**

*30-60-90 triangles are the best triangles.*

*Or not *impossible*. You could always just derive the sides of a 30-60-90 triangle using trigonometry. But this will waste valuable seconds.

As you can see, the only difference between the two triangles is that the length of each side of the second triangle has been doubled. This means that the sides of the second triangle *have the same ratio to each other as do those of the first.* For example, 2:3:5 is equal to 4:6:10. Here's how the ACT-bot tests this:

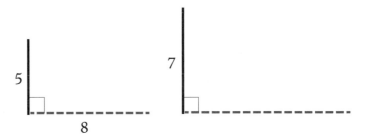

A 5-foot pole casts an 8-foot shadow. How long is the shadow cast by a 7-foot pole at the same time of day?

First off, whenever you see two straight lines at a right angle, go ahead and draw the third line to create a triangle. This "hide the triangle" trick, believed to be invented by standardized-test-creating Neanderthals, is one of the oldest in the world.

Now that you've created two triangles, let's solve this similar triangle problem by creating an equation that compares the similar lengths. The trick here is to put the similar sides on the same sides of the fraction: $\dfrac{5}{8} = \dfrac{7}{x}$

Cross multiply to find that the shadow is 11.2 feet.

**Let's Play**

## SIMIL∆R TRI∆NGLES

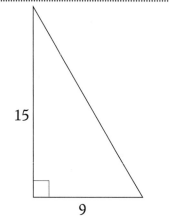

**1.** Jeremiah built this splendid triangle out of blocks. His little brother, Nazir, loved it so much that he wanted to build the same triangle. But he is smaller, and he can stack up only 5 blocks. How long should the base be, to make a similar triangle?

    **A.** 1
    **B.** 2
    **C.** 3
    **D.** 4
    **E.** 5

## SIMIL∆R TRI∆NGLES

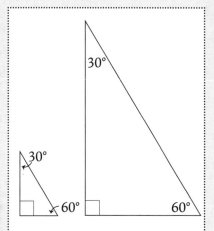

**2.** In the 2 similar right triangles above, the hypotenuse of the larger triangle is 6. If the larger triangle is 3 times larger than the smaller, what is the perimeter of the smaller triangle?

    **A.** 2
    **B.** $2 + \sqrt{3}$
    **C.** 4
    **D.** $3 + \sqrt{3}$
    **E.** 5

**Answers: 1.** C; **2.** D

Remember, if two triangles share the same angle measurements, they're similar.

—Ava

## Nightmare Similar Triangle Problems

That shadow problem did an *okay* job of hiding the similar triangles, but the ACT-bot, especially toward the end of the section, can get downright *nasty* with the whole "disguise the similar triangles" game. Here are the two most common ways of hiding similar triangles:

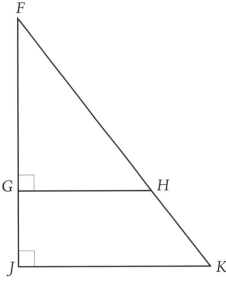

Don't be afraid to draw on the images. Extending parallel lines or writing in known angles might be all you need to discover a hidden relationship.

—Jon

In the first diagram, *ABC* is a smaller, similar version of *CDE*, but flipped on its head. In the second, *FGH* is a smaller, similar version of *FJK*. Find the similar triangles to make solvable proportions in the following nightmare problem:

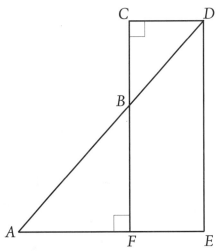

If *FE* = 4 and *AE* = 10 and *AB* = 9, how long is *AD*?

For this nasty beast, we need to recognize the hidden "similar triangle" shape, which reveals that triangle *AFB* and triangle *BCD* are similar.

**Famous Triangles**
- The pyramids at Giza
- Doritos
- The Bermuda Triangle
- The Eiffel Tower (kinda)
- One of the non-marshmallow Lucky Charms
- Those things outside of the Louvre Museum
- Did we already say Doritos? We did already say Doritos.

Using the information we are given, we know that the base of $AFB$ is 6, because $AE$ is 10, and $FE$ is 4. We know that $CD$ is also 4, because it is the same length as $FE$! If $AB$ is 9, then we can set up our ratio: $\frac{AF}{AB} = \frac{CD}{DB}$. Fill in the ratio with the known lengths: $\frac{6}{9} = \frac{4}{DB}$. Cross multiply to find that $DB = 6$. Add $DB$ to $AB$ to get our answer: 15.

## AREA OF A TRIANGLE

Sick of triangles yet? Never fear, you have only one task left: finding the area of a triangle. Luckily, this ain't too bad. **The area of a triangle is $\frac{1}{2} \cdot base \cdot height$.** Your job is to find the base and the height.

In the equilateral triangle below, $AC = 2\sqrt{3}$. What is the area of $\triangle ABC$ if $BD$ is perpendicular to $AC$, and $AD = DC$?

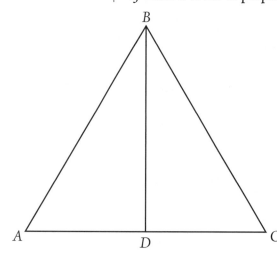

Okay, we admit it, this problem is a little nightmarish, but we wanted to bring together a few triangle concepts and group them all in one problem. If this strikes you as a real head-scratcher, remember that every piece of information in the problem is important. The fact that the triangle is equilateral means that angle $DAB$ is 60 degrees, which in turn means that triangle $ADB$ is a 30-60-90. If the small side $(AD)$ is $\sqrt{3}$ (because it is half of $AC$), then side $BD$ must be $\sqrt{3} \cdot \sqrt{3}$, because that's how 30-60-90 triangles *always* work. If $BD$ is 3, then our height is 3, because $BD$ is the height of the triangle. So the *area* $= \left(\frac{1}{2}\right)(3)(2\sqrt{3}) = 3\sqrt{3}$.

✳Everyone
else calls
them obtuse
triangles.

—Zack

Many of the more challenging problems involving the area of a triangle use what we call *leaning triangles.*✳ Like this:

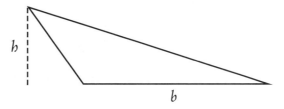

Just remember to drop a straight line from the highest point of the triangle to the "ground" or level of the base of the triangle. This line is the height. Try it out:

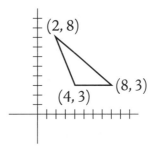

What is the area of the triangle above?

In this problem, we just need to measure the distance from that top point (2, 8) to the base of the triangle, which lies along $y = 3$. From 8 down to 3 is a distance of 5, which is our height. To find the base, we just count from the $x$-point of one end of the base (4), to the $x$-point of the other end (8). So our base is 4, and our area is $\frac{1}{2} \cdot 4 \cdot 5 = 10$.

Let's try a couple of tough triangle problems:

## NIGHTMARE TRIANGLES

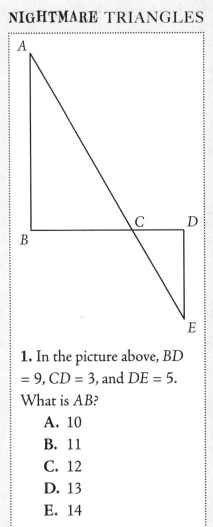

**1.** In the picture above, $BD = 9$, $CD = 3$, and $DE = 5$. What is $AB$?

   **A.** 10

   **B.** 11

   **C.** 12

   **D.** 13

   **E.** 14

## NIGHTMARE TRIANGLES

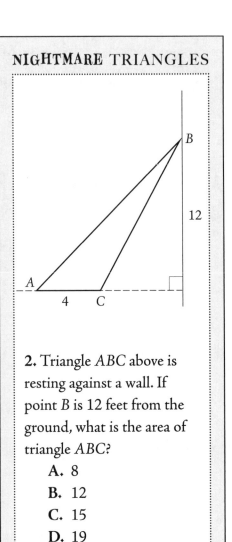

**2.** Triangle *ABC* above is resting against a wall. If point *B* is 12 feet from the ground, what is the area of triangle *ABC*?

   **A.** 8

   **B.** 12

   **C.** 15

   **D.** 19

   **E.** 24

* The candy corn may be the better bet, unless you want to get cited for vandalism and destruction of property. "No officer, I swear! I was just studying for the ACT!"

    —Zack

**Answers: 1.** A; **2.** E

    And *we are done with triangles forever!!!!* Actually, they are going to come back when we talk about trigonometry, but, whatever, for now *we are done with triangles forever!!!!*

    Do yourself a favor—go outside and find something in the shape of a triangle (like a "yield" sign or a piece of candy corn) and throw it in the trash.*

## RECTANGLES

You know how some movies have love rectangles? Like in *Twilight 2: More Twilight,* how the girl loves the vampire who loves the werewolf who loves Frankenstein who loves the girl? Well, those love rectangles would not be possible without real rectangles.

### How to Play

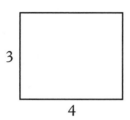

To find the perimeter of a rectangle, add the four sides. Another way of saying this is: The perimeter of a rectangle = 2(*base*) + 2(*height*). A frequent sloppy error is to see this diagram ... and add only 3 + 4. Don't do this.

The **area** of a rectangle = *base · height*. So the area for the above rectangle is 12.

### Let's Play

Let's say you are confronted with the following problem:

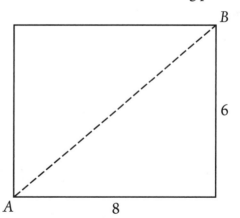

In the rectangle above, what is the length of the fastest route from *A* to *B*?

Do you:

**A.** Run screaming to the Ozarks, never to return.

**B.** Change your name and hide in a pillow fort.

**C.** Use triangles to solve the problem.

We know that choices A and B are tempting, but allow us to suggest C. This requires you to see that diagonal as the hypotenuse of a triangle with the base as one leg and the height as the other. Then $6^2 + 8^2 = c^2$. Use algebra to determine that $c$, which is the path we are looking for, is 10.

## PARALLELOGRAMS AND TRAPEZOIDS *

Like rectangles, parallelograms and trapezoids have four sides. Unlike rectangles, parallelograms and trapezoids are *oddballs*, and require different strategies to determine their areas.

**How to Play**

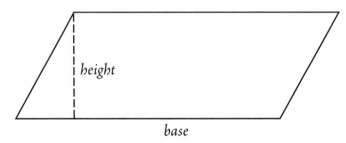

base

This deviant shape is a **parallelogram,** because opposite sides are parallel, but interior angles are *not* necessarily all 90 degrees. In order to find the area of this shape, you multiply the base and the height. The catch with a parallelogram is that the height might require some mathin' to find.

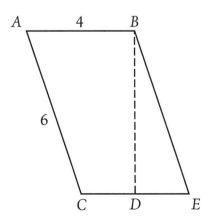

$BD$ is the height of parallelogram $ABCE$. If $DE = 2$, what is the area of $ABCE$?

To determine the height of the shape, we need to see that triangle $BDE$ is a right triangle. That means that this problem (like most problems in life) can be solved with the Pythagorean theorem. We know that $BE$ is the same length as $AC$ and is the hypotenuse of the right triangle, so $2^2 + B^2 = 6^2$. $B = 4\sqrt{2}$, which

---

*\* I believe it was Anaxagoras who discovered the relationship between the number of syllables in the name of a shape and the level of difficulty in finding its area.*

*—Jon*

**Little-Known Math Fact**

*"Parallelograms" was originally the name of a fiber-rich kids' cereal, until Math bought the rights to the name.*

gives us our height for the parallelogram. Multiply that by the base and we get $4\sqrt{2} \cdot 4 = 16\sqrt{2}$.

As poorly behaved as that shape was, it's got nothing on the following:

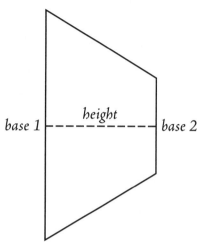

That, my friends, is a **trapezoid.** A trapezoid is a quadrilateral with exactly one set of parallel sides, or bases. To find the area of a trapezoid, multiply the height and the average of the two parallel lengths. Try it out:

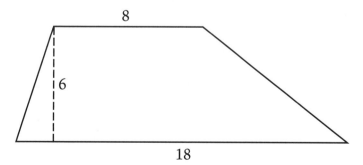

What is the area of the trapezoid above?

The average of the two bases is $\frac{8 + 18}{2} = 13$. Multiply that by the height to get the area: $13 \cdot 6 = 78$.

Let's try a few:

## PARALLELOGRAM

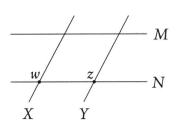

**1.** In the diagram above, lines *M* and *N* are parallel, and are separated by a constant perpendicular distance of 5 units. If *w* and *z* are points of intersection, and segment *wz* is 6 units long, what is the area of the parallelogram formed within the 4 lines?

   **A.** 30
   **B.** 36
   **C.** 40
   **D.** $42\sqrt{3}$
   **E.** 50

## TRAPEZOID

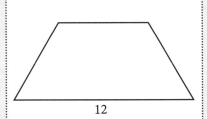

**2.** In the trapezoid pictured above, the top is half the length of the base. If the base is 12 units long and the area of the whole trapezoid is 45, what is the height of the trapezoid?

   **A.** 4
   **B.** 5
   **C.** 6
   **D.** 7
   **E.** 8

**Answers: 1.** A; **2.** B

One shape left, geometricians!

## CIRCLES

Ah, circles! Without circles, our cars would go clumping down the street on octahedral wheels; we would scratch our tongues on the jagged edges of our triangular lollipops; our square Hula-Hoops wouldn't work, so there'd be discarded Hula-Hoops everywhere, blocking up the streets and causing traffic jams. Thank goodness for the circle!

The only (only!) downside of the circle is that the ACT-bot can use it to create some pernicious questions.

### How to Play

The first step in any circle problem is to find the radius. This is so important that it deserves the ol' bold-caps treatment, followed by six exclamation points: **THE FIRST STEP IN ANY CIRCLE PROBLEM IS TO FIND THE RADIUS!!!!!!**

The **radius is the distance from the center of the circle to its circumference.** The **diameter is twice the radius,** or the distance from a point on the circumference to the opposite point, passing through the center of the circle.

The **circumference** of a circle $= (2\pi)(radius)$. The **area** $= (\pi)(radius)^2$. Once you've found the radius, in other words, you're good to go. Let's do this:

A circle is inscribed in a square with a side length of 6.

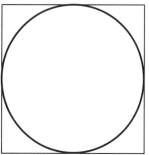

What is the circumference of the circle?

If each side of the square is 6, then the diameter of the circle must be 6 as well, which means that the radius is 3. Plug this into

> If you are given the diameter in a problem, I recommend immediately rewriting half of it as the radius; the radius is used much more often (almost exclusively) in geometry, and this might keep you from accidentally using the diameter when you only wanted the radius.
>
> —Jon

the circumference formula to find that the circumference of the circle is $6\pi$.

The ACT-bot has also been known, in certain moods (just kidding, its only mood is lust for destruction) to talk about **central angles** and **arcs.** A central angle has its vertex at the center of a circle and defines an arc of equal measure on the circle's circumference.

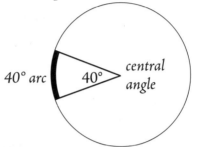

You might also see an **inscribed angle,** which is created by extending two straight lines from a point on the circumference of the circle across the circle. As in:

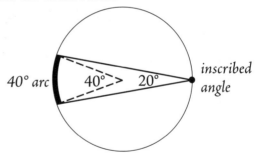

As you can see, the inscribed angle above is 20°. Whoa, that's half of the central angle and arc! Can that be true? Yes, it's always true. So true, there's even an equation: inscribed angle = $\frac{1}{2}$ central angle = $\frac{1}{2}$ arc. Try this problem:

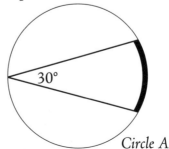

*Circle A*

**Famous Circles**

- Stonehenge
- The One Ring to Rule Them All
- Pennies—oh, and quarters. And dimes. And ha'pennies . . .
- Honey Nut Cheerios
- Full Moon–Shaped Stickers

If the radius of *Circle A* is 12, what is the length of the bolded portion of the circle?

This is a secret two-step problem. First, let's use that 30-degree inscribed angle to see that the corresponding arc is $2 \cdot 30 = 60°$. So the bold section of the circle must be $\frac{60}{360}$ or $\frac{1}{6}$ of the total circumference. We can find the circumference using the circumference formula with our radius $(2)(12\pi) = 24\pi$. Take a sixth of the total circumference to find the answer: $4\pi$.

Try a couple:

CIRCLES

**1.** The square inscribed in the circle above has an area of 25. What is the area of the circle?

  A. $8.5\pi$
  B. $10\pi$
  C. $12.5\pi$
  D. $14\pi$
  E. $16.5\pi$

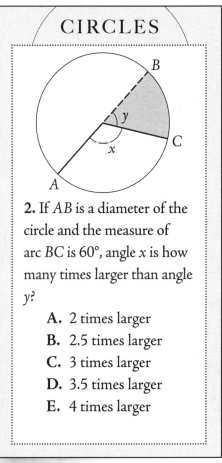

CIRCLES

**2.** If *AB* is a diameter of the circle and the measure of arc *BC* is 60°, angle *x* is how many times larger than angle *y*?

  A. 2 times larger
  B. 2.5 times larger
  C. 3 times larger
  D. 3.5 times larger
  E. 4 times larger

**Answers: 1.** C; **2.** A

So, those are our geometry basics. Let's move on to some of the more challenging geometric problems, which involve taking these shapes onto the coordinate plane.

## Coordinate Geometry

In elementary school, teachers like to introduce second graders to coordinate geometry by giving them Peg-Boards and rubber bands. The kids are told to make shapes by stretching the rubber bands around the pegs. *Oh my gosh*, all second graders think. *Coordinate geometry is the Best. Math. Ever.*

But coordinate geometry, like everything else in life, is not quite as simple as it looked in second grade. Instead, coordinate geometry applies the techniques of function graphs to normal geometry. Remember that the graphs of functions were all about "seeing" equations in *xy*-planes? Well, coordinate geometry is all about "seeing" geometric shapes from the equations that create those shapes. The equation is the math-style expression of the shape, and moving back and forth between the visual shape on the *xy*-plane and the equation that determines that shape is the name of the game. Let's start simple.

### THE LINE

In coordinate geometry, the line is the basic unit.

### How to Play

The formula for a line is most often expressed as $y = mx + b$. *B* stands for the *y*-intercept, or the point at which the line crosses the *y*-axis. In this illustration, the line crosses the *y*-axis at $(0, 7)$, so $b = 7$. So far, here is the equation of our line:

$$y = mx + 7$$

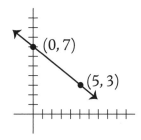

**$M$ is the slope of the line.** The slope of a line is defined as

$$\frac{\text{rise} \left(\text{amount it moves up or down from point } A \text{ to point } B\right)}{\text{run} \left(\text{amount the line moves left or right from point } A \text{ to point } B\right)}$$

and is typically expressed as a fraction. If we look at the first point on our line $(0, 7)$ and the second $(5, 3)$, we see that the line has moved down 4 spaces, from 7 to 3, so the "rise" is $-4$. We see that it has moved to the right 5 spaces, from 0 to 5, so the "run" is 5. Our slope, or $m$, is $-\frac{4}{5}$. Here's the final version of the equation of the line:

$$y = -\frac{4}{5}x + 7$$

There is a shortcut to finding a slope. Let's say you know two points on a line: $(x_1, y_1)$, for the one point, and $(x_2, y_2)$, for the second point. You can find the slope with the equation:

$$slope = \frac{y_2 - y_1}{x_2 - x_1}$$

## Let's Play

A line (not shown), passes through the points $(2, 7)$ and $(5, -3)$. What is the slope of the line?

Just plug those points into the slope equation: $\frac{-3 - 7}{5 - 2} = -\frac{10}{3}$

Knowing the equation of the line allows us to do some awesome things that we could never do just by looking at the line.

**Little-Known Math Fact**

*"Rize Over Run" was a popular dance move in 1993.*

✳ If it helps you remember it, consider the fact that $y_2 - y_1$ is the rise and $x_2 - x_1$ is the run.

—Zack

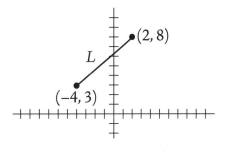

In segment $L$ above, what is the $y$-intercept?

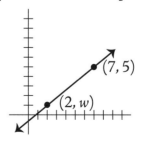

This problem would be wicked tough to eyeball. At best we could say "something like 6ish?" ✳ In response, the ACT-bot would cackle and then blast you with an ion ray. But we can use the equation of the line ($y = mx + b$) to find the exact $y$-intercept. First off, let's find that slope using the slope equation:

$$\frac{8 - 3}{2 - (-4)} = \frac{5}{6}$$

So our equation is now $y = \frac{5}{6}x + b$. To find $b$, just pick any coordinate, and plug the $y$ value and $x$ value into the equation. Let's use the second point $(2, 8)$ and plug it in:

$$8 = \frac{5}{6}(2) + b$$

$$8 = \frac{5}{3} + b$$

$$\frac{19}{3} \text{ or } 6.\overline{3} = b$$

So our $y$-intercept is $6.\overline{3}$. Thank goodness we didn't say 6ish, right?

Another great way to use line and slope equations:

The above line passes through points $(2, w)$ and $(7, 5)$. If the line has a slope of $\frac{4}{5}$, what is point $w$?

✳ Even if "6ish" is as far as you get, it would probably allow you to rule out two answer choices.

—Ava

To solve for $w$, plug all of the points into the slope equation, and solve it as if it were a standard algebra problem:

$$\frac{5 - w}{7 - 2} = \frac{4}{5}$$

$$\frac{5 - w}{5} = \frac{4}{5}$$

$$5 - w = 4$$

$$w = 1$$

Try a few out for yourself:

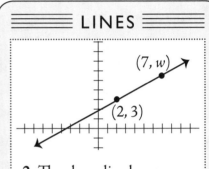

$$\equiv \text{ LINES } \equiv$$

**1.** If a line passes through the points $(3, 4)$ and $(5, 7)$, what is its $y$-intercept?

   **A.** −2

   **B.** −1.5

   **C.** −1

   **D.** −0.5

   **E.** 0

$$\equiv \text{ LINES } \equiv$$

$(7, w)$

$(2, 3)$

**2.** The above line has a $y$-intercept of 2. What is $w$?

   **A.** 5

   **B.** 5.5

   **C.** 6

   **D.** 6.5

   **E.** 7

**Answers: 1.** D; **2.** B

The ACT-bot can make things more complicated in two ways: It can introduce parallel or perpendicular lines, or it can ask about the midpoint between two points or the distance between two points. If you see any of these concepts, crumple your test, leap up on your desk, and spike the crumpled test like a football.*

Joking! Don't do that. Read this instead:

*They give out lots of bonus points for assertiveness, right?

—Zack

**Little-Known Math Fact**

*You know how in cop shows, the detectives always refer to criminals as "perps"? That's cop slang for "perpendiculars," because criminals run perpendicular to the law.*

## Parallel and Perpendicular Lines

A parallel line runs alongside the original line like a railroad track.* Parallel lines have the same slope, but *not* the same $y$-intercept. Try this out:

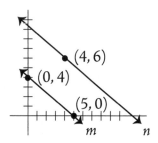

Line $n$ runs parallel to line $m$ and passes through the point $(4, 6)$. What is the $y$-intercept of line $n$?

Remember that parallel lines have the same slope. We can find the slope of line $m$ using the coordinates of the two points provided. Do that:

$$\frac{0 - 4}{5 - 0} = -\frac{4}{5}$$

This means that the slope of *both* lines is $-\frac{4}{5}$. Just as in the previous problem, we can then find the $y$-intercept of line $n$ using the slope and the coordinates of the one point provided:

$$6 = \left(-\frac{4}{5}\right)(4) + b$$
$$6 = -3.2 + b$$
$$9.2 = b$$

So, our $y$-intercept for line $n$ is 9.2.

Perpendicular lines, on the other hand, intersect each other at 90-degree angles. This means that they have opposite slopes, or, to say the same thing in more complicated words, their slopes are negative reciprocals of each other. Like this:

Slope: $\frac{4}{5}$; perpendicular slope: $-\frac{5}{4}$

Slope: $-\frac{3}{2}$; perpendicular slope: $\frac{2}{3}$

Slope: 4; perpendicular slope: $-\frac{1}{4}$

Got it? Then try this out:

*Also like railroad tracks, parallel lines are owned and controlled by Cornelius Vanderbilt.

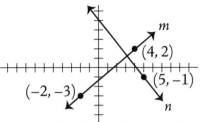

Line *n* is perpendicular to line *m*. What is the slope of line *n*?

First, let's use the slope equation to find the slope of line *m*. $\frac{2 - (-3)}{4 - (-2)} = \frac{5}{6}$. The slope of line *n* is the negative reciprocal of the slope of *m*: $-\frac{6}{5}$.

## Midpoint and Distance Problems

Both midpoint and distance problems require that you plug coordinate points into formulas. The best strategy here is either to memorize the formulas or to train a parrot to repeat the formulas, then place this parrot outside the window of the testing center. Your choice.

The coordinates for the midpoint between one point $(x_1, y_1)$ and another point $(x_2, y_2)$ are: $\left( \frac{x_1 + x_2}{2}, \frac{y_1 + y_2}{2} \right)$

In other words, we are taking the average of the two *x*-coordinates and the average of the two *y*-coordinates.

What is the midpoint between the points (3, 2) and (7, 4)?

*x*-coordinate: $\frac{3 + 7}{2} = 5$

*y*-coordinate: $\frac{2 + 4}{2} = 3$

The midpoint is (5, 3).

The distance formula is a bit hairier. We recommend going ahead and tattooing it on your forearm. In later life, you can tell people that you "just really love the distance formula. Always have. Always will." (If you later regret the tattoo, you can just tattoo "I regret this," with an arrow pointing at the formula.)

Distance formula: $\sqrt{(x_1 - x_2)^2 + (y_1 - y_2)^2}$

RAWK!
$\sqrt{(X_1 - X_2)^2 + (Y_1 - Y_2)^2}$
DISTANCE! RAWK!

If you forget the distance formula, remember that it's just a variation of the Pythagorean theorem. Sketch a right triangle with the difference in *x*-values as the base, the difference in *y*-values as the height, and the line connecting the two points as the hypotenuse, and solve for the hypotenuse with the PT. That's your answer!

—Jon

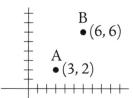

What is the distance between point A and point B?

Plug those points into the distance formula:

$$\sqrt{(3-6)^2 + (2-6)^2}$$

$$\sqrt{(-3)^2 + (-4)^2}$$

$$\sqrt{9 + 16}$$

$$\sqrt{25}$$

5 = distance

Try some out for yourself:

## D I S T A N C E

**1.** Luann and Lou live on the Great Coordinate Plains (which are in Illinois). Luann lives at (3, 12), while Lou lives all the way out at (7, 15). Luann invites Lou over for a date. Lou is excited, but lazy. He decides to calculate the distance first. What is the distance between their 2 houses?

   **A.** 4.25

   **B.** 5

   **C.** 5.73

   **D.** 6

   **E.** 6.83

## MIDPOINT

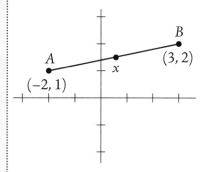

**2.** In the plane above, what are the coordinates of point x, if it lies exactly midway between points A and B?

   **A.** (1, 0.5)

   **B.** (0, 1)

   **C.** (0.5, 1)

   **D.** (0.5, 1.5)

   **E.** (1, 1)

**Answers:**

**1.** B; **2.** D

## CIRCLES

You've seen circles, sure. But have you ever seen one *drawn on a coordinate plane?* Prepare to have your world turned upside down.✳

Check this out:

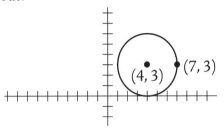

✳ This will be the most exciting thing you see today until your friend Snapchats you a picture of her lunch.

—Jon

## How to Play

First you need to know that the formula for a circle is:

$$(x - h)^2 + (y - k)^2 = r^2$$ ✳ ✳

Looks tough? Well, it's actually not that bad. We know that $x$ and $y$ simply refer to the coordinates for any point on that circle. The new elements are $h$, $k$, and $r$. What do you think $r$ stands for? Rhythm? It's not rhythm, that's a ridiculous guess. It's the *radius*, the unwavering, always-the-same distance from the center to the points around the circle.

So $r$ is the radius. The main thing to notice here is that the equation doesn't exactly say $r$. It says $r$-squared. So to find that part of the equation, find the radius and square it.

Look at the circle graphed above. What's the radius? Well, if you travel 3 over from the center at $(4, 3)$, you hit $(7, 3)$ on the circumference. That's the radius. You have $r$, which is 3, so $r$-squared is 9.

But what about $h$ and $k$? Easy. The point $(h, k)$ denotes the center of the circle. For the circle graphed above, the center is at $(4, 3)$. That means $h = 4$ and $k = 3$. The key thing to notice about $h$ and $k$ is the fact that the equation says $x$ **minus** $h$ and $y$ **minus** $k$. So even though our circle's center is at positive 4 and positive 3, the equation will need to read $(x \text{ **minus** } 4)^2 + (y \text{ **minus** } 3)^2 = 9$.

✳✳ All of the graphing circle problems will use this equation, so don't forget it. Once you know the radius and center coordinates, just plug them in for $r$, $h$, and $k$ and you have the equation.

—Zack

If the $x$ or $y$ coordinate of the circle's center were negative, $h$ or $k$ would turn positive. So the equation for that circle is $(x - 4)^2 + (y - 3)^2 = 9$.

Try this:

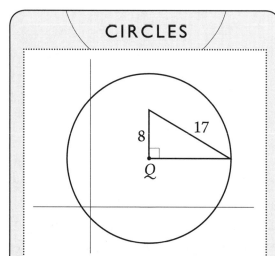

## CIRCLES

In the above diagram, point $Q$ is the center of the circle. What is the formula for the circle?

**A.** $(x - 8)^2 + (y + 8)^2 = 169$

**B.** $(x - 8)^2 + (y - 10)^2 = 169$

**C.** $(x + 10)^2 + (y + 8)^2 = 225$

**D.** $(x - 10)^2 + (y - 8)^2 = 225$

**E.** $(x + 10)^2 + (y - 8)^2 = 225$

**Answer:** D

**Nightmare Circle Problems**

Because the equation of a circle is not as well known as, say, the equation of a line, your average nightmare circle problem will have circle formulas as answer choices. This looks scary if you don't know the formula. But you do! So answer this problem:

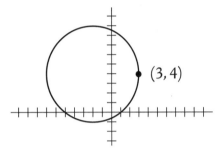

The above circle has a radius of 5, and the point shown is the rightmost point. Which of the following gives the formula for the circle?

**A.** $(x + 3)^2 + (y - 4)^2 = 9$
**B.** $(x + 4)^2 + (y - 5)^2 = 25$
**C.** $(x + 2)^2 + (y - 4)^2 = 25$
**D.** $(x - 2)^2 + (y - 4)^2 = 25$
**E.** $(x + 3)^2 + (y - 5)^2 = 16$

This problem tests your knowledge of the circle formula, pure and simple. If you can remember that the equation is always set equal to $r^2$, then we know that we are looking for 25, and can eliminate answers A and E. Then we need to find the center. If (3, 4) is the rightmost point, we know that it is at the same height as the center, so the $y$-value of our center must be 4. The $x$-value of the center needs to be 5 units in from the outer edge, or $-2$. So our center is at $(-2, 4)$. Plug this into our formula to see that C is the answer.

## PARABOLAS

The last shape of the geometry section is the parabola. Have we saved the best for last? You better believe it!

### How to Play

A parabola can be either vertical or horizontal, so let's take them one at a time. First, let's talk about vertical parabolas, which can either look likes smiles or frowns.

The shape below is a vertical parabola. Here's how it works: The lowest point is called the **vertex,** here at (2, −4).

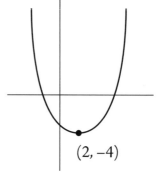

$(2, -4)$

If the vertex is $(h, k)$, then the equation goes a little something like this (actually, it goes exactly like this):

$$y - k = a(x - h)^2$$

So, the formula for the above vertex would be $y + 4 = a(x - 2)^2$. But wait a second, what is that $a$? So glad you asked!

The $a$ determines how fat or skinny a parabola is. If a parabola has been pigging out on Krusty Krispy Pork Kracklins, it starts to look like this:

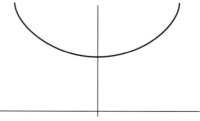

A fatty parabola has a really small $a$-value. (You would think that a fatty parabola would have a big $a$-value, but the Math gods, they are cruel.) That hefty fella up there probably has an *a*-value of $\frac{1}{8}$ or $\frac{1}{9}$. But if the same parabola takes up judo or, better yet, Super Judo (like normal judo, but, you know, super), it can eventually look like this:

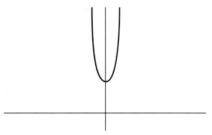

A skinny parabola has a larger *a*-value. The above Super Judo champion might have an *a*-value of 8 or 9. ✳

The last thing you need to know is that a positive *a*-value orients the parabola upward (smile, a new frozen yogurt store opened in your town!), while a negative *a*-value orients the parabola downward (frown, the frozen yogurt store is a front for the black market organ trade).

Now, horizontal parabolas can either look like someone smiling while lying on his or her side, or someone frowning while lying on his or her side:

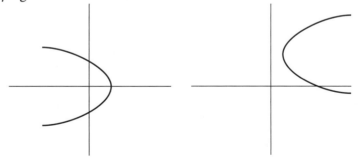

Horizontal parabolas have a slightly different equation: You just switch the *x* and *y*.

$$x - h = a(y - k)^2$$

### Some Fun Parabolas

- The Gateway Arch in Saint Louis
- All smiles
- All frowns
- The graph depicting the popularity of ironic trucker hats from 2000 to 2013
- The letter *U*
- Hills
- Bald heads

Again, $(h, k)$ are the coordinate points for the vertex of the parabola, while *a* determines the width of the parabola. Just like the previous example, the smaller the *a*-value, the fatter the parabola. A positive *a*-value means the parabola opens to the right, and a negative *a*-value means it opens to the left.

### Let's Play

Parabola problems are not terribly common on the ACT, but you might see one. More likely than not, the problem will be testing your awareness of the equation. And because the basic equation of the parabola is nightmarish enough, the following can count as both standard and nightmare parabola problems.

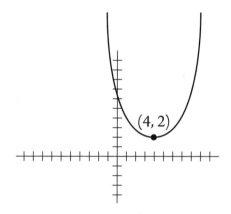

1. In the graph above, the parabola has the standard equation $y - k = a(x - h)^2$. What is $h \cdot k$?
   A. −8
   B. −6.5
   C. 0
   D. 2.5
   E. 8

Looking at the graph, we are given the vertex of the vertical parabola at $(4, 2)$. All we need to know to solve this problem is that the vertex is always $(h, k)$, so here we simply need to multiply $4 \cdot 2 = x$. Our answer is E. A totally simple problem, right? Sure, as long as you remember how the formula works.

Other problems might test how a change in the equation might change the graph:

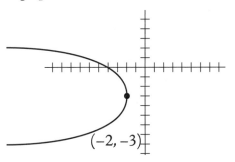

**2.** The parabola above has the formula $x - 2 = -2(y + 3)^2$. How would the parabola change if the graph were altered to $x - 2 = \frac{1}{2}(y + 3)^2$?

    **A.** It would flip on a vertical axis.

    **B.** It would get wider.

    **C.** It would flip on a vertical axis and get wider.

    **D.** It would stay the same width but move up.

    **E.** It would stay the same width but move down.

What has changed in the equation? The $a$-value has gone from negative to positive, and changed from 2 to $\frac{1}{2}$. That means two things have happened: Going from negative to positive means that the parabola now opens to the right, instead of the left, so it flips on the vertical axis. And the smaller $a$-value means that it is much wider. The answer, then, is C.

Let's do one. This is the last geometry question, so savor it!

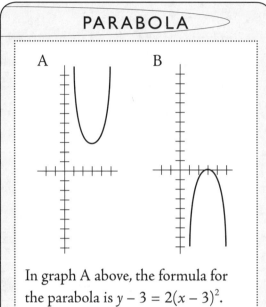

PARABOLA

In graph A above, the formula for the parabola is $y - 3 = 2(x - 3)^2$. Which of the following could be the formula for the parabola in graph B?

**A.** $y = 2(x + 3)^2$

**B.** $y = -2(x - 3)^2$

**C.** $y + 3 = \frac{1}{2}(x - 3)^2$

**D.** $y + 3 = 2(x - 3)^2$

**E.** $y - 3 = -\frac{1}{2}(x + 3)^2$

**Answer:** B

## Three Scary Words: Logarithms, Trigonometry, and Matrices

Just say them out loud. Logarithms. Trigonometry. *Matrices!* Sends shivers up your spine, right? While the names sound like bad news, we have three pieces of good news: 1.) There are only two or three problems involving logarithms, between three and five problems involving trigonometry, and maybe two (but usually one) problems involving a matrix. 2.) The logarithm, trigonometry, and matrices questions on the ACT are very basic. 3.) Logarithms, trigonometry, and matrices are not as scary as they sound.

## LOGARITHMS: EXPONENT PROBLEMS FROM SPACE

Imagine, if you will, an alternate American past. After landing on the moon, the nation became so enthusiastic about space travel that it dedicated more money to galactic exploration. In 1972, we established our first lunar colony, from which we expanded to Mars, then Venus by 1989. From there, we were able to explore deeper space, charting the rocks and gaseous clusters near Alpha Centauri. Then, in 2003, we made contact with intelligent alien life: the Logarithmoids.

Logarithmoids look like purple kittens, but they are as intelligent and conversant as humans. (Cute, right?) They quickly learn standard American English, which they speak with a slight lisp. (*So cute!*)* After about six months of communication, we realize that the Logarithmoids are very similar to us, with one essential difference: They write exponent problems in a crazy, alien way. Here's how they do it:

| Normal American Exponent Problem | Logarithmoid Exponent Problem |
| --- | --- |
| $6^3 = 216$ | $3 = \log_6 216$ |
| $5^5 = 3{,}125$ | $5 = \log_5 3{,}125$ |
| $4^{\frac{1}{2}} = 2$ | $\frac{1}{2} = \log_4 2$ |
| $3^{-2} = \frac{1}{9}$ | $-2 = \log_3 \frac{1}{9}$ |

In other words, if $y = x^z$, then $\log_x y = z$.

## How to Play

It is likely that you will see a logarithm problem with one value (either $x$, $y$, or $z$) missing. Just rewrite the problem in good ol' American exponent form (while whistling "The Star-Spangled Banner"), and the answer will be clear:

---

> WE WUV MAF!

---

\* I think logarithms are easiest said aloud. If you have the equation $\log_x y = z$, you should say to yourself, "What number $z$ do I have to raise $x$ to in order to get $y$?"

—Zack

*They also consume their weakest children. But they do it in the most adorable way!

If $\log_4 64 = x$, what is $x$?

Rewrite it: $4^x = 64$. $x$ must be 3, because $4^3 = 64$.

This could be a bit tougher if the exponent is a fractional or negative exponent. Like this:

If $\log_{625} x = \frac{1}{4}$, what is $x$?

Rewrite it: $625^{\frac{1}{4}} = x$. Remember that this is the same as $\sqrt[4]{625} = 5$. So $x = 5$.

### Nightmare Logarithm Problems

There *might* be one or two tougher logarithm problems on the test. These will require that you know logarithm rules. Just as logarithms are exponents from space, so too are logarithm rules just exponent rules from space.

Assuming that we are talking about logarithms with the same base:

Rule 1: $\log_b x + \log_b y = \log_b xy$

so: $\log_4 3 + \log_4 6 = \log_4 18$

Rule 2: $\log_b x - \log_b y = \log_b \frac{x}{y}$

so: $\log_4 6 - \log_4 2 = \log_4 3$

Rule 3: $y \cdot \log_b x = \log_b x^y$

so: $2\log_4 3 = \log_4 9$

Let's try one together:

If $\log_4 16 = 2$ and $\log_4 x = y$, what is $\log_4 16x$?

Remember the first rule. If we are multiplying two logarithms of the same base, this is the same as adding the answers. So if $\log_4 16x = \log_4 16 + \log_4 x$, then this is the same as $2 + y$, which is our answer.

A helpful similarity between exponents and logarithms is that the _base_ of an exponential expression (the number that's being raised to a power) will be the _base_ of its logarithmic equivalent (the little number next to the logarithm).

—Jon

## Calculator to the Rescue

But wait a second: Can't you just use the [LOG] button on your calculator to solve these questions? Here's the problem: That [LOG] button is actually $\log_{10}$, meaning it assumes that you are solving for logs in base 10. We recommend translating the question back to exponents, *then* using your calculator.

Let's try a few together:

**1.** If $\log_x 12 - \log_x 4 = \frac{1}{2}$, what is the value of $x$?

   **A.** 2

   **B.** 3

   **C.** 4

   **D.** 9

   **E.** 12

Combine the two logs using the subtraction rule:
$\text{Log}_x(\frac{12}{4})$, or $\log_x 3 = \frac{1}{2}$
Now translate this log statement into Earth exponent-ese:
$x^{(\frac{1}{2})} = 3$, or $\sqrt{x} = 3$. Square both sides to get 9, our answer.

**2.** If $2\log_2 3 + \log_2 x = -1$, what is the value of $x$?

   **A.** $\frac{1}{18}$

   **B.** $\frac{1}{9}$

   **C.** 0

   **D.** 9

   **E.** 18

First, use the multiplication rule to get rid of the 2 in front of that first log:
$2 \cdot \log_2 3 = \log_2 3^2 = \log_2 9$
Then use the addition rule to add your two logs:
$\log_2 9 + \log_2 x = \log_2 9x = -1$
Translate into exponent form:
$2^{(-1)} = 9x$, $\frac{1}{2} = 9x$, $x = \frac{1}{18}$, which is our answer.

## Little-Known Math Fact

*To a mathematician, the concept of a "log cabin" is very confusing.*

## TRIGONOMETRY:
## THE RETURN OF THE TRIANGLE

Here's the bad news: The ACT-bot drops two to four trigonometry questions at the end of the Math section. Here's the good news: The trigonometry on the ACT is very basic. So stick around.

### How to Play

In order to understand ACT trigonometry, you have to do one thing, and one thing only: Imagine a right triangle. Like this one.

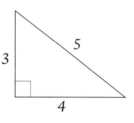

Here we have a basic 3-4-5 triangle. In order to make it a trig-ready triangle, we need to add some labels. First, pick either of the non-right angles, and give it a name. Let's call it "Bob," because we've used "*x*" a million times, and we're sick of "*x*."

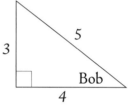

Next, we need to label the **hypotenuse** of the triangle. That's the one across from the right angle. Then, we need to label the side that is **adjacent,** or next to Bob. Finally, label the side that is **opposite,** or across from Bob.

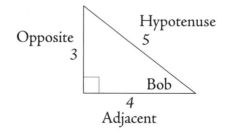

Feast your eyes on that triangle. Certified 100 percent trig-ready!

Using a trig-ready triangle, we can talk about three trigonometric functions. Scary words, I know, but super simple. Here they are:

The **sine** of angle Bob = $\dfrac{\text{(the opposite side)}}{\text{(the hypotenuse)}} = \dfrac{3}{5}$

The **cosine** of angle Bob = $\dfrac{\text{(the adjacent side)}}{\text{(the hypotenuse)}} = \dfrac{4}{5}$

The **tangent** of angle Bob = $\dfrac{\text{(the opposite side)}}{\text{(the adjacent side)}} = \dfrac{3}{4}$

"Hold up!" you say. "That's not so simple. That's like *three* things to remember!"

Well, lucky for you, there is a trigonometry cheat code. Repeat after me:

"**SOH-CAH-TOA.**" Sine is **O**pposite over **H**ypotenuse, **C**osine is **A**djacent over **H**ypotenuse, **T**angent is **O**pposite over **A**djacent.

Cool, right? Don't thank us for that cheat code. Thank Abraham Lincoln, who we believe invented it.

**Sine, cosine,** and **tangent** allow us to do a lot of things, but the most important for the purpose of the ACT is the ability to use one trig function (like cosine) to find another trig function (like tangent).

## Using One Trig Function to Find Another

Here is the most common ACT trigonometry problem:

If $\sin y = \dfrac{8}{17}$, what is $\tan y$?

To solve it, we need to follow four steps: Build it, label it, complete it, and find the answer.

### 1. Build it.

First, let's build a right triangle. Then pick a non-right angle and call it $y$.

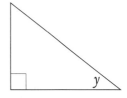

## 2. Label it.

Label the **hypotenuse,** the **opposite** side, and the **adjacent** side. Remember SOH-CAH-TOA? So if sine of $y$ is $\frac{8}{17}$, and sine is opposite/hypotenuse, then the opposite must be 8, and the hypotenuse 17.

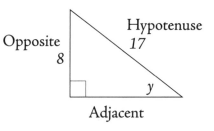

## 3. Complete it.

Use the Pythagorean theorem, which, using our trig labels, becomes "opposite squared + adjacent squared = hypotenuse squared." Use this formula to fill in the last side of the triangle.

$$8^2 + b^2 = 17^2$$
$$64 + b^2 = 289$$
$$b^2 = 225$$
$$b = 15$$

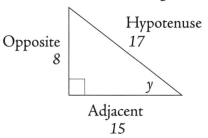

## 4. Find the answer.

With all three sides filled in, we can get the **tangent** of $y$, using SOH-CAH-TOA. If the **tangent** is the opposite/adjacent, then the tangent of $y$ is $\frac{8}{15}$.

Try a couple yourself:

## TRIGONOMETRY

**1.** If $\tan p = \frac{12}{5}$, $\sin p =$

A. $\frac{13}{12}$   B. $\frac{12}{13}$   C. $\frac{7}{15}$

D. $\frac{5}{12}$   E. $\frac{5}{17}$

## TRIGONOMETRY

**2.** If $\cos w = \frac{7}{25}$, $\tan w =$

A. $\frac{7}{24}$   B. $\frac{1}{3}$   C. $\frac{24}{25}$

D. $3\frac{3}{7}$   E. $3\frac{4}{7}$

# TRIGONOMETRY

**3.** If $\sin x = \dfrac{40}{41}$, $\cos x =$

**A.** $\dfrac{3}{41}$     **B.** $\dfrac{6}{41}$     **C.** $\dfrac{9}{41}$

**D.** 1     **E.** $\dfrac{41}{40}$

**Answers: 1.** B; **2.** D; **3.** C

### Nightmare Trigonometry

Bot Boy toughens up trig problems in two ways: It either makes problems based on one of **two famous trig identities,** or it expects that you understand the **trig graphs** and how they relate to **trig equations.**

First, let's look at the identities. You're going to need to memorize these, or tattoo them on the back of the head of the person who will sit in front of you during the test:

**Identity 1.** $\tan x = \dfrac{\sin x}{\cos x}$

This one's not so bad: Wherever you see an equation with a "tan $x$" in it, just rewrite it as " $\dfrac{\sin x}{\cos x}$."

Often, problems including "tan $x$" will involve dividing by a fraction, as in:

$$\left(\frac{\sin x}{\cos x}\right) \div \left(\frac{\cos x}{\sin x}\right)$$

If you remember to flip the denominator and multiply, this ends up giving you $\dfrac{\sin^2 x}{\cos^2 x}$, which—because of that first trig identity—is the same as $\tan^2 x$.

**Identity 2.** $\sin^2 x + \cos^2 x = 1$.

Always. That means that $\sin^2 x + \cos^2 x + 23 = 1 + 23 = 24$. This also means that $\sin^2 x = 1 - \cos^2 x$. Any time you see a sin or cos multiplied by itself, you should think of this rule.

You can remember the tangent identity by remembering SOH-CAH-TOA, i.e., if you divide $\frac{O}{H}$ by $\frac{A}{H}$ (sin x by cos x) you get $\frac{O}{A}$, which is tan (x).

—Jon

Let's take these rules out for a spin with two nightmare-level questions:

1. $\dfrac{\sin x}{\cos x} + \dfrac{\cos x}{\sin x} =$

First, let's treat this like a normal fraction problem and find a common denominator before we add:

$$\frac{\sin x \sin x}{\cos x \sin x} + \frac{\cos x \cos x}{\cos x \sin x} = \frac{\sin^2 x + \cos^2 x}{\cos x \sin x}.$$

Based on rule 2, that equals $\dfrac{1}{\cos x \sin x}$, which is our answer.

2. If $\dfrac{\tan x}{\sin x} = 3$, what is the value of sin $x$?

Let's use the first rule to rewrite that division problem as $\dfrac{\sin x}{\cos x} \div \sin x = 3$. Our sin $x$'s will cancel, leaving us with $\cos x = \dfrac{1}{3}$. Once we have that, we can just draw our triangle, and use the Pythagorean theorem to find that $\sin x = \dfrac{(2\sqrt{2})}{3}$, which is our answer.

Now for the graphs:

Wanna see boring, old sine and cosine turn into sleek, bold curves? Just set each one equal to $y$ on your graphing calculator and you'll get a visual. These equations will look like this:

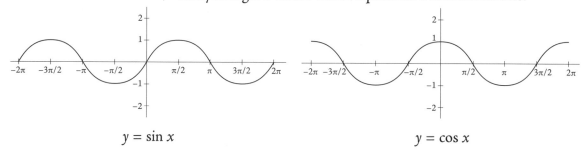

$y = \sin x$              $y = \cos x$

Now, a few things to notice about these two graphs:
**Similarities:**
+ Both curves go up and down around the $x$ axis.
+ Both range up to 1 and down to −1 on the $y$ axis.
+ Both waves repeat themselves after traveling $2\pi$ along the $x$ axis.

**Differences:**
- Standard sine curves start at the origin $(0, 0)$ and go up.
- Standard cosine curves start at $(0, 1)$ and go down.

All of this changes, of course, when you add other numbers into the equations you're graphing. A particularly grumpy ACT-bot can mix in as many as four additional numbers—we'll call them A, B, C, and D—into the standard sine and cosine equations. That may sound tough, but our brains are conveniently designed by nature to handle exactly four different pieces of information at a time! So let's break them down!

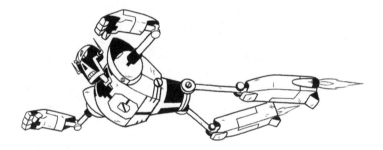

Here's where the bot will insert those new, nasty numbers:
$y = A\sin B(x + C) + D$ or $y = A\cos B(x + C) + D$

A and D appear most often on the ACT, but let's get a handle on what each one does to the standard graphs.

A stands for "amplitude" because it amps the graph up (and down). Use A to stretch or squeeze the graph vertically up and down. Check out the graphs:

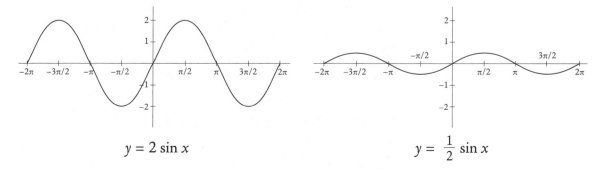

$$y = 2 \sin x \qquad\qquad y = \frac{1}{2} \sin x$$

**Quick Tip**

If a question tells you that "the range of $y = (t)\sin x$ is $-12 < t < 12$" it's telling you that $t$ (which, in this case, is standing in for A) has to equal 12.

Try making A much bigger or much smaller on your calculator and see how the graph changes.

B stands for "bulkier." Okay, that's not true, but it is a helpful way to remember that B stretches or squeezes the graph horizontally (from side to side).

When you add a B in the mix in front of the $x$, the B *divides* how long it takes for the graph to start repeating itself. Wuzza-*who*now? Don't worry, in practice this just means that if B is a big number, then your curve compresses like an accordion. Make B a tiny number, and your curve stretches out like a slow ocean roll. Here's a simple example:

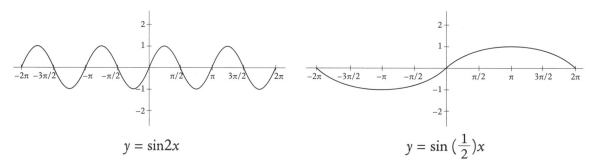

$$y = \sin 2x \qquad\qquad y = \sin \left(\tfrac{1}{2}\right)x$$

Try entering large and small B values on your calculator to see how they squeeze and stretch the graph.

So far, A and B have stretched and squeezed the graphs—A up and down and B left and right.

So what's left for C and D to do? C and D *shift* the whole graph up and down and left and right.

C moves the graph C units to the left. If we add $\left(\tfrac{\pi}{2}\right)$ to $x$ in the sin graph, the whole graph slides over half $\pi$ units to the left so that it looks exactly like . . . a cosine curve. That's deviant and probably won't happen on the ACT, but this will:

D shifts the whole graph up or down D units. Add a 3 to the end of your equation and the whole graph shifts up from the $x$ axis to the $y = 3$ axis. Similarly, set D = −1, and the whole graph will move down 1. Check it out:

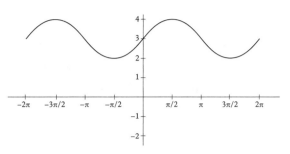

$$y = \sin x + 3$$

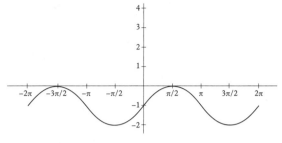

$$y = \sin x - 1$$

Here's a quick review of all four:

+ A stretches or squeezes the graph up and down.
+ B stretches or squeezes right to left.
+ C shifts the graph over left or right.
+ D shifts the graph up or down the y axis.

Note that the horizontal changes—B and C—behave counterintuitively: The *bigger* you make B the *shorter* and *more compact* your curve gets, and a *positive* C value shifts the graph toward negative territory.

Try out this practice problem:

## TRIGONOMETRY

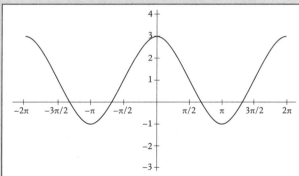

Which of the following gives the formula for the graph above?

   **A.** $y = \cos x$

   **B.** $y = \sin x$

   **C.** $y = 2\cos x$

   **D.** $y = 2\sin x + 1$

   **E.** $y = 2\cos x + 1$

**Answer:** E

The first matrix you ever do will be <u>awesome</u>. However, the ones that follow will be progressively more disappointing and forgettable.

—Jon

## MATRICES

Have you ever seen that movie *The Matrix*? Rockin' movie, right? With the super slo-mo bullets and the mind-bending reality shifts and the high-jumping kung fu, it's so *boss*. Well, guess what, film fan, the mathematical matrix is just as boss.

### How to Play

Check this.

$$\begin{bmatrix} 2 & 4 & 6 \\ 3 & 5 & 9 \end{bmatrix} + \begin{bmatrix} 7 & 2 & 5 \\ 5 & 2 & 4 \end{bmatrix}$$

While this might look strange and possibly scary, you are just adding the top left cell (2) of the first matrix to the top left cell (7) of the second matrix, the top middle cell of the first (4) to the top middle cell of the second (2), and so on to get:

$$\begin{bmatrix} 9 & 6 & 11 \\ 8 & 7 & 13 \end{bmatrix}$$

This is the same for subtraction as well. Try one yourself:

$$\begin{bmatrix} 7 & 3 \\ 12 & 8 \end{bmatrix} - \begin{bmatrix} 5 & 7 \\ 6 & 4 \end{bmatrix}$$

Subtract within each cell to get: $\begin{bmatrix} 2 & -4 \\ 6 & 4 \end{bmatrix}$

That's about as cool as slo-mo bullets, right? Yep. It's exactly as cool as slo-mo bullets.

### Nightmare Matrices

The ACT-bot has one very rare, but very dreadful weapon. Think of this as its electrically-charged-poison-dart-that-is-also-somehow-a-piranha. That's right, we're talking about multiplying matrices.

The general rule for multiplying matrices is to multiply the terms from each row (across) of the first matrix by the terms in each column (down) of the second matrix. We know, we know—it's a headache to think about, let alone remember and use on a

## Calculator to the Rescue

To solve the sample problem, press (2nd), (x⁻¹) to get to the matrix menu. Scroll across to "Edit" and press (ENTER), then change matrix A to a 3 x I by pressing (3), then scrolling over and replacing the second number with (1). Press (ENTER), then replace the three numbers within the matrix by typing (3) (ENTER) (2) (ENTER) (1). Quit the menu by pressing (2nd) (MODE). Enter the matrix menu again, scroll across to "Edit," and this time scroll down to B, press (ENTER), and change it to a I x 3. Press (ENTER) and insert the numbers 4, 3, and 8 into the matrix. Quit the menu. Finally, enter the matrix menu again, and simply press (ENTER). An [A] will appear on your screen. Press multiply, re-enter the matrix menu, scroll down to [B], and hit (ENTER). Your screen should read [A] x [B]. Press (ENTER) to get your answer.

test. Hopefully you won't have to, but just in case, here's what we mean:

$$\begin{bmatrix} 3 \\ 2 \\ 1 \end{bmatrix} \times \begin{bmatrix} 4 & 3 & 8 \end{bmatrix}$$

To solve the problem, we take the term from the first row of the first matrix (3) and multiply it with each term from each column to create the first row of our answer matrix: $\begin{bmatrix} 12 & 9 & 24 \end{bmatrix}$. Then we repeat with the second row of the first matrix (2), and finally the last (1), to produce the final answer matrix:

$$\begin{bmatrix} 12 & 9 & 24 \\ 8 & 6 & 16 \\ 4 & 3 & 8 \end{bmatrix}$$

One thing to notice about multiplication problems is that the answer is going to have only as many rows as there are in the first matrix, and only as many columns as there are in the second.

When it comes to matrices, the ACT is not going to get much harder than this, except perhaps by replacing some of the numbers with variables.

Try it out:

---

### MATRICES

$$\begin{bmatrix} 3 \\ 2 \end{bmatrix} \times m = \begin{bmatrix} 12 & 3a & 6a \\ 8 & 2a & 4a \end{bmatrix}$$

Which of the following matrices could be $m$?

A. $\begin{bmatrix} 4 & a & 2a \end{bmatrix}$

B. $\begin{bmatrix} a & 2a & 4a \end{bmatrix}$

C. $\begin{bmatrix} 6 \\ 2a \end{bmatrix}$

D. $\begin{bmatrix} 3 \\ a \end{bmatrix}$

E. $\begin{bmatrix} a & 4a \end{bmatrix}$

---

**Answer:** A

## Hooray!

Guess what? You just finished the entire Math section! And it was really long! After you give yourself a major pat on the back, take yourself out for ice cream, then a romantic walk, ending in a slow paddleboat ride in which you stare into a mirror, marveling at your own intelligence and perspicacity. After that, the best thing to do is to practice with Math sections from *The Real ACT Prep Guide*. Think of your math brain as a muscle. The more you use it, the more flexible and strong it gets. One of the best things about the *The Real ACT Prep Guide* is that it provides explanations for *every math question*. Look at every math error you correct as an opportunity to replace a broken math part of your brain. In other words, view every incorrect math problem as an opportunity to *never get that kind of problem wrong again*.

But before you look at any practice sections, or any math at all, give yourself a break: Go play some Hydro-Monopoly Xtreme. (Remember that joke? That was over 100 pages ago! We've been through so much math together.)

## PARTY FAVOR!

As a takeaway gift for finishing the Math chapter, we'd like to give you this handy list of all the math formulas we discussed. Cut it out, laminate it, and hang it on a string around your neck until you have the formulas memorized. You're welcome!

### THE THREE QUADRATIC EQUATIONS

$$(x + y)(x - y) = x^2 - y^2$$
$$(x + y)(x + y) = x^2 + 2xy + y^2$$
$$(x - y)(x - y) = x^2 - 2xy + y^2$$

### PYTHAGOREAN THEOREM

$$a^2 + b^2 = c^2$$

### AREA OF A TRIANGLE

$$\frac{1}{2} \cdot \text{base} \cdot \text{height}$$

### PERIMETER OF A RECTANGLE

$$2(\text{base}) + 2(\text{height})$$

### AREA OF A RECTANGLE

$$\text{base} \cdot \text{height}$$

### AREA OF A TRAPEZOID

height · (average of the lengths of parallel sides)

### CIRCUMFERENCE OF A CIRCLE

$$2\pi r$$

### AREA OF A CIRCLE

$$\pi r^2$$

### INSCRIBED ANGLES, CENTRAL ANGLES, ARCS

$$\text{inscribed angle} = \frac{1}{2} \text{ central angle} = \frac{1}{2} \text{ arc}$$

### FORMULA OF A LINE

$$y = mx + b$$

### SLOPE OF A LINE

$$\frac{y_2 - y_1}{x_2 - x_1}$$

### MIDPOINT FORMULA

$$\frac{x_1 + x_2}{2}, \frac{y_1 + y_2}{2}$$

### DISTANCE FORMULA

$$\sqrt{(x_1 - x_2)^2 + (y_1 - y_2)^2}$$

### CIRCLE FORMULA

$$(x - h)^2 + (y - h)^2 = r^2$$

### VERTICAL PARABOLA

$$y - k = a(x - h)^2$$

### HORIZONTAL PARABOLA

$$x - h = a(y - k)^2$$

### TRIGONOMETRY

SOH-CAH-TOA

# CHAPTER 6

# The Reading Test

## Because "The Movie-Watching Test" Would Have Been Too Much Fun

*Caution: Intense laser focus might burn books.*

# You Know How to Read

Just like driving, reading is something you think you can accomplish without any effort. Ninety-five percent of the time this is true. But the ACT is the other 5 percent. Pay attention when reading—and driving, too!

—Ava

You've read before, right? Of course you have. You're reading this right now. And we assume you've read a couple of other things, too, like the novelization of *Fast & Furious 6* and some back issues of *Glorious Puppies*.

In the Reading section, the ACT-bot tests your ability to comprehend what you read. It presents four reading passages and asks 10 questions per passage. To answer these questions, you have to do the same things you've been doing since second grade: recall information, summarize the main ideas of passages and paragraphs, and make inferences about the author's meaning.

Here's the good news: You've been reading for most of your life. Unlike every other section on the ACT, the Reading section does not ask you to demonstrate any unfamiliar skills.

Here's the bad news: Even though you've been reading for most of your life, you do not necessarily read *well*.

Try reading this sentence:

> The green boxer punched the purple boxer in the nose.

As soon as you read that sentence, you see an image in your mind's eye. It doesn't matter that you've never heard of a green or a purple boxer; your brain supplies the image and the meaning so quickly that it seems to work by magic. Of course, this isn't magic; it's just that you started reading sentences like this in elementary school, so your brain creates the image automatically.

Now try this:

> Allagash framtoomed so zebbishiously that vellreuntin quay abismo.

Compare the experience of reading that gibberish sentence with the previous simple sentence. Perhaps for the first time in quite a while, you had to *sound out* some of the words because they were unfamiliar. As likely as not, no image popped into your head. You were simply faced with puzzling words and had to sound them out.

Now let's try a passage, taken from a real book, *Blindness and Insight: Essays in the Rhetoric of Contemporary Criticism*, written by the cultural critic Paul de Man:

> After associating the essential thinness of allegory
> with a lack of substantiality, Coleridge wants to
> stress, by contrast, the worth of the symbol. One
> would expect the latter to be valued for its organic
> or material richness, but instead the notion of
> "translucence" is suddenly put in evidence.

Did that passage make you want to throw your head into the trash? Of course it did, and it's not just because the words are somewhat difficult. "Translucence," "substantiality," or "allegory" might be unfamiliar or half-familiar words, but *most* of the words in the passage are words that you know. The problem here is that the passage is expressing a complicated thought. Your brain cannot immediately generate an image or meaning for the sentence. Instead of one boxer punching another, our brain gives us an "Error no. 1606b: Image not found. Please contact Customer Service" screen.

Even on a second read, the passage becomes something like:

> After associating the blah blah blah of allegory
> with a blah blah blah, Coleridge wants to stress,
> by contrast, the worth of the symbol. One would
> expect the latter to be valued for its blah blah blah,
> but instead the notion of "blah" is suddenly put in
> evidence.

We might understand about 60 percent of the words in the sentence, but those "blah blah blahs" are essential to the meaning. In order to answer an ACT question about this passage, we need to minimize the "blah blahs." We need to become better readers.

Which sucks, because we thought we already knew how to read.

*And unlike a '90s computer, you can't fix your brain by beating it with the palm of your hand. Trust me, I've tried.*

—Jon

## A Few Thoughts on "Test Reading"

Standardized tests like the ACT have been around for a long time. And for all that time students have gotten really frustrated by reading sections. And why wouldn't they? These students have been reading forever, and they think they know how to read! When they take a reading section and score lower than they expected, they are caught totally off guard, so they come to the same conclusion: "Reading a passage for a standardized test must be a *different activity* from reading a book or magazine article."

An entire bookshelf's worth of test-preparation tomes agree with the kids: Test reading is different from normal reading, and it should be approached in a different way. The books propose a wide range of strategies. The Princeton Review, for example, recommends that kids read the questions first, then underline relevant phrases in the passage, *then* read the passage and answer the questions. Other books recommend that students underline key phrases as they read, or jot down small summaries of each paragraph along the margins, or read only the first and last sentences of each paragraph.*

Some of these strategies are interesting, others are mediocre, and some are completely bananas, but they *all* share the same, underlying idea that test reading is different from normal reading. We would like to make a radical suggestion: The only way to conquer the Reading section is to use the same skills that you should use in your standard, everyday reading. Clever strategies or "tricks" are tempting because they seem like a quick fix. But the only way to truly and consistently raise your Reading score is to become a better reader.* *

But what does that mean?

---

\* My recommendation is that you sing all of the sentences backward to the tune of "Follow the Yellow Brick Road" from *The Wizard of Oz*. That way, you're sure to find any hidden meanings.

—Zack

\* \* That's right, folks. The only way to get better is by <u>trying</u>. We're just as upset as you are.

—Jon

## Lean-Forward Reading

WHY WOULD YOU SAY THAT?!

The next time you're in a library or study hall, take a look around. First, take a look at the High-Achievemotrons (you know who they are). Notice how they're sitting? More often than not, these kids are curled over their books and notebooks and laptops as if they were mother hens protecting their chicks. Their pencils are a blur of activity. Their fingers pound their keyboards into complete submission.

Now, see if you can spot a Who-Carezoid. This might be difficult, because Who-Carezoids don't often hang out in libraries or study halls. But if you can catch one, he or she will definitely have his or her feet up on a table; headphones in the ears; the chair tipped back on two legs, cool-kid style; a bizarre assortment of textbooks, magazines, and electronics scattered around haphazardly. (If you think you are a Who-Carezoid, you are wrong. The fact that you are reading Chapter 6 of a test-prep book means that you do care, at least a little.)

Now, here's the interesting thing. If you were to ask both the High Achievemotron and the Who-Carezoid what they were doing, they would both say: "I'm reading." But it's immediately obvious to anyone with eyes that these two types of students are engaged in *very* different activities. Your Who-Carezoid is scanning the words on a page, mixing the information with whatever else is in his or her mind (or on his or her iPhone), and letting complicated passages or unfamiliar words drift by as if they didn't exist. The High-Achievemotron is a lot more careful, following the thread of a main idea, noting when the passage sets off in a separate direction, and rereading a confusing sentence or paragraph. The High-Achievemotron is almost *talking* to the passage as she reads, asking questions as she goes along, raising her eyebrows when she spots something surprising, and underlining an interesting or important detail.

Obviously, we are talking about stereotypes here. Some Who-Carezoids are a lot better at hiding their lack of engagement than in our portrayal, and a lot of kids *look* like they are studying hard when they are really thinking about all of the mind-destroying dubstep music they are going to create as soon as they save up enough money for equipment. But in general, you want to start reading like a High-Achievemotron. And the way to do this is to "lean forward," to *actively engage* with whatever text you have in front of you.

That means you have to develop the Five Habits of Lean-Forward Reading.

## The Five Habits of Lean-Forward Reading

*If you do this during the test, don't let the proctor think you're talking to him or her— that could be bad.*

—Zack

## I. TREAT READING LIKE A CONVERSATION

Everything you read is *someone telling you something.* So react the same way you would to a real person! Ask questions as you go. Make sure you are following the thread of what the author is saying. Allow yourself to be surprised, puzzled, or offended. As you read, don't be afraid to laugh, or scowl, or even mutter, "Oh, go soak your head, you goon, you." The more engaged you are with the words on the page, the more you are absorbing, inferring, and understanding what you read. If people are looking at you with concern and fear while you read, then you're doing it right.

## 2. BE INTERESTED IN WHAT YOU READ

Do you remember your entire biology textbook? No? Well, do you remember the part about sex? Thought so. From U.S. history, do you remember the East India Company's ad valorem tax on British imports? Not so much? How about when Sam Adams dressed up as a Native American and dumped chests of tea into Boston Harbor? Facts and passages stick in our minds and engage our imaginations *when we find them interesting.* If you are going to become an engaged reader who retains information, then you have to *train your mind to be interested in what you are reading.*

Pretend the passage is a story from your best friend, and you have to pay attention even if it's not interesting.

—Ava

This is tough! But with practice, it is possible to make yourself *more interested* in what you are reading. Here's how it works: For the time that you are reading, *pretend* that you are fascinated by what you are reading. It sounds crazy, but we can totally trick our brains for short periods of time, which is all we need for the few minutes it takes to read a passage. Try it out on some boring articles or passages. The following paragraph, for example, is literally about watching paint dry. It is *incredibly* boring, far more boring than anything on the ACT. But we want you to *pretend* that you love it. How? Well, try this out: Pretend that you want to become a very rich, very famous paint inventor (these exist, maybe). Once you understand how paint dries, you will use this knowledge to become a trillionaire! Try it out:

> When amateurs talk about paint "drying," they are usually making a rather embarrassing mistake. When we look at a wall, we are looking at a coat (or multiple coats) of paint that have both dried *and* cured. The drying process can be said to be complete when the wall does not leave a trace of paint on our clothes or hands. But it is only cured, and thus *truly dry*, when we cannot leave a scar in the paint by pressing on it. How long does the drying and curing process take? This is a complex question, and it requires a complex answer. There are two popular forms of wall paint: latex and oil-based paints. Latex is famous, in paint-drying circles, for drying from the *outside in,* which means that it can appear dry long before it is totally *cured.* Oil-based paints, on the other hand, dry from the *inside out,* and so are usually cured at around the same time that they dry. We haven't even begun to talk about temperature and humidity, the Zeus and Hades, if you will, who rule over the realm of drying paint. We'll save that discussion for a later date.

Who knows? By giving a seemingly dull subject a chance, you might find that it *actually* interests you.

—Jon

\* If you don't understand something, no big deal. But don't be too proud to admit it. Notice and fix the problem.

—Zack

Were you fascinated the entire time? If not, you need to practice *pretending* to be interested in what you are reading.

## 3. ADMIT WHEN YOU ARE CONFUSED OR DISTRACTED \*

Read this passage, from the German philosopher Georg Hegel's famously difficult *Lectures on the Philosophy of World History*:

> The sole end of history is to comprehend clearly what is and what has been, the events and deeds of the past. It gains in veracity the more strictly it confines itself to what is given, and—although this is not so immediately evident, but in fact requires many kinds of investigations in which thought also plays a part—the more exclusively it seeks to discover what actually happened.

For about 99.99 percent of the world, those sentences are difficult to understand. Maybe you picked up that the passage is talking about history, and that history has an "end" or goal, and something about "veracity." In other words, bits and pieces might stick, but the overall meaning is clouded by a general sense of *huh?!?* The important thing here is to realize that you are not expected to understand everything immediately, but you *are* expected to go back, reread, and puzzle through the tough parts. Read it again.

Did you pick up anything new? The passage is about the goal of history, which is to present "what actually happened." That makes sense, right? This passage seems to be saying, in very complex language, that "history achieves its goal when it presents what actually happened." This is not a terribly complicated thought, but it is expressed in a complicated way. Do not let your brain *give up* on a sentence or passage because it *sounds* complicated. Admit to yourself that the sentence is tough, swallow your pride, and *try it again*. Similarly, you might zone out while reading a sentence or passage. Just admit to yourself, "Okay, during that last paragraph I was thinking about the jumbo bag of Chex Mix Muddy Buddies Cookies & Cream that I'm going to buy as soon as I finish studying. I need to read that again."

## 4. PAY ATTENTION TO DIRECTION WORDS

Every written passage has a shape. It might begin by making a point, then emphasize this point, then raise a possible objection, then explore this objection before demonstrating why the objection is wrong, etc. In order to follow along with the passage, we need to be aware of the shape. We do this by paying extra attention to "direction words." Words or phrases like *therefore, so we see, because of this,* and *also* move an idea forward, while terms like *however, surprisingly, but,* and *on the other hand* introduce a new, contrasting idea or an objection. Direction words should appear in bold in your mind, because they give you a sense of the shape of the passage and can act as guideposts, leading you from the beginning to the end.

## 5. SUMMARIZE AS YOU GO

After each paragraph, or at the conclusion of a new idea, quickly summarize in your head what you've just read. There are two reasons to summarize: 1.) It helps you incorporate each new paragraph into the overall idea of the passage. If a new paragraph does *not* seem to fit, then you need to revise your understanding of the main idea. 2.) It helps you notice when a paragraph is challenging, or when you might have lost focus. If you cannot summarize the paragraph, you have to read it again! (Some tutors and prep books recommend that you jot down a one- or two-word summary next to each paragraph. If you feel that you can do this without taking too much time, then go ahead. Make it part of the way you read. But *do not* try to do this for the first time when you take the test, as it risks slowing you down.)

I like putting labels next to each paragraph: "argument," "evidence," "counter-argument," stuff like that.

—Ava

## Patience, Young Grasshopper: Training to Become a Master Reader

While I never trained with Grandmaster Irate Dachshund, I did work with Sifu Incensed Poodle.

—Zack

Here at *Up Your Score*, we're big into kung fu movies. We love the spinny kicks and the cartwheel punches, the terrible dialogue, and the hammy acting. But our favorite part of kung fu movies is always the training scene montage. You see, most kung fu movies have at least one character who, in order to save his (or, more rarely, her) village from rapacious warlords, needs to learn a kung fu style. So he (or, less frequently, she) travels to a remote mountaintop to find the master of some technique with a name like Sunburned Cobra or Irate Dachshund.

When the hero arrives on the mountaintop, the master is usually doing some everyday activity, like washing the dishes. The hero scoffs, but then he notices that *the master is doing the dishes with only his pinkies!!!* He stops scoffing, asks for the master's help, and begins his training.

It begins with a boring and pointless activity, like grooming the master's cat. Then the hero moves on to something more sophisticated, like grooming two cats. And these cats have *seriously* matted hair. The hero complains to the master: "What's with the cats? My village is going to be destroyed by rapacious warlords in three weeks; I don't have time to groom your cats." The master shakes his head and says, "You do not yet have eyes to see. You are grooming cats *and* not grooming cats." The hero continues and gets better at grooming. Eventually, he is told to groom the sheep, then the cows, and finally the horses. As he moves from animal to animal, the hero begins, in spite of himself, to

Becoming a better reader will help you not only on the Reading section. It'll also help you on the English section (by exposing you to grammatically and stylistically correct writing), the Science section (by helping you understand cause-and-effect relationships), and the Math section (by helping you make sense of those daunting word problems).

—Jon

\*You *could* start off with Kanye West's Twitter feed, but, let's be honest, do you really want to?

—Jon

enjoy grooming. Within a week, he takes pride in the speed and vigor with which he grooms even the tangliest llama. A day later, the master calls the hero into his room.

Inside is a wooden dummy.

"Destroy the dummy," the master instructs.

The hero goes for it. He smashes his palm against the dummy, nearly shattering his wrist. Nothing happens. The hero swings around and whirls his foot against the dummy's head. A loud crack rings out, but the dummy barely wobbles.

The master smiles coyly. "*Groom* the dummy."

Puzzled, the hero makes a grooming motion across the dummy's chest. It explodes in a million splintered pieces! The hero is shocked. The master chuckles.

"You have mastered Well-Groomed Llama Style. I have nothing left to teach you. Go save your village."

There is so much wisdom in these scenes. They show us how *becoming skilled at something requires practice*, and that *the best way to succeed is to learn to enjoy practicing*, and that *after practicing, performing at a high level feels effortless*.

To become a master of reading, then, you need to do the exact same thing. Practice the Five Habits of Lean-Forward Reading. Do so with our trademarked "Progressive Reading Strategy," which has a money-back guarantee to save your village from warlords:

**1. Every day, read one editorial or op-ed (which stands for "opposite the editorial page" but is always an opinion piece) from either *The New York Times*, *The Economist*, or *The Wall Street Journal*.** Editorials are opinionated, informative, engaging, and, above all, short. Reading one will take about 10 to 20 minutes, and it will greatly increase both your reading ability and your background knowledge.

**2. Read two engaging articles per week. Start off with something manageable, from *Sports Illustrated* or *Time*.** Pick a topic that you think you will enjoy. If the article gets dull, practice your ability to pretend that it is interesting.\*

**Veritas Reader**

At Veritas, getting kids to read often and read hard is the backbone of the work we do. We have students use the Veritas Reader, a great free resource for interesting essays, articles, and book excerpts that are organized by subject, length, and difficulty. Check it out at reader.veritastutors.com. In our sessions, we discuss the assigned reading with our students to help them discover unexpected and challenging ideas. We know that reading makes you smart, and that a gain in reading ability translates—100 percent of the time—to a gain in test scores.

If you want, you can read your book on an e-reader. That way you can still feel the cold, comforting touch of technology while you read.

—Jon

**3. Read one difficult article per week.** This is where you stretch yourself. Pick a feature article from *The New Yorker, Harper's Magazine, The Atlantic, Wired,* or *Scientific American.* The Veritas Reader (see sidebar at left) and the website Arts and Letters Daily (aldaily.com) are also great places to find interesting, challenging articles. Your goal, at first, is to wrestle with and attempt to understand at least half of an article. After a couple of weeks, you should be able to work your way through an entire article.

**4. Always be reading a personal book.** You can start with something that you are certain you will enjoy, like *The Hunger Games.* But soon you should challenge yourself to try more sophisticated contemporary fiction, nineteenth-century fiction, or nonfiction bestsellers—or even some popular philosophy or history. This, for many people, sounds like the toughest requirement. Who has the time, in this day and age, to sit down and read an unassigned book? But here's the thing: If you can find a book that you *enjoy* reading, it won't seem like work at all, and it will make you a much better reader! Here's what we recommend: Go to the library or bookstore. Before you borrow or buy a book, give it a 15-page trial. If, after 15 pages, you are not enjoying the book, *put it down and try another.* If it does capture your attention and your interest, then you're good to go. We also suggest that you make reading your last activity before going to sleep. Instead of watching a television show or going online, read some pages of your book. This is a great habit to build your reading, and it is guaranteed to help you fall asleep!

As you practice, always remember that the most frustrating moments of reading are the moments where you are making the greatest gains. Sometimes reading *should* be exasperating, difficult, and confusing. Every time that you are forced to reread, look up a complex word, or struggle to understand a new concept, you are becoming smarter by expanding your vocabulary and familiarizing yourself with more complex ideas.

## Finally, the Real Deal: Tips for the Reading Section

Now that you have an understanding of how to make yourself a better reader, it's time to talk about the ACT-bot and the actual test. Let's start with some large-scale strategies before getting into the specific types of Reading passages.

### CHECK YOUR KNOWLEDGE AT THE DOOR

Hey, you know all that stuff you know? All of those facts and opinions and statistics and jokes and recipes for bacon banana bread? For the 35 minutes that you are taking the Reading section, we want you to put all that stuff in a box and put it away in the closet. Don't lose it, because you'll probably need it later. But for now, get rid of everything in your brain.

One of the biggest mistakes that people make on the Reading section is to use their outside knowledge when answering the Reading questions. **The ACT-bot is testing you on what the passage says; it does not require any outside knowledge.** In fact, as we will see later, one of the ACT-bot's most *common* tricks is to provide reasonable, even factually correct answers that were *not* in the passage, and thus wrong.

This is why so many questions begin with "according to the passage" or "according to the author." It's like your grandma always used to say: "All that gull-pluckin' knowledge is gonna get you in a heap o' trouble."

Did your grandma not say that? That's probably for the best, because that is a terrible thing to say, except in this particular instance.

"Wait, wait," you may be saying. "I thought the ACT was all about testing our knowledge. Now you want us to *not* use it? Isn't that stupid?" Well, no.

You see, this idea of *sticking to the text* is one of the most important skills you can develop before college. In college, you are going to be wrestling with very complicated books that are filled with intricate and subtle arguments. Bringing in outside opinions is a classic freshman error. The ability to understand what an author is saying, without cluttering his or her ideas with your own ideas, will make you a much more perceptive and accurate reader. So, much as it might pain us to say it, the ACT-bot is right to test reading this way.

## KNOW YOUR SPEED

The ACT-bot asks you to handle four passages in 35 minutes, thus giving you a little less than nine minutes per section. With only 10 questions per section, this would give you a little less than a minute per question, which is not too bad. But, oh wait, *you have to read and understand an entire passage before you can even head into the questions.* Yikes!

This news might make you so nervous that you rush out and buy one of those how-to-speed-read books. But hold on a second. For one, speed-reading techniques don't work for most people. Believe us, we've tried. Also, even when speed-reading *does* work, you sacrifice comprehension and information retention in favor of speed. This is *terrible* for the ACT, which is going to test you on both your comprehension and your information retention after you read the passage. So that's out.

The best strategy here is to get out your copy of *The Real ACT Prep Guide* and practice with real tests. Set a timer, work through a section, and see how far you get by the time the buzzer rings. Get a sense of your natural pace and, if necessary, try to speed things up bit by bit. Don't start zooming right away. Instead, gradually increase your speed with each new practice Reading section. As you practice and get used to the types of passages and questions, your speed will increase. Just make sure to keep your eyes on the timer.

The key thing to remember here is to take as much time as necessary to understand the passage, then increase your speed while handling questions. If you race through the passage, your odds of correctly answering questions drop dramatically. (Don't worry, we're going to go into more detail on both reading and answering questions later on.)

*It is helpful to time how long you take on each *type* of passage. This way, you can identify your strengths and weaknesses as far as the passage types go, knowing which ones you can hurry through in order to bank time for tougher sections.

—Jon

## Read the Intro Paragraph!

Each Reading passage comes with a one- or two-sentence introduction. These usually tell you the title of the book, article, or magazine from which the passage is excerpted and the date of publication. Who cares, right? Clever test takers, that's who. A careful reader can scour these introductory sentences for extra information. The title of the article, for instance, will often help you figure out the main idea of the passage. The name of the magazine can give you context clues to determine which details in the passage are most important. And the date of publication will help you determine whether certain words are being used in an older or a more current way. Reading the intro will take you four seconds, and could really help you out!

## KNOW YOUR FAVORITE SECTIONS

Different folks enjoy reading different things. Chris will read *anything* written about the Civil War, while Ava eats up articles about soap chemistry, Zack enjoys vegan cookbooks, and Jon has a separate closet for all of his historical fiction and J. R. R. Tolkien. Know which of the four passage types (Prose Fiction, Social Science, Humanities, and Natural Science) is likely to be your favorite, and *do that section first*. Save your least-favorite section for last.

Why? Because the fourth section is likely to be the most rushed. Due to the insane time constraints, we often find ourselves skimming the last few questions. If you have to rush, it's better to rush on the passage where you are most likely to screw up anyway, right?

## LEAVE THE BORING/COMPLEX SECTIONS FOR LAST

No matter which section is your favorite, *any* type of Reading passage can be difficult or extra-boring. Chris, for example, loves the fiction passages, but even he grimaces when the passage is an excerpt from some nineteenth-century novel of manners like *Dame Croxbury's Most Unfortunate Mid-Afternoon Cotillion*.

You will know if a passage is insanely complex or dull after two sentences. If you can tell that the passage is going to be a challenge, skip it and leave it for the end. Again, the idea here is that a difficult passage is going to eat up precious time that could be spent handling questions on a later, easier passage. Remember, they're not going to award you more points for answering tougher questions correctly. No matter how hard the question is, each right answer is worth one raw score point. There are no difficulty level multipliers. Skip the tough passage and handle it after you've made sure to rack up points on the easier passages.

But what if *all* of the passages are boring and complex? Well, then you're just going to have to bite the bullet and go in any

Don't forget: It is your job to pretend to be interested in the passage! If you find it mind-numbingly boring, then you aren't doing your job.

—Zack

Another option when you come across a difficult question is to tear up your test and run screaming out of the test center and into oncoming traffic . . . but you should probably just skip and come back.

—Jon

Save questions that ask about the whole passage for last. You'll know much more after you answer all the detail questions.

—Zack

order you prefer. Whatever you do, don't waste too much time thinking about which passage to attack first. Just dive in and get swimming.

## SKIP AND COME BACK

After you have read and comprehended a passage using the Five Habits (see page 238), you are going to answer the questions. The strategies for answering questions will be discussed in detail below, but as a general strategy, within each passage *you must skip and come back to difficult questions.*

Think about it: Every question refers back to the passage, right? If a question is difficult or you can't decide between two tempting answer choices, skip the question, wrestle with two more, then come back. These two new questions are going to require that you think about the *same* passage, so when you come back to the tough question, you will be more of an expert.

As we've discussed, another great advantage of skipping and coming back is that it saves you time. Instead of sitting there furiously "working," biting your cuticles, and scowling at the page, you just move on.

Finally, skipping and coming back in the Reading section will help you guard against frustration. If a problem gives you trouble, you just calmly and quickly skip it, instead of dwelling on how stupid you must be for not solving it.

Bonus reason to skip and come back: These questions don't go from easiest to hardest. The first question could be the most difficult. You'd be a Goofy Gulliver to answer the hardest question first, when answering all the others and rereading the passage as you go will make you much likelier to get that first, hard question right.

## So Many Different Types of Passages

As we mentioned earlier, the ACT-bot is going to unleash four different types of passages (though the second and third are awfully similar): Prose Fiction, Social Science, Humanities, and Natural Science. Unfortunately, these passages require different kinds of reading techniques.

### PROSE FICTION

Prose Fiction passages are excerpts taken from novels, novellas, and short stories. Take this excerpt, from the fake novel *Bloody Bayou Rose*:

> Georgina, who'd had just about enough of Bertrand's prevaricating, closed the lid of Rose's snuffbox with extra vigor. If he wanted something, he would have to come out and ask her.
>
> "Is it time for lunch?" Bertrand nervously fingered the doily on Rose's bed stand. If he were to be born again as an animal, Rose had once said, Bertrand would be an old sheep. Georgina agreed. He had an old sheep's listlessness, its thoughtless acceptance, without excitement or trepidation, of life's unfolding. Georgina much preferred chickens and billy goats, animals that were more likely to get into forbidden places and ruin things.
>
> Still, if Bertrand were to ask her, perhaps she would respond. An old sheep might be a dull companion, but he's a companion nonetheless.
>
> "Lunch ain't for another hour and you know it," Georgina said.

As we can see, the Prose Fiction passage will often dump us in the middle of a scene, without introducing the characters or telling us much about them. More often than not, it will present us with a relationship, hint at unstated feelings, desires, or motivations, and present a more or less clear setting. It might contain obscure vocabulary words that require context to understand.

The Reading section is, famously, one of the hardest sections to teach. After all, how do you teach a kid how to read if she already knows how to read? What we do is enforce good reading by finding challenging but interesting articles and making our clients read *at least two* of them per week. We ask them to write about the main idea and the structure and tone of the article to make sure they fully understand it. We know our students, so we guide them to the right challenges and turn them into readers.

While reading a fiction book for fun, you would never make crazy assumptions about the characters. That would be stupid. Don't do it on the ACT, either.

—Jon

*If you must know, "prevaricate" means "to evade the truth," or "equivocate."

Because the Prose Fiction passage does not give us all the information we need, the questions are going to rely heavily on *inference*, which is our ability to read between the lines.

So what *do* we know? We get the names of three characters: Georgina, Bertrand, and Rose. The only mentions of Rose (aside from the title) are "Rose's snuffbox," "Rose's bed stand," and "Rose had once said," all of which imply that, while the other characters might be in Rose's room, Rose herself may not be present. Georgina must be in Rose's room with Bertrand.

And who are Georgina and Bertrand? We have no idea. What do they want? We're given a few clues. Georgina is fed up with Bertrand's "prevaricating." If you don't know what that means (and the ACT-bot is hoping that you don't), then you know only that she is fed up with him.* There's another clue at the end of the passage. She is waiting for Bertrand to ask her *something*, and she thinks he could become a *companion*.

We also know that Georgina thinks that Bertrand is listless and dull, and that Bertrand is nervous. The trick with the Prose Fiction passage is to use these clues to infer what's going on *without going too far*. We can't prove, for example, that Georgina is waiting for Bertrand to propose *marriage*. There are no clues to back this up. But we can safely say that Georgina is waiting for some kind of proposal, either of a friendly or romantic nature, and that she is getting sick and tired of waiting.

We also have to infer the author's opinion. In this passage, the author gives us Georgina's thoughts but none of Bertrand's. Perhaps the author is more sympathetic to Georgina? Again, we have to be careful. The author presents Georgina as somewhat impatient, with a tendency toward chaos (she likes "chickens and billy goats"), which is not necessarily good. We can safely say that the author is writing from Georgina's perspective but is not necessarily fond of either character.

We have to realize that reading between the lines does not mean making up crazy stuff. You can't, for instance, conclude that

Georgina sees Bertrand as a good provider, based on the fact that she thinks of him as an "old sheep," and sheep produce wool. Or that the question about lunch implies that Bertrand is poor and starving.✳ It would be more reasonable to infer that she finds Bertrand to be as boring as an old sheep, because this is based on the evidence of the words "without excitement."

Making inferences in the Prose Fiction passage is about maintaining a balance: You use your imagination to fill in blanks, but you don't use it to make things up. Reading between the lines is *almost* like making a guess, but only based on what the passage actually says. Be careful not to fabricate plot elements that you cannot back up with clues from the passage.

✳ Or that Rose's snuffbox implies that she is a powerful cocaine baroness and will soon return to her room after a shootout with the FBI.
—Zack

## SOCIAL SCIENCE AND HUMANITIES

The Social Science and Humanities passages are similar to each other. Both are like reading you've done in history, social studies, or economics classes. Social Science passages are more likely to discuss history and economics, while Humanities passages lean toward art history, literary criticism, and biography. Take a look at this excerpt from the imaginary book *Powder Keg: America from 1855 to 1861.*

> The story of John Brown's headstrong and hopeless raid on Harpers Ferry—in which Brown, two of his sons, and 19 other men captured and held an armory for one day before they were defeated by the U.S. Marines—is well known. But the true measure of the man requires a broader historical lens. After all, without an understanding of Brown's long involvement in militant abolitionism, we might too hastily conclude that he was simply insane, or that he was so incensed by his desire to end slavery that he lost his grip on reason.
>
> Nothing could be farther from the truth. Brown cut his teeth in the fields of Kansas in the

mid- to late 1850s, a period so violent—it was popularly known as "Bleeding Kansas"—that it is now seen by historians as an important precursor to the Civil War. There, Brown learned that small, violent actions, even when unsuccessful tactically, could advance the larger goal of earning abolitionism a more prominent place in public discourse.

Like most Social Science and Humanities passages, this excerpt presents information and uses potentially new terms that require context in order to understand, especially if you've never seen them before. It is also typical that this passage uses the information in order to make an argument.

What's the main idea here? John Brown learned in Kansas that violent actions like the raid on Harpers Ferry could have an impact even if they are unsuccessful in the short term. The trick is to fit each fact into the overall story or argument. Here, we need to fit Harpers Ferry and Bleeding Kansas into the author's argument.

What is that argument? Looking at our direction words can be a big help. First, we are given a summary of the raid, "but" we need more information to really understand Brown. "After all" we don't want to "too hastily" call Brown insane. "Nothing could be farther from the truth," because once we see that he had experience with these kinds of tactics, we see that the raid, even if Brown knew it would fail, was not insane or pointless. These direction words guide us through the argument.

Finally, we should quickly summarize the argument: Many people misunderstand the popular historical figure John Brown and should learn more about his background and the times in which he lived.

In Social Science and Humanities passages, we always want to maintain our understanding of the overall point. We want to ask those Lean-Forward questions: How does each fact fit into the main idea? Are there any surprises, contradictions, or sudden

The Natural Science passage is the one in which the ACT-bot will most likely try to trick you into using your own knowledge rather than the facts explicitly stated in the text.

—Jon

changes in direction? How has the author organized the passage and why? After all, these are essentially the questions the ACT-bot is going to be asking you.

## NATURAL SCIENCE

The Natural Science passage will be similar to material in your science textbook or popular science magazines. Like this excerpt from the not-real article "The Oldest Organisms" from *Shut Up, It's Science*, a magazine we wish existed:

> The vast majority of life on this planet is either aerobic (like you, me, the pandas, and the giraffes) or photosynthetic (like the trees and the grass and the bushes and the shrubs). But just as every rule must have an exception, so must life allow for the existence of other types of organisms. Chemoautotrophs are able to eschew traditional phototropism by oxidizing iron in order to gain an electron. This electron earns them the power that plants typically harness from photons in natural sunlight.
>
> We usually think of these iron guzzlers as outliers, but we might more accurately call them our great-great-great-great grandparents. Recently, scientists have claimed that chemoautotrophs might have been the first organisms on Earth. Given their natural habitats, this hypothesis makes sense.

Science passages primarily like to intimidate you with new terms. But don't be a fraidy cat! These terms will either be explained somewhere in the passage or they will not be tested. Though it may initially seem otherwise, the ACT-bot, at least in the Natural Science section, does *not* require that you bring in outside knowledge. And although the Science passages can be the scariest at first glance, you have only two jobs:

**1. Keep track of the facts.** Most of the questions are going to ask you what the passage said. You just need to go find the answer.

Don't be afraid if the answers for a Natural Science reading question are not phrased the same way as in the text. The ACT-bot enjoys rephrasing scientific details to make them less obvious (and sometimes, less science-y).

—Jon

That said, sometimes the answer is copied verbatim from the passage, which is nice.

—Ava

**2. Understand the logic of the scientific phenomenon or process.** Questions are going to ask you *how* the phenomenon or process works, so keep track of the cause and effect because, as we'll see, this is tested very explicitly.

Here, we are introduced to chemoautotrophs in comparison to traditional plants and animals. We are told that chemoautrotrophs gain an electron from a process called "oxidation" (again, you don't have to know what this is) and use this electron to power themselves. Scientists are now hypothesizing that these organisms might be the oldest on Earth, because of where they live. The skill here is to strip away the technical terms as best you can, and summarize as you go. Use those direction words, like "but" and "what's puzzling" and "recently," as guideposts to help you through the passage.

In general, your task in the Natural Science passage is to be brave. Do not let the sesquipedalism* of the passage scare you away. Once you have figured out the general sense of what is being said, Natural Science questions tend to be the most straightforward in the Reading Test. For instance, a question about this passage might read: *Oxidization replaces which common process to acquire an electron?* As long as you've wrestled with the passage, the answer is readily available: Oxidation replaces photosynthesis. If you haven't understood the passage, it sounds very complex.

More so than any other passage on the Reading Test, then, the Natural Science passage requires that you determine the meaning of the passage *before* you head into the questions.

*Sesquipedalism* means "an abundance of long words," which of course you already knew.

## Finally, a Trick: The General Strategy

So far, we've discussed how you should read *in general,* and then how you should read *each type of passage.* There were no tricks, no gimmicks, and barely any strategies. We told you about the Five Habits of Lean-Forward Reading, and told you to practice, practice, practice.

Well, from here on out, it is all about *strategy.* The ACT-bot constructs reading comprehension questions in order to test whether or not you can read like a pro. But after seeing approximately one quadrillion reading comprehension questions, we know the ACT-bot's tricks. We know the *types* of questions the bot is most likely to ask; we know how to anticipate the questions; we even know how to smell wrong answers from a mile away. And guess what? We're going to show you *all* of that. Let's start with the big gun: The General Strategy.

### THE GENERAL STRATEGY, or, How to Smash Reading Questions into Pathetic Little Pieces and Send Each Piece Running Home to Mama

Used correctly, the General Strategy will destroy about 80 percent of the Reading questions. Later, we'll tell you some more sophisticated strategies that you can use to mop up those remaining brutal questions.

Okay, so after you've read the passage with Lean-Forward Reading (asking questions, summarizing, following the direction words, and rereading complex or extra-boring parts so that you understand everything), you're ready to hit the questions. Follow these six steps:

### I. Read the question.

Goes without saying, right? No! It goes *with* saying! Fifty percent of the mistakes in the Reading section come from misreading the question. If you know you are a sloppy reader, *read it twice.* If you are a careful reader, *read it twice anyway.* It will only take three extra seconds and possibly save your score.

Pay attention to words like "not," "except," and "agree" (or "disagree"). A second read means you are more likely to pick up on these bad boys.

—Jon

When a question specifically refers to a section, I like to go back and put brackets around it. That helps me focus on the relevant parts.

—Zack

## 2. Scan the relevant section of the passage.

If the question explicitly refers to a section of the passage, *go back and read it again.* The answer has to be in the passage, *not* in your brain. So go back and find the answer! Some questions, on the other hand, ask about the main idea of the passage. To answer these questions, you might not need to reread any particular section, but take a look over the passage as you . . .

# 3. ANSWER THE QUESTION YOURSELF BEFORE READING THE ANSWER CHOICES.

Why did we write that in extra-big caps? Because it is the most important step, as well as the step that most test takers either forget or ignore. After you've read the question and reread the relevant section of the passage, you must come up with your *own* answer to the question. The ACT-bot is about to hit you with four answer choices that are *designed to tempt you.* Unless you have your own idea about the answer, you will be at the mercy of the answer choices. In a tough question, *every answer* will sound reasonable. They will pollute your brain with their trickery. *Do not let this happen.* Come up with your own answer, so that you can move through the answer choices with a purpose: to find the answer that is closest to your own answer. If you *cannot* come up with your own answer, then you know you need to skip that question and come back later.

## 4. Go through the answer choices quickly, handing out "MAYBEs" and "NOs."

Again, a good Reading question will have four tempting answer choices. Each answer choice is like a pit of quicksand or an octopus's tentacles—or, rather, it's like *a pit of quicksand filled with grasping octopus tentacles!* The more time you spend with an answer choice, the deeper you sink into the quicksand and get tangled in the tentacles. So we want you to read each answer choice *quickly*, give it two seconds (tops!) of consideration, and decide whether it is MAYBE right (if it is, write "M" next to the letter), or if it is definitely wrong (in which case either write "N" or "No" or cross it out—up to you). Notice how we are *not* looking for the right answer. Rather, we are quickly cutting away all of the obviously wrong answer choices. ✳

### 5. Compare your "MAYBEs."

This is a crucial and often-overlooked step. Once you've separated the chaff (the NOs) from the wheat (the MAYBEs), you need to *compare* the MAYBEs. How are the two answers different from each other? This will help you focus in on exactly what an answer choice is saying and how it differs from the other tempting choices.

### 6. Pick the correct answer or skip.

If one answer is obviously, totally correct, then pick it. If you have time, go back to the passage and find *proof* that the answer is correct. If you can't find proof, or you cannot decide between your two MAYBEs, then you must skip. At first, this is going to feel awful. You are *so* close. But if you're not certain, you need to get used to skipping. After all, skipping is *not* admitting defeat; rather, it is giving yourself the opportunity to look at the problem again with fresh eyes. Wrestle with two more problems, and then come back.

Let's try this out: Read this passage, excerpted from Robert Hughes's documentary series, *The Shock of the New*:
> The essence of the early modernist experience
> was not the inventions; most people weren't
> affected by a prototype in a lab or an equation on a
> blackboard. Not yet. No, the important thing was

✳ If you can't comfortably hand out any "NOs," you may not have understood the question. Similarly, if all the answers seem like "NOs," you may need to reread the question. The important thing is not to get flustered by what looks like four right (or four wrong) answer choices. Take a deep breath and skip and come back.

—Jon

a sense of an accelerated rate of change in all areas of human discourse. It provided the feeling of an approaching millennium, a new order of things, as the nineteenth century clicked over into the twentieth. The end of one kind of history and the start of another.

First, let's make sure that we're using Lean-Forward Reading. There are some tough terms there, like "early modernist experience," but we can use context to help us figure them out. We are talking about the time when "the nineteenth century clicked over into the twentieth," so early modernists must belong to that time period.

And what exactly is the passage saying? Use those direction words to move through the idea. It says that people did *not* experience "inventions" or "equations"; rather they experienced an "accelerated rate of change." In other words, they might not have cared about one invention or idea, but they all felt that the times were a-changin'.

Let's tackle the question:

### Step 1: Read the question.
*Which of the following best expresses the experience of an early modernist?*

Did you read the question *twice*? Good. Notice how we are *not* giving you the answer choices. That's because we want you to get used to handling questions the right way, without just jumping to the answer choices.

### Step 2: Scan the relevant section of the passage.
If we head back to that excerpt, we read that "the important thing was a sense of an accelerated rate of change in all areas of human discourse . . . the feeling of an approaching millennium, a new order of things. . . ."

You want the answer
choices? YOU CAN'T
HANDLE THE
ANSWER CHOICES!

—Jon

## Step 3: Answer the question yourself.

So how would we answer the question? We could paraphrase the passage and say that early modernists felt that the world was changing more rapidly and that society was moving into a new era.

## Step 4: Go through the answer choices quickly, handing out NOs and MAYBEs.

A. *Horse-drawn carriages had been replaced by early automobiles.*

Maybe. This seems like a change, right? Move on.

B. *Laboratories were experimenting with an increasing number of prototypes.*

No. The passage mentions both laboratories and prototypes, but as examples of how people did *not* experience change. Move on!

C. *New modes of living were replacing each other with increasing speed.*

Maybe. The wording here is complex and loopy, and we don't want to get sucked in, but it could work. Move, move, move!

D. *Discomfort at the ending of one age and the onset of a new, unfamiliar age.*

No. This answer could be correct if it didn't contain the word *discomfort*, which is not implied in the passage.

## Step 5: Compare your MAYBEs.

Okay, so we are left with A and C. How are they different? Let's take a closer look at the two answer choices. A is about the change between one form of technology and another, while C is saying, in more abstract terms, that new things are more quickly replacing each other. Let's take our MAYBEs back to the passage. We read that "the essence . . . was not the inventions," which seems to

Correct answer choices won't introduce new information from outside the passage. Even if the new information fits with the purpose of the passage, you can eliminate them.

—Jon

counter answer choice A. Later on, the passage talks about "an accelerated rate of change," which makes C the more likely answer choice.

(Now, it is quite possible that you won't *love* the answer you are left with. That's okay. Your job is simply to pick the *best* answer from the ones provided. If you've definitely eliminated three answer choices, the fourth one has to be correct.)

### Step 6. Pick the correct answer choice or skip.

Because we were able to find evidence to support C and evidence to eliminate A, we're feeling pretty confident that we can pick answer choice C. If we weren't so confident, we would skip it (circle the number of the question to remember that you need to come back) and come back two questions later.

"Hold up," you might be saying, "you expect me to go through *all that* for *every question*? That will take up too much time, and I won't be able to get through the section."

In a word: yes. We *do* want you to go through *all* of those steps *every time* you tackle a Reading question. But we want you to practice the strategy until it becomes second nature. What you'll find is that, with a little practice, you can whip through these steps and, what's more, *they will actually save you time.* Instead of allowing yourself to get sucked in by the tentacle-filled quicksand of a tempting answer choice, you will go through your answers quickly. Instead of thinking really hard, you will compare your MAYBEs and bring them back to the passage. Instead of scratching your head and squinting in concentration, you will skip and come back.

The General Strategy works because it has built-in phases for you to double-check, to reread, and to compare answer choices. Because it doesn't allow you to dillydally while you "work" on a problem, it ultimately saves you tons of time.

**Quick Recap of the General Strategy**

**Step 1:** Read the question.

**Step 2:** Scan the relevant section of the passage.

**Step 3:** Answer the question yourself.

**Step 4:** Go through the answers quickly, handing out NOs and MAYBEs.

**Step 5:** Compare your MAYBEs.

**Step 6:** Pick the correct answer choice or skip and come back.

## The Torturer's Tools: Know the Question Types

The General Strategy, once you've had some practice, should help you defeat most of the questions on the Reading section. But it also helps to know the types of questions you'll encounter, and the kinds of wrong answer choices that the ACT-bot relies on.

First, let's look at question types. For the sake of clarity, all of the example questions will be based on the following passage, excerpted from a made-up biography of made-up painter Severine Duramplace, with the made-up title *Severine: The Prophet of Nobody's Time*:

> Duramplace was not the first—nor would he be the last—artist to wager his career on the success of a musical genre. The young philosopher Friedrich Nietzsche sang the praises of the composer Richard Wagner, for example, and many American abstract impressionist painters in the late 1950s explained their obscure canvases as depictions of experimental jazz. But Duramplace was unique in his dedication to polka.
>
> Though he was born shortly after the First World War, Duramplace calls to mind an earlier figure: the romantic young man of fin de siècle Europe. Like those sighing, pining, emotive adolescents of the 1880s and '90s, Duramplace found something he loved and bestowed upon it all of the meaning that a more measured person might reserve for a broader range of ideas, people, and things. To him, polka was not simply the highest and most earnest expression of beauty, it was the *only* expression. From the age of 16, he exclusively painted polka dancers, polka musicians, and, later in life, still lifes of polka instruments. It was unfortunate, then, that he began his career as polka entered its steep decline in popularity.

*We know this passage is pure fiction because polka is timeless.

—Zack

## Question Type: **What did the passage say?**

Many of the questions in the Reading section will ask you to choose the answer choice that *most accurately paraphrases* an idea or sentence from the passage.

> *Based on the information in the first paragraph, which of the following best summarizes the relationship between abstract painters and experimental jazz?*

First, go back to that section of the passage and come up with your own answer. Here, we might say: Abstract artists were trying to make paintings that visually evoke the sound of experimental jazz.

## Question Type: **What did the author mean?**

These are your *inference* questions, and they are slightly more difficult. The ACT-bot is going to ask you to think about a complex portion of the text, and boil it down to a main idea.

> *The author would most likely characterize Duramplace's interest in polka as:*

We have to read the whole second paragraph to determine the author's opinion of Duramplace's polka obsession. In that paragraph, the author compares Duramplace to "romantic . . . sighing, pining, emotive adolescents," and contrasts him with "a more measured person." We don't want to go too far and conclude that the author *dislikes* Duramplace or thinks that he is *stupid*. We can safely say that he finds Duramplace's love of polka to be too extreme, perhaps unbalanced. We will be looking for answer choices that reflect this safe inference that is based on the clues in the passage.

## Question Type: **How was this word used?**

These are your *vocab-in-context* questions. The ACT-bot will either pick a word that it hopes you don't know, or pick a word that you do know, but that's being used in a rare or unusual way.

*This type of question might seem more subjective. It's not! Find details from the text to support your answer.*

*—Jon*

Again, these questions require that we provide answer choices. But we still want you to come up with your own answer first!

In the passage, *fin de siècle* most nearly means:

**A.** poetic.

**B.** musically exciting.

**C.** overly emotional.

**D.** at the end of the century.

If you know what "fin de siècle" means, then this question will be easy. But if, like 94 percent of the world, you've never seen that term before, you have to use surrounding information in order to figure it out. So: We know that "fin de siècle" is being used as an adjective to define Europe. What else does the passage say about Europe that can help us out? In the next sentence, we are told that these romantic young men were living in the 1880s and 1890s. Really, this is the *only* other information we are given that has to do with time and place, so it is our only clue. We know that there has to be some context clue, so let's use it! Answer choice D is the only one that makes sense.

Notice how we could read A, B, or C back into the passage, and none of them (except maybe B) would sound ridiculous. That's because the ACT-bot intentionally picks answer choices that could make sense, and that's why these questions can be so tough. The trick here is to *pick an answer choice that clearly corresponds to context clues in the passage.*

**Question Type: Why did the author write this way?**

These are your *structure* questions, in which the ACT-bot asks why the author is making his or her point in a particular way, and not in some other way.

> *The author mentions the "romantic young man of fin de siècle Europe" in order to:*

The ACT-bot is asking about the purpose of the comparison between Duramplace and the "romantic young man." Again, this requires that we go back to the paragraph to understand why the author is using this comparison. Our answer: to show that Duramplace is overly emotional in his attachment to polka music.

"Why did the author write this way" questions can also refer to the author's *tone*. Tone questions are doozies for two reasons: 1.) Much like inference questions, tone questions require finesse. We don't want to go too far. 2.) In coming up with terms to describe the tone of a passage, the ACT-bot likes to throw in rare, 10-dollar words.

Take a look at the following question. We will provide the answer choices, because they are essential. But we still want you to answer the question *yourself* before you read the choices!

The author's tone in the passage can best be described as:
A. laudatory.
B. measured.
C. snide.
D. querulous.

To find an author's tone, it is helpful to ask the question, "How does the author feel about his or her subject?" As we've discussed before, the author writes that Duramplace is overly emotional and reckless in his attachment to polka music. But the author also describes Duramplace's misguided affection as "unfortunate," which seems more pitying than critical. We want to be careful, then, and not rush to say that the author is *only* critical or *only* praising. We can safely say that he is somewhere in between. Looking at our choices, then, we can eliminate "laudatory," which is another word for strong praise, and "snide," which means sarcastic. "Querulous," which means complaining, seems too negative, which leaves us with "measured."

But wait. What if you don't know what some of those tone words mean? "Querulous," for example, is not a word that you frequently hear in conversation or even read in magazines or newspapers. There are two things you should do: 1.) Rely more heavily on those words you *do* know, and either choose or eliminate them. 2.) Familiarize yourself with this list of frequently tested but obscure tone words. Each definition is followed by an example sentence written in the tone described.

## A Few Key Tone Words

**ADMONISHING** *Definition:* Reprimanding. *Example:* How could you have deleted my recordings of *America's Next Top Model* after I left notes to save them on the TV, the fridge, the microwave, and the dog?

**ANALYTICAL** *Definition:* Reasoning. *Example:* Monica's extreme sadness was due partly to her general lack of emotional self-control and partly to her having painfully stubbed her toe.

**APATHETIC** and **REMISS** *Definition:* Not caring, negligent. *Example:* Your asthma inhaler? I put it under a thing in some room somewhere. I'm not really sure.

**CALLOUS** *Definition:* Without compassion. *Example:* Did you read that hilarious article about all those puppies getting terrible cases of puppy flu?

**COMPLACENT** *Definition:* Self-satisfied. *Example:* I know that some people struggle to understand philosophy, but it's always come naturally to me. Some of us are just better equipped, I guess.

**CYNICAL** *Definition:* Believing in only the worst of human nature or events. *Example:* Bianca sneered at the idea that a summer spent volunteering would be worthwhile.

**DETACHED** *Definition:* Uninterested or disconnected. *Example:* Everyone is dead. Also, there is a new Tyler Perry movie opening on Friday that looks pretty good.

The ACT-bot will sometimes ask for the definition of a simple word and give four answer choices that are all technically correct. The key is to review the word in context and pretend like you've never heard it before in your entire life, allowing you to come up with a _single_ definition that works for the word _in the passage_.

—Jon

**EBULLIENT** _Definition:_ Full of happy energy. _Example:_ LOOK AT THIS WEBSITE I FOUND!! IT'S GOT PHOTOS OF KITTENS DRESSED AS THE CAST OF THE AVENGERS!!!!

**EQUIVOCAL** _Definition:_ Ambiguous, difficult to interpret. _Example:_ I've decided once and for all to come out in favor of more deliberation that will eventually address the question of whether or not I will go out on a date with you.

**FACETIOUS** _Definition:_ Reacting to a situation with (often inappropriate) humor. _Example:_ Hey, look on the bright side. Now that you've been expelled, you have plenty of time to develop your TV-watching skills.

**INCREDULOUS** _Definition:_ Disbelieving. _Example:_ The entire season of _The Voice_ is available on Hulu? Right, and they've discovered a way to make zero-calorie salted-caramel cupcakes.

**JOCULAR** and **MIRTHFUL** _Definition:_ Playful, amusing, lightly and inoffensively humorous. _Example:_ Dame Oxenburg had always suffered from a surfeit of curiosity. She tiptoed about the parlor like a dormouse, nibbling a corner of each finger sandwich before tea.

**LAUDATORY** _Definition:_ Praising. _Example:_ Your vaudeville performance was wonderfully droll! I chortled so merrily that I had to be escorted out of the theater.

**MOROSE** _Definition:_ Gloomy, bad-tempered. _Example:_ I spilled my coffee this morning—the first of the many inevitable failures that characterize each and every day of my life.

**PEDANTIC** _Definition:_ Intended to instruct or preach, often in an unneeded or annoying way. _Example:_ You told me to "Watch out for that _train_," when actually it was a _cable car_ that almost ran me over. There *is* a difference, which I would be more than happy to explain.

**WHIMSICAL** *Definition:* Fanciful, capricious, playful. *Example:* As a child, he liked to imagine that his bed was situated on the back a great blue whale, and at night he would descend to the depths of dreams, passing starfish, dolphins, and seahorses.

## Become the Monster: How to Create a Reading Question

 **What Do Tutors Do?**

We make our students *write their own reading questions*, then we give these questions to other students we're working with and have them answer them. This gives our students a real insight into what it is like to try and trick a reader by creating answer choices that are *very close to correct* but not quite correct. It makes them much better at spotting wrong answers.

*Though for Uncle Merle, this was just an excuse to take his clothes off and eat trash.

We've given you a number of weapons with which to attack the Reading Test, but, as Uncle Merle used to say, the best way to catch a possum is to think like a possum.* So let's take a look at how the ACT-bot builds a wrong-answer trap out of quicksand and malevolence. This knowledge will enable you to more easily sense a wrong answer choice when you read it.

Start by reading this excerpt from a not-real history textbook with the not-real title *Ancient Peoples and the Stuff They Did and Why They Did That Stuff*:

> The habits of the Batiringi seem, to our eyes, quite strange. But as is often the case with nomadic peoples, especially those living in arid environments, many social structures and cultural practices can be traced back to topographical and climatological causes. The famous Batiringi dance—depictions of which have been preserved in 5,000-year-old cave paintings—can be interpreted only when we realize that these movements were performed as expressive complaints to Bukkot, the lazy god of rain. And the Batiringi practice of hopping from one foot to the other instead of walking only makes sense once we realize that the sand was incredibly hot. This also explains why Trau'Obiso, the legendary inventor of the first grass shoes, is referred to by the honorific

"Ba'antu Kal," which can be roughly translated as "Thank the gods for that guy."

Here's the question:

*According to the passage, geographical facts can aid our understanding of cultures because . . .*

Now, let's pretend that we are the ACT-bot. First, we need to become much nastier. Imagine the town pool in summer. Do you want to cement it over and turn it into an orthodontist's office? Good. Now let's ramp it up. Imagine the Coachella music festival: Everyone is loving it—they're holding hands, singing along, and looking at each other with wide smiles and warm affection. Do you want to cut the power to the stage and instead recite a full ACT test, answer choices and all in a merciless monotone? Yes? Okay, I think you're ready.

The first step is to come up with a correct answer:

*Seemingly strange behaviors can be understood as responses to weather and land conditions.*

The next step is to *hide the right answer in vague language:*

*Behaviors can be understood within the context of prevalent conditions.*

Isn't that just a terribly vague, boring sentence? It's perfect! But that's the easy part. Much more difficult (and fun, if you are evil) is creating wrong answers that tempt the test taker. ✳

### Wrong #1: Reasonable answer that's not in the passage

These are the most common wrong answers. They sound totally reasonable. They might even be *correct* in the real world. But *the passage did not say it.*

*Researchers can apply the methods of geographical and climatological science to cultural artifacts such as wall paintings.*

✳ If you've already invented terribly difficult ACT questions for fun, you may or may not be a dangerous robot. You should get yourself checked out.

—Jon

Or you may be a future <u>Up Your Score</u> guest editor. In which case you should check us out.

—Ava

This answer choice is tempting because *it might actually be true.* It seems likely that researchers *do* use other scientific methods to confirm or test their historical theories. But this is not what the passage is talking about!

The main way to unmask these answer choices is to *go back and make sure your answer choice is based on the passage.* (This is a great check for *any* answer you pick.)

## Wrong #2: Answer that is in the passage but doesn't answer the question

These wrong answers are designed to trigger that part of your brain that says, "Oh! I remember that!" The ACT-bot is hoping that the thrill of recognition will override your reasoning. Like this:

> *Arid environments adversely affect motor processes like walking and dancing.*

Sure, the passage says this about the Batiringi, but is this *why* geographical facts help us understand cultures? No, it is too specific. The ACT-bot is hoping that you will think, "Oh, this is *totally* in the passage," and ignore the fact that it does not adequately answer the question.

The best way to be on your guard against these questions is to *be suspicious of any choice that includes words from the passage.* This does not *necessarily* signal that the answer choice is wrong, but it should make you nervous.<sup>＊</sup>

## Wrong #3: Contrary to what the passage says

These answer choices are puzzling. They say the *opposite* of what the passage says, and yet they often tempt even the sharpest, most attentive test takers. This is because they are clearly *related* to both the question and the passage. They can also make you doubt whether you understood the passage correctly, which makes them particularly gnarly.

＊ As if you weren't nervous enough already.
—Jon

*Group behaviors provide us with an insight into past weather conditions.*

Here, they've taken the right answer and flipped the logic. Instead of weather and land conditions affecting our understanding of behaviors, the behaviors are now affecting our understanding of the weather. Again, both parts of the answer choice seem to be in the right ballpark, but the cause-and-effect logic has been flipped. The ACT-bot *loves* to do this.

If you are in a situation where you are left with two answer choices, with opposite cause-and-effect relationships, you should skip and come back. With a clear head, go back to the passage and reread the relevant section.

## Wrong #4: Too extreme

These are particularly nefarious wrong answers. Basically, they are correct answers that go a little too far.

*The practices of ancient societies can be understood only when geographical factors are taken into consideration.*

This is almost the same as our correct answer (it's even phrased better, making it more attractive) except we threw in that "only." That little word makes a world of difference! The passage is not saying that the habits of the Batiringi can be understood *only* with reference to the surrounding land and weather. That's taking it too far.

In order to see extreme answers coming, be on the lookout for the following words: *only, most, none, never, always, exclusively, solely, without exception,* etc.

As you take practice Reading tests, try to spot wrong answer types. Is that answer choice reasonable but not in the passage? Is it too extreme? Or has the logic of the answer choice been flipped? If you do this, you'll be a much more savvy test taker.

If you find yourself justifying an answer with, <u>well, he could have meant this</u> . . . , walk away! Too extreme!

—Ava

## Moving Forward

We've told you everything you need to know to ace the Reading section. But the most important thing, for this section more than any other, is to practice. Develop the Five Habits of Lean-Forward Reading with increasingly challenging books, articles, and newspapers. Take timed Reading sections to get a sense of your reading speed.

It is crucial that you take practice tests, of course, but simply taking a practice test will not necessarily improve your score. The crucial thing is to *look at the questions that you answer incorrectly.* Ask yourself: How did this question trick me? What type of wrong answer choice did the ACT-bot use? What type of question was it? If I misread a section of the passage, how did I misread it?  Every time you go back and find out *how* the ACT-bot tricked you, you are becoming a stronger test taker. Finally, use the practice tests to hone your skipping and coming back skills, so that you don't become bogged down in the tentacle-filled quicksand.

✳ This is good advice for any section or practice test.

—Zack

# CHAPTER 7

# The Science Reasoning Test

## In Which Reasoning Is Tested Far More Than Science

*Murgg and Shpluk: The Fathers of the Scientific Method*

**D**o you remember every fact you ever learned in biology class? How about chemistry and physics?

If you answered "yes," you are not being entirely honest.

*Nobody* remembers everything they learned in biology, chemistry, and physics. Those classes are packed full of facts, names, types, processes, and formulas. What's worse, they present you with facts that you will very rarely discuss, read, or hear about outside the classroom. For the vast majority of students, exposure to science facts begins and ends in school.※

All of which makes the Science Reasoning Test very scary indeed. Take a look at this paragraph, which is very similar to a real ACT passage:

> Scientists used a $1 \times 10^4$ ohm resistor and a capacitor with a capacitance of $1 \times 10^3$ farad. At the beginning of the experiment, the capacitor was not charged. The scientists closed the switch and started a timer simultaneously at time zero. At that time and at 20-second intervals thereafter, the scientists wrote down the voltage across the capacitor. The data is recorded in Table 1.

Bone chilling, right? You start reading and are like, "Cool, I know what a scientist is," and then you're hit with "ohm" and "capacitor" and "capacitance" and freakin' "farad"?!?!?! *Four* words

you've probably never even *seen* before, in the first *sentence?!?*

It's a scary section, all right, and the ACT-bot is all about scaring you. But here's the secret about the Science Reasoning section: It is *much* more straightforward and predictable than it seems. Let's talk about why.

※ Well, that's just depressing.

—Ava

## What the Science Reasoning Section Says It Tests

If you were to ask the ACT-bot what exactly is in the Science Reasoning section, here is what it would say: "Science stuff."

More specifically, it would say that it tests biology, chemistry, earth and space science, and physics. If you were to look at an ACT and flip to any passage, you would agree. The terms in any given passage fall into one of those four concept areas. So far, so awful.

The ACT-bot would also reveal that the Science Reasoning section is broken down into seven passages:

+ Data Representation (three passages, five questions each)
+ Research Summaries (three passages, six questions each)
+ Conflicting Viewpoints (one passage, seven questions)
+ Total: 40 questions in 35 minutes

The different types of passages can be arranged in any order—there is no hierarchy of difficulty, so the easiest passage might come at the end. But *there is something sneaky going on here. . . .*

## What the Science Reasoning Section *Really* Tests

It's a reading test, basically, but with not-so-pretty pictures and complicated-sounding words.

—Ava

In truth, the *type* of passage is *much* more important than the content of the passage. While the passage might be about solar flares or the dispersion of carbon atoms in the ozone, it is *really testing* whether or not you can:

1. Interpret graphs (for the data representation questions).
2. Follow the logic of an experiment (for the research summaries questions).
3. Analyze an argument (for the conflicting viewpoints questions).

And that's it. In other words, the Science Reasoning section *pretends* to be about science, but it *actually* tests reasoning. This is great news. All of those scary words (*ohm, capacitance,* etc.) are like a spooky ghost costume draped over a bunch of questions

When the ACT-bot uses a complicated scientific term, there is almost always a sentence that defines it verbatim.

—Ava

about tables and graphs and logic. In most passages, understanding the science terms will be completely unnecessary. Once we remind ourselves how to interpret graphs, follow experiments, and analyze arguments, we can throw our old science textbooks in the trash and still rock the Science Reasoning section. (Then we should probably take those science textbooks out of the trash and sell them online, because money is money and chocolate éclairs don't pay for themselves.)

"Hold up," you might be saying. "Can that *possibly* be true? There's *no science* explicitly tested in the *whole* section?"

Okay, we're exaggerating a tiny bit. There might be one or, at *most*, two questions that require knowledge of scientific facts. For example, they might ask you a question that requires you know that a lipid bilayer is a semipermeable membrane, or that the valence number of an atom refers to the number of bonds that an atom can form with other atoms.

But these questions are so rare that it seems unwise to review *all of science* in order to get *one* question right. If you come across a real science question and can't remember what you learned in class, it's smarter to eliminate ridiculous answer choices and take a guess.

* Usually these questions are pretty easy—different schools have different curricula, so the bot can't assume that any given student has studied every aspect of science.

—Zack

So the only thing we have to do in this chapter is learn how to work with graphs, experiments, and arguments! Piece of cake. The reality is that this section, if approached correctly, can be one of the most straightforward sections on the test. If you focus, there is a good chance that you can pull out a great score on this section. But first, let's talk about general strategies.

# Overall Strategy: Go, Go, Go!!!

I find the Science section the hardest, not because it tests difficult material but because it gives you so little time to work. Moving quickly is *the* greatest challenge.

—Jon

## Top Four Psych-Up Slogans

4. My mind is even sharper than my pencil.

3. For country! For family! For getting into BU early decision!

2. Make educated guesses, not war!

1. I am test taker. Hear me roar!

*They were awful, violent, cannibalistic monkeys; don't feel bad for them.

If you've taken a Science Reasoning Test, the first thing you probably noticed is that you're given a ludicrously short amount of time to get through the section. You have seven passages in 35 minutes, or five minutes per passage. Most of the passages (four of them, to be exact) have six or seven questions, which means you have *less than a minute per question*. And, oh yeah, you *also* have to read a passage *as well as* interpret data before you can even *answer* the questions!

And did we mention that the Science Reasoning Test is the last or next-to-last section of the ACT (depending on whether you're taking the "optional" Writing Test)? This means that you will be both mentally and physically exhausted by the time you *begin* the section.

What this boils down to is that you have to get psyched up and go *fast*. There are two ways to do this:

1. Drink so many energy drinks that you enter an alternate time-flow, which buys you an extra hour for the section.
2. Move through the section strategically.

We had monkeys try the first strategy a couple of times, but they always had heart attacks before we entered the alternate time-flow.* So let's go with the second option.

First and foremost, you need to recapture some energy before launching into the section. The best way to do this is to take a deep breath and remind yourself that this section is as clear-cut as the ACT gets, and if you can just stay with it, you'll do well. Pop a hard candy into your mouth, summon up your inner triathlete—and get ready to power through.

Now, let's talk about the best way to approach the Science Reasoning Test. First, you need to **pick your battles.** As we mentioned, the seven passages are not arranged in order of difficulty, so the later passages can be easier than the first ones. Glance at a passage before you dive into it, and decide whether

Several people, including teachers and past test takers, told me that you should skip the passage and dive right into the questions, _then_ go hunting for the answer in the passage and the graphs. My intuition told me that this was a ludicrous idea. I didn't do it, and neither should you.

—Jon

Your reading practice (remember that?) will definitely help you with the stuffy writing in the Science section.

—Zack

you want to spend time on it now or later. This does _not_ mean that you should read all the passages, then decide which one to attack. Rather, we want you to glance at the first passage, determine whether or not it looks gnarly, then commit to solving it or move on. Do this for each passage as you move through the section. No sense wasting time on a brutal passage (where you're more likely to get a few wrong) if it means you won't have time for an easier passage at the end.

When you _do_ read a passage, take all the time you need to understand the text, charts, and graphs. Your inclination may be to rush through it, but you need a clear understanding of the passage in order to master this section. (More on _how_ to understand passages in a moment.) Once you feel like you understand what's going on, speed through the questions. Most of the questions in this section, you'll see, are _very_ straightforward. They might ask you to read a graph, compare two graphs, or explain why an author came to a particular conclusion. If you've grasped the passage, these questions should take very little time to answer. It's not at all uncommon for a test taker to spend three minutes deciphering a passage and then blaze through all of the questions in two minutes.

That being said, know that the introductory paragraphs are often intentionally intimidating. You do not need to understand exactly what the intro is saying; instead you can replace foreign terms with "(some kind of)" or a variation thereof. Let's try this out on the same scary passage we saw earlier:

> Scientists used (some kind of) resistor and a capaci-whatever with (some quality) of (some number). At the beginning of the experiment, the capaci-whatever was not charged. The scientists closed the switch and started a timer simultaneously at time zero. At that time and at 20-second intervals thereafter, the scientists wrote down the voltage across the capaci-whatever. Their data is recorded in Table 1.

The only thing we have to know is that a switch was closed in the capaci-whatever and a timer was started. Every 20 seconds, they recorded a voltage. Without worrying about the big words, we can see that the problem has to do with the changes in voltage through some kind of machine at regular intervals of time. Once you've understood that, you'll be able to read the charts and tables, and answer all of the questions.

And remember, it is crucial that you **skip and come back** within each passage. All of the questions in a passage refer to the same charts, tables, and summaries. If a question is difficult, skip it. When you go back to the tough question, you will be more familiar with the material.

Now, let's take a look at the three types of passages that you will confront.

## Data Representation

Data representation passages are all about charts and graphs. These problems initially look very scary, especially if you're not a subscriber to *Charts and Graphs Quarterly*. The ACT-bot will do its best to try and dig up types of graphs that you haven't seen before. It might even throw in two or three graphs and ask you to find information using more than one of them. It may also ask you to make predictions and generalizations based on the information in the graphs.

This might seem like a lot, but all of this boils down to one thing: You need to be able to "tell the story" of the graphs. Once you can do this, the questions will become some of the least complicated ones on the entire ACT.

The best way to understand how these passages work is to go *backward*, to start with a story and then create a graphic representation. To do this, we're going to reach way back into our memories. . . .

Here's a secret: Even Chris, now a renowned and somewhat grizzled author of *Up Your Score*, used to be young. When he was fresh out of college, becoming a test-prep book author was still beyond his wildest dreams. Instead, he worked at the Disney Channel, in its research and development department. At that time, Disney wanted to create a brand-new tween pop group, and it was his job to determine what kind of group would sell the most records. *

So, he did what any member of a research and development department would do: He created nine different groups, put them onstage in front of a thousand tweens, and recorded the decibel level of the audience's shrieking while each band played a three-minute song.

Here were his nine groups, organized by band name, musical genre, and the gender of the band members:

**2 Real 2 Go 2 Bed**—rap/hip-hop; boys and girls
**Gold-Plated Pencils with Diamond Erasers**—rap/hip-hop;
  boys only
**Tweety and the Text Messagettes**—rap/hip-hop; girls only

**Hee Haw, Y'all**—country and western; boys and girls
**Aww Shucks, More Big Trucks**—country and western;
  boys only
**Cowhide iPhone Case**—country and western; girls only

**Shut Up, Everyone**—punk rock; boys and girls
**Expletives NOT Deleted**—punk rock; boys only
**I Will Punch Your Smile**—punk rock; girls only

To graph the reaction to each band's performance, we've created a basic coordinate plane. The *x*-axis is time, while the *y*-axis is the decibel level of shrieking. Each line corresponds to a band. Here, for example, is the graph of the hip-hop groups:

I've always found it easier to look at the graphs/diagrams before attacking the wordy bits. Most of the time the questions only concern the relationships between variables, which you can often figure out just by following the patterns in the table or graph.

—Ava

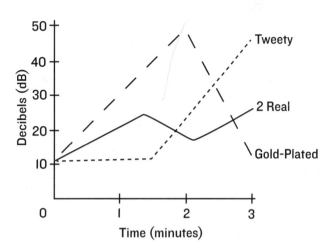

So how do we "tell the story" of this graph? Well, just like in a story, a change is happening through time. Here, the crowd started to cheer for 2 Real, then seemed to lose interest, but after the two-minute mark regained their enthusiasm and cheered louder than ever. Gold-Plated Pencils caused a more dramatic spike in screaming, but right before the two-minute mark experienced a massive drop-off. Tweety had the most interesting trajectory, causing almost no increase for a full minute and a half, then enjoying the most dramatic spike in volume of all the rap groups.

Of course, this story has a lot of holes, and it's important to note those as well. We don't yet know *why* Gold-Plated Pencils lost their audience. Maybe the band forgot the words, or a member of the band fell off the stage. ✳ Maybe there was a fire drill. As it stands, this graph presents no more information than the level of screaming as the band played for three minutes.

The most basic—and the most common—data representation question will look like this:

> Which band had the most enthusiastic reception, measured in dB, at the two-minute mark?

To answer this question, we need to realize two things: the minutes are located on the *x*-axis, while the "enthusiastic reception," or volume, is located on the *y*-axis. So you first go to

✳ This would probably add to my excitement.

—Zack

The nice thing about the Science section is that it's full of clear-cut instructions for verbally inclined people and full of pretty pictures for pictorially inclined people.

—Ava

the two-minute mark on the *x*-axis, then look up to see which band corresponds to the highest point on the *y*-axis, which is clearly Gold-Plated Pencils. There are plenty of questions that really are this simple, we swear to Veritrax, the Norse god of honesty.

But that question was simple only because we had taken the time to "tell the story" of the graph. We understood exactly what it was saying, and *then* answered the question.

But obviously the ACT-bot has not completely fallen asleep at the Destructo-Wheel. It can mix things up and make things more complex by throwing in two data representations. Like this:

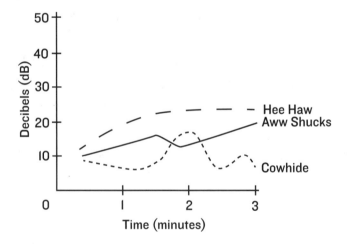

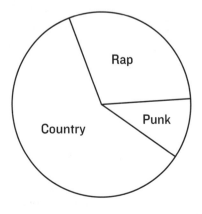

Audience members' choice of genre that makes them dance instead of shriek

Assume that no matter which band is chosen, it will undoubtedly play no actual music and instead star in three made-for-TV movies entitled (Band name)-Camp: The Power of (Generic Attribute).

—Jon

Here, we're presented with two new pieces of information, both of which contribute to our story. Looking at the first graph, we can see that Hee Haw caused the volume to rise and then level off, while Aww Shucks had a brief dip before continuing their modest upward trajectory. Finally, Cowhide wavered the most and ended with the lowest volume.

Before we look at the pie chart, let's go ahead and compare those country performances with our hip-hop performances from the first graph. With the exception of Gold-Plated Pencils, the hip-hop groups generated a *much* louder reaction than the country groups. It wouldn't be silly to imagine, then, that our new Disney pop sensation is more likely to be a hip-hop group than a country band.

Now let's go back to that pie chart.* It measures the choice of music that makes the audience want to dance instead of shriek, by recording the percentage of the audience that is dancing. Clearly, country music won. This alters our story: Perhaps the audience was more interested in dancing during the country music, and so did not expend as much energy in shrieking.

The ACT-bot is likely to test us on all of this information by asking:

> Based on the audience's reaction to the country groups, a Disney executive has decided to cut them from the roster of musicians. Is this a smart decision?

Because we've already told the story of the new graphs, we recognize that the question is intentionally vague. The "audience's reaction" could be either shrieking *or* dancing. So our answer would have to be something like this:

> No, because the dB level alone does not provide enough information to make this decision.

*It's a key-lime pie chart, BTW. With real key limes that our Uncle Morris brought back from his vacation in Florida.

Finally, let's look at one last graph, in which responses to the question, "What is your favorite type of music?" were plotted on a

On all types of graph interpretation questions, you'll benefit from coming up with an answer <u>before</u> looking at the answer choices to avoid being enticed by one of the ACT-bot's devious answer-choice schemes.

—Jon

scatter-plot graph, with the y-axis corresponding to the music type, and the x-axis corresponding to the age of the respondent.

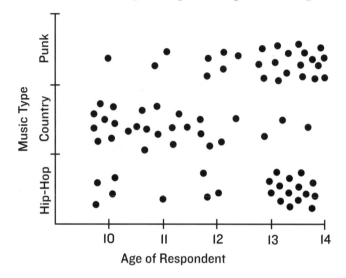

What's the story here? We can see that lots of 10- and 11-year-olds like country music, but as the respondents get older, they seem to split between punk music (which is unpopular for younger kids) and hip-hop (which kids seem to like, lose interest in at ages 11 and 12, then take up again at 13).

The toughest types of questions might ask you to make **predictions** based on the information. As in:

The bigwigs at Disney have decided not to focus on the teenybop audience. They want to create a group that will be popular among 16- and 17-year-olds. Which genre of music should they invest in?

The answer, using this graph, should continue the trend that we see in the graph. This is a little complicated, because hip-hop experienced a dip. But *in general*, both hip-hop and punk experience an upward trend. So the answer would look like:

The higher-ups should create music in either the punk or hip-hop genre.

But if the ACT-bot is feeling particularly cataclysmic (and it usually is), it might also ask you to make a **generalization** based on all of the data provided. As in:

> Disney wants to invest in a band that will garner profits for at least five years. Which band should it sign?

Looking at all of the graphs and charts that we have available, we have to synthesize a lot of information to come to a decision. We know that the rap groups, especially Tweety, concluded their performances with the loudest screaming. But remember that the country groups might have encouraged dancing, rather than singing. Then again, country music's popularity tails off once kids become teenagers, and Disney wants the band to make a profit for at least five years. So we're going to have to go with Tweety. Another pop supergroup is born! ✳

(While Chris enjoyed working in research and development, he found that, after a year, listening to tweens shriek all day grew a little tiresome.) ✳✳

Before moving on, we should note that graphs are also really helpful for **eliminating ridiculous answers.** Many data representation questions will ask you about a graph and then present you with four numerical answers corresponding to numbers on the graph. At least two of these answers are usually *way* off. Even if the problem is giving you trouble, if you can eliminate these (cross them out!), then skip and come back, you're going to be just fine.

✳ And disappears after one short month of popularity.
—Jon

✳✳ Coincidentally, he got out of teaching for similar reasons.
—Zack

## Research Summaries

Three of the Science Reasoning passages will be research summaries. These will present you with one or more experiments, then ask you questions about the plan, the hypotheses, and the results of those experiments. But what they're *really* testing you on is whether you know how the scientific method works. So, without further ado, we present a short play:

**A Scientific Drama**

**Murgg and Shpluk: The Fathers of the Scientific Method**

*Interior Cave, Day*

*Shpluk, a gray-haired Neanderthal, is sleeping in a corner of the cave. He snores like a caveman.*

*Murgg, a younger Neanderthal, enters the cave holding a stick, one end of which is on fire. He is very pleased with his stick.*

*They both speak with the British accents that were typical among Neanderthals.*

**Murgg:** Shpluk, I say, *do* have a look at this.

**Shpluk:** (*Without opening his eyes*) Can't you see I'm sleeping, Murgg? You're being frightfully rude.

**Murgg:** You can't be sleeping and talking at the same time. Besides, I'm quite sure you'll want to see this.

*Reluctantly, Shpluk sits up.*

**Shpluk:** What . . . what is it?

**Murgg:** I haven't the foggiest idea! I was walking across the plain, holding this stick up over my head—

**Shpluk:** Why?

**Murgg:** Why what?

**Shpluk:** Why walk around holding a stick over your head?

**Murgg:** (*Considers*) Why not?

**Shpluk:** Good point. Continue.

**Murgg:** —when all of a sudden I hear a loud KRAKOOM and I'm hit by one of those beastly zigzags, or whatever they're called.

**Shpluk:** They're called "beastly zigzags."

**Murgg:** That's right. So I'm knocked out cold, but when I come to, the stick is like this. I call it "fire."

**Shpluk:** Fire is very shiny. (*Walks closer to the stick*) And bright. And warm. (*Investigates*) Do you think it's . . . food?

**Murgg:** I *do* think it's food! At least I rather *hope* it's food, because I so *adore* food.

**SHPLUK:** Me, too. Give it here!

*Shpluk takes the flaming stick. He cautiously sticks out his tongue and slowly brings it to the flame.*

**SHPLUK:** YOOOOOWWWWWCH!!!

**MURGG:** Too salty?

**SHPLUK:** It bit me!

**MURGG:** Are you sure? Perhaps you haven't developed your palate. It took you months before you were able to enjoy a spot of muskrat vomit.

**SHPLUK:** No, it hurts!

**MURGG:** Perhaps it's the *stick* that hurts, and not the fire? Every time I try to eat a stick, it hurts.

**SHPLUK:** (*Considers*) Maybe . . .

**MURGG:** I have an idea!

**SHPLUK:** What's that?

**MURGG:** Let's figure this out by inventing science.

**SHPLUK:** Invent a whole new way of thinking? Now? Before supper?

**MURGG:** Why not? We're always inventing groundbreaking ways of behaving. Why, just this morning we invented art.

**SHPLUK:** (*Whining*) But I'm still *tired* from inventing art.

**MURGG:** This is much simpler. And you've already done half of it. Here's how it works. We've observed a *phenomenon:* The fire hurt your tongue. Based on that *phenomenon,* you've made a *hypothesis:* that fire hurts you every time you touch it, and that it hurts *more* than a stick alone.

**SHPLUK:** (*Wistfully*) If only me dad could see me now, making a hypothesis based on a phenomenon. He once said I'd amount to something, right before he died from forgetting to eat.

**MURGG:** Anyway, now that we've observed a phenomenon and made a hypothesis, we need to design an *experiment* to test it. Here's where things get fun!

Muskrat vomit:
a British delicacy
to this day.

—Jon

**SHPLUK:** I'm not having fun; my tongue hurts.

**MURGG:** Well, look at all the fun *I'm* having. An experiment is where we *test* to see whether a hypothesis is true. Here, we're testing the hypothesis that fire itself hurts. We'll do this by testing whether touching fire-on-a-stick hurts more than touching a normal stick. Here, we are calling the normal stick a *control*, because in both instances, you will touch the stick.

**SHPLUK:** *Me?!?* Why do *I* have to touch it?

**MURGG:** Why *not* you?

**SHPLUK:** (*Considers*) Good point.

**MURGG:** As I was saying, the *control* is the *normal* situation: you touching a stick. The *variable* is the fire. We call it *variable* because it *changes*. In one instance there is fire; in one instance there is no fire. This ensures that we are testing only *one* thing: fire.

*Shpluk raises his hand.*

**MURGG:** Yes, Shpluk?

**SHPLUK:** All these new terms are stupid and I hate them.

**MURGG:** Duly noted. Your reactions to the stick and to the fire-on-a-stick will be our *results*, and we will *analyze* these results posthaste to determine whether the hypothesis proved correct, or whether we need to alter our hypothesis.

**SHPLUK:** Very good.

*Murgg picks up a normal stick from the cave floor.*

**MURGG:** Now go ahead and touch this stick.

*Shpluk is hesitant at first, then touches it.*

**SHPLUK:** Quite nice, actually. I rather like a good stick-touch.

*Murgg holds out the flaming stick.*

**MURGG:** Now touch the fire-on-a-stick.

**SHPLUK:** This is going to be fun! I think I'm going to prefer being a scientist to being an artist!

*He touches the fire, leaps back in pain.*

**SHPLUK:** *Blast* you, science! Hurt me finger, science did!

**MURGG:** Very interesting. I'm analyzing the results now . . . and . . . fire-on-a-stick hurts more than a normal stick! Fire hurts! Hypothesis proved correct!

**SHPLUK:** Great for you. All this science has made me hungry. (*Reaches for the flaming stick*) Give us a bite of that lovely fire.

**MURGG:** (*Pulls the stick away*) I don't know, Shpluk; recent studies have shown that fire eating can result in charbroiled gums—a painful and sometimes deadly condition.

**SHPLUK:** (*Scowling*) Stupid science.

*Curtain.*

As you can see, the scientific method is one in which we test a hypothesis by developing an experiment. We determine a control and a variable in order to ensure that we are testing only *one* thing.

Research summary passages will present us with a—you guessed it—summary of a research experiment. Whereas in data representation passages you had to "tell the story," here you have to find the scientific method that determines the experiment.

To do this, first read the passage, then answer these questions in your head:

1. What are they testing? What are the controls and variables?
2. Do they have a hypothesis? (They might not state a hypothesis, but you might be able to guess what their prediction would be, based on the design of the experiment.)
3. What are their results? What can we conclude based on the experiment?
4. Are there any flaws in the experiment, or ways to improve it? Let's take a look at an example:

At the Nutz for More Dough Donut Laboratories, scientists are trying to determine the ideal size of a doughnut. To do this, they've developed the following experiment:

Seventy-three subjects are seated, one at a time, in the center of a room. To the subject's left, a counter stands 4 feet off the ground. To the subject's right, a set of 7 stairs leads up to a similar counter, which we'll call the right counter (Rc). On the left counter (Lc) one glazed doughnut measuring 6 inches in diameter and 1 inch in thickness is placed on a plate.

On the Rc, doughnuts of six ascending sizes, starting at 6" x 1", are placed on separate plates. The subject is asked to choose and eat one doughnut, either from the left or right counter. The results are tabulated below.

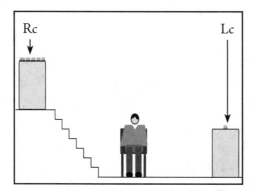

| Doughnut dimensions | # of subjects who chose doughnut |
|---|---|
| 6" x 1" (normal, on Rc and Lc) | 1 (from Lc) |
| 7" x 2" (large) | 3 |
| 10" x 3.5" (x-tra large) | 8 |
| 12" x 5" (Moby Dick) | 31 |
| 14" x 7" (Big Bang) | 27 |
| 24" x 10" (Simply Outrageous) | 3 |

Doughnuts. Yum.

—Ava

So let's break this experiment down to its scientific method.

### I. What are they testing? What are the controls and variables?

Here, the scientists are testing what *size* doughnut will appeal *more* than an average-size doughnut. They've decided to use stairs as an impediment to the larger doughnuts, with the intention of learning whether a larger doughnut will exert enough appeal to overcome the impediment. The control here is the availability of normal-size doughnuts on both counters. The variable, the thing that is changing, is the increasing size of the doughnuts at the top of the stairs.

## 2. Do they have a hypothesis?

The hypothesis is not explicit in the design of this experiment, but we can guess that the scientists are anticipating that more people will brave the stairs for larger doughnuts.

## 3. What are their results? What can we conclude based on the experiment?

Looking at the table, we can see that only one subject chose a normal-size doughnut on the left counter. Larger doughnuts caused more people to walk up the stairs to claim them, until the 14" x 7" Big Bang doughnut, which proved less popular than the 12" x 5" Moby Dick. When the subjects were offered the 2-foot-across, 10-inch-high Simply Outrageous doughnut, only three (very hungry) subjects decided that yes, they did in fact want more than 4,000 cubic inches of doughnut in their bellies.

So we can conclude that 12" x 5" seems to be closest to the most tempting size for a doughnut.

The scientists felt that the original name of the "Simply Outrageous" doughnut, the "Type 2 Diabetes," might dissuade some participants from choosing it.

—Jon

## 4. Are there any flaws in the experiment, or ways to improve it?

Totally. For one, stairs might deter some people, but this does not mean that they are considered obstacles by everyone. Maybe some respondents thought, "Hey, if I climb some stairs, then I won't have to feel as guilty about eating a foot-wide doughnut." In other words, one could argue that the stairs made the larger doughnuts seem *more* attractive.

Also, we have no idea who these people are. The scientists could have recruited subjects from the "Big-Doughnut-Lovers Convention," for all we know. Such a small sample size (73 people) hardly seems like an objective measure, especially if we know nothing about them.

Once we've done the hard work of figuring out the scientific method, the questions are very clear-cut.

Most experiments have some possibility of error and/or room for improvement, so you should be able to come up with at least a couple of answers if they ask.

—Jon

A few of the questions in any research summary will ask you to interpret graphs and tables, much like in a data representation passage:

1. Based on the results in the experiment, a doughnut with a diameter of 13" and a width of 6" would most likely be chosen by how many subjects?

   A. Between 6 and 11
   B. Between 12 and 26
   C. Between 27 and 31
   D. Above 32

We see that the doughnut described falls in size between the Moby Dick and the Big Bang, so it will logically be chosen by between 27 and 31 subjects. C is correct.

Other questions might ask you about the scientific method underlying the experiment.

2. Given the design of the experiment, which of the following could have been a basic assumption?

   A. When it comes to doughnuts, people prefer some flavors over others.
   B. Larger doughnuts are preferable to smaller doughnuts.
   C. People would always rather not walk up stairs.
   D. People will always choose only one of two doughnuts.

This question is a bit tougher. The design of the experiment does not alter the flavor of the doughnut, which eliminates choice A. The aim of the test is to determine *whether* people prefer larger doughnuts, so it cannot be assuming that people always prefer larger doughnuts, which eliminates B. Finally, in the experiment, the subject is explicitly told to choose only one doughnut, so the

scientists are not *assuming* that the subject will choose one, eliminating D. This leaves C, which is the correct answer choice, because using stairs as an *obstacle* means that the scientists assume that people would always rather not walk up stairs. (This is a silly assumption, as for all they know "walking up stairs" could be the hot new fitness craze.)

Finally, the ACT-bot will probably ask a question about tinkering with the experiment. Here, we just need to ask ourselves how the tinkering would affect the scientific method of the experiment:

3. Suppose the scientists varied the size of both the doughnuts to the right *and* the doughnut to the left. Would this improve the experiment?

A. Yes, because the subject would be able to choose the preferred size of the doughnut without the interference of an obstacle.

B. Yes, because the greater range of choices would help the subject make a more informed decision.

C. No, because the subject would be given too many choices, and the risk of confusion would jeopardize the experiment.

D. No, because the experiment would lose its control, and the scientists would not be able to isolate the variable and arrive at a conclusion.

When we take out the consistent placement of a 6" doughnut to the left of the subject, we remove the control from our experiment. The answer, then, is D. These questions, again, will seem more complicated if we have not done the initial work of determining the scientific method of the experiment.

Congratulations! You're two-thirds of the way through the Science section. Before we move on to the last type of reading passage, let's take a little break to appreciate everything science has done for us.

> Pay attention to the answer choices' accurate use of scientific terminology, like "control," as a hint to a correct answer, but don't be drawn in by any old sciency-sounding word.
>
> —Jon

## TOP FIVE SCIENTIFIC INNOVATIONS

5. **Radioactivity.** In the 1880s, Polish scientist Marie Curie helped discover radioactivity. She became the first woman to teach at the University of Paris and the first woman to win the Nobel Prize. Then, after drinking a vial of radioactive juice, she transformed into Marie Fury, the first woman to shoot fire bolts out of her palms.

4. **Large Hadron Collider.** In 2008, the world's largest and highest-energy particle accelerator was built beneath the Franco-Swiss border. There, thousands of scientists gather everyday to watch large hadrons smash into each other. "Oh, my gosh," they say, scribbling excitedly on their science pads. "Did you see when it went *kra-BLAMmo?!?* It was all like *shprakow-plarakarakaBOOM!*" An article summarizing their findings, entitled "You're Never Gonna Believe How Hard These Things Collide with Each Other," will be published in the October issue of *Nature*.

3. **Baking Soda Volcanoes.** If you add red dye to the vinegar, it looks *exactly* like lava. Fun!

2. **Earth's Orbit Around the Sun.** In 1543, Copernicus suggested in his book *On the Revolutions of Heavenly Spheres* that the Earth revolved around the sun. The reaction was immediate and passionate: "Oh, does it? How *interesting*! You know what else is interesting? We're all dying at age 28 from plague, smallpox, and the common cold. Seriously, a breeze comes through the window and we immediately die. We deliver our babies using *wooden tongs*. I have a total of two teeth and I'm coated in pestilent sores. But yeah, that's really cool about the Earth and the Sun and whatever . . ."

1. **Double Stuf Oreos.** It is well known that scientists work by staring out the window, waiting for a flash of inspiration to hit them. Well, one night in the mid-1980s, one such

scientist was hit by a flash *so inspiring,* he almost fell off his chair: What if, instead of the normal amount of "stuf" in an Oreo cookie, we throw caution to the wind and *double down* on the "stuf"? With tears of joy still wet on his cheeks, the scientist called Nabisco and proposed his idea. In response, the president of Nabisco got so excited he slipped into a coma, but his replacement ushered in the development process. Their invention heralded the modern era of having twice as much "stuf" crammed into our cookies.

Thank you, science!

## Conflicting Viewpoints

This is another section where you should check your knowledge and opinions at the door.

—Jon

One passage in the Science Reasoning section is going to present two or (occasionally) three arguments about a phenomenon or theory. The ACT-bot doesn't care about which argument is more convincing. It's just going to test you on how the arguments are constructed and how they relate to each other.

You should handle these passages in the same way you handled the data representation and research summary passages: Figure out the passages first, then blaze through the questions.

So read the arguments, then follow these steps:

1. Find the disagreements and agreements between the arguments.
2. Within each argument, locate the evidence and support for each thesis.
3. Advanced move: Can you spot any assumptions?

If you can get through the first two steps, then you're ready to head to the questions. If you can tackle the third step, then you're ready to *rock* the questions. Let's try it out.

First off, read the arguments, duh.

*Scientist 1*

It used to be commonly held that the luminescence of a firefly served as a warning signal to predators. This was based on simple observation. We've long noted the pleasant, atmospheric illumination of firefly larvae, colloquially referred to as "glowworms." This trait, combined with the known toxicity of the larvae, convinced scientists that the glow functioned as a sort of traffic sign: "Don't eat me, I'm poisonous!" It was a small leap to assume that the bioluminescence of adult fireflies served a similar purpose.

But as so often happens, further observation forced us to change our theory. Scientists in North America have noted repeated patterns or "pulses" of bioluminescence that occur only during mating seasons. We now give the firefly a bit more credit. Instead of seeing the light as a warning sign, we now think of bioluminescence as the firefly's version of flirting.

*Scientist 2*

Of all the vexing results of the Darwinian revolution in biology, possibly the most irritating is this notion—cherished by scientists across the world—that every aspect of life must have an evolutionary purpose. Those stripes on a cat's tail? They must hypnotize some sort of field mouse, allowing the cat to pounce. That peculiar song of the blue-throated swallow? It must communicate a nearby source of food. We've gotten to the point where a teenager, waking up to find a new pimple on his nose, can be comforted by the scientifically approved notion that acne will somehow vouchsafe his genetic continuance.

Take fireflies, for example. Scientists bend over backward to explain the firefly's bioluminescent displays, but the truth is that there is *no way* to determine whether or not the bug has any purposive control over its own shiny rump. As any American child knows, if you capture a few fireflies in a jar, you can make them light up by shaking the jar. Does this mean that the light is an expression of fear? Of anger? Of stress? Maybe . . . or maybe not. There is no way of knowing! Until we can find a way to inhabit the mind of the firefly, we will not be able to answer this question. And any attempt otherwise is a futile effort to impose order on an orderless universe.

OH, BUZZ OFF.

Mark the places where passages disagree. It'll help you zero in on the answer to those questions.

—Ava

## Step 1: Find the disagreement.

In these passages, the authors clearly disagree over the purpose of a firefly's bioluminescence. Scientist 1 believes that fireflies use their light to attract mates, while Scientist 2 disagrees, asserting that we'll never discover the purpose of a firefly's bioluminescence.

## Step 2: Locate the evidence and support for each thesis.

Here is where we get into the meat and potatoes of the conflicting viewpoints section, and it's helpful to pause for a second and ask ourselves: What *is* an argument?

The answer, of course, is that an argument is a table.

The thesis of an argument is its main point, the big idea, the whole enchilada. But when you make an argument, you don't just say your idea over and over again (unless you are five years old, which would be incredible because reading a test-prep book is a really impressive feat for a five-year-old). No, you *base your argument* on evidence, or ideas. The thesis, then, is a tabletop, and each leg is a supporting piece of evidence or a supporting idea.

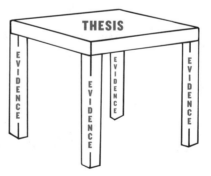

Scientist 1's thesis is that *fireflies use bioluminescence primarily as a means of attracting a mate*. What's her evidence? Her main piece of evidence is the observation that fireflies emit certain pulses only in the mating season. Thus, she believes we can conclude that their lights are used for mating.

Scientist 2's thesis is that *we cannot know the purpose of bioluminescence unless we inhabit the mind of the firefly.* He supports this conclusion by presenting a phenomenon (a firefly lighting up when shaken), then giving a number of conflicting explanations (fear, anger, anxiety) in order to invalidate all of them.

Now, if we only get this far in analyzing the two arguments, then we are ready to begin tackling the questions. But you might have forgotten one thing: The ACT-bot is a techno-devil that wants to melt your eyes into a delicious dipping sauce for his panini, which are made from your brains and shattered dreams and also focaccia bread. To this end, the ACT-bot is going to ask a number of questions about the *assumptions* of each argument. If you have time, it's useful to try and locate some of those assumptions before heading into the questions.

### Step 3 (Advanced): Can you spot any assumptions?

An assumption is an unstated logical step. Take a look at these two statements:

> The grocery store is selling pastel-colored M&M'S. It must be springtime.

In order for me to conclude that it is springtime, based on my observation of the candy, I am assuming that pastel-colored M&M'S are sold in my grocery store only in springtime. This is not stated, but it must be true in order for the statement to be accurate. The reason we look for assumptions is that assumptions are often the hidden "weak spots" of arguments.

In Scientist 1's passage, we can restate the argument like this:

> Fireflies pulse in a particular way only during mating season. The sole purpose of bioluminescence is to attract a mate.

Here, the assumption is there is no purpose of bioluminescence other than to attract a mate. Why is this a "weak spot"? Because that *assumption* is totally stupid! Bioluminescence might be used

Before the advent of seasonal foods like pastel-colored M&M'S and the Shamrock Shake, people kept track of the year through mathematics and astronomy . . . barbarians!

—Jon

to attract a mate, but that doesn't mean attraction is the *only* purpose. Perhaps bioluminescence has a number of purposes, of which mating is only one. And here's an alternative conclusion: Maybe the fact that a firefly pulses its light in a particular way during mating season is a coincidence. Perhaps it's for something else entirely, like to complain, "Sheesh! All this mating is exhausting."

Locating an assumption in an argument is a great way to find the *weak spots* in an argument. This is a classic move in debate and in logical reasoning. It's one of the reasons why this section is more of a *reasoning* test than a science test.

Let's restate Scientist 2's argument:

> We cannot know what the firefly is thinking. We cannot know the purpose of bioluminescence.

So does the first sentence *necessarily* imply the conclusion? Nope! The author is *assuming* that the firefly has direct, conscious control of its butt lights. But isn't it possible that the butt lights *do* have a purpose, regardless of what the firefly is thinking?

Now that we've located the assumptions for both arguments, we're prepared to move swiftly through the questions.

The most basic type of question will ask you about something one scientist said:

1. Scientist 2 would most likely agree that the patterns on the fur of a fox are evidence of:
    A.  nothing more than the random outcome of chance.
    B.  an adapted trait, helpful for camouflage.
    C.  an inherited trait, useful for maintaining warmth.
    D.  proof of Darwin's theory of evolution.

Knowing that Scientist 2 is opposed to interpreting biological traits as evolutionarily beneficial, we can only go with answer choice A.

Other questions will ask you to think about how one author would disagree or agree with the other.

2. Scientist 1 might respond to Scientist 2's claim that we can never know the intent behind an insect's behavior by saying that:

   A. the primitive brain structure of insects makes them an easier subject of psychological study.

   B. observing behavior patterns allows scientists to draw conclusions about behaviors independent of any intent.

   C. Scientist 2 lacks the imagination necessary to think like an insect.

   D. Scientist 2 is essentially correct.

The trick here is to pick the answer that not only best responds to Scientist 2's point, but the one that is most similar to Scientist 1's argument. Because Scientist 1 makes her point about insect behavior with reference to an observation, answer choice B is the closest to her argument.

Another popular question type introduces new evidence and questions how the authors would react. These questions are often secretly testing the *assumptions* in each argument.

3. Recently, scientists have observed that fireflies make a certain pattern of light pulses only in the presence of certain types of prey. How would Scientists 1 and 2 address this new data?

   A. Scientist 1 would reject the observations as faulty; Scientist 2 would claim that the data proves his conclusion.

   B. Scientist 1 would test to see if mates were also present during these pulses; Scientist 2 would accept the conclusion that bioluminescence calls attention to prey.

   C. Scientist 1 would claim that the data proves her conclusion; Scientist 2 would claim that no conclusions could be made regarding the purpose of the light pattern.

The worst mistake to make is to mix up the two scientists. Doing so would make choice D seem incorrect and choice A seem more viable.

—Jon

**D.** Scientist 1 would consider allowing for more than one purpose for bioluminescence; Scientist 2 would claim that no conclusions could be made regarding the purpose of the light pattern.

The question gets at one of the assumptions of Scientist 1: that the bioluminescence can have only *one* primary function. This data would force her to allow for more than one function. Scientist 2, however, could continue to write off the data, claiming that no amount of observation can get at the purpose behind a behavior. Answer choice D, then, is correct.

And that's all you need to know!

We're almost over and out for the Science section. The two most important things to remember are: 1.) Skip and come back—if a quick glance at a passage makes you want to stab yourself with your pencil, move on to the next one, then come back. Do the easier passages first. 2.) Take your time figuring out the passages, then move quickly through the questions.

Our last, essential piece of advice is to *practice, practice, practice*. Unlike every other section of the ACT, the Science Reasoning Test is nothing like your school homework. In order to get used to this section of the test and to build up speed, there is no better strategy than to take a lot of practice Science Reasoning sections. And, as always, the best place to find Science Reasoning sections is in real tests in the *The Real ACT Prep Guide*.

## It's Party Time, Science Style

Guess what, Science Master (who is actually just a Reasoning Master who is no longer afraid of scary science words)? You're done with this section! It's time to CELEBRATE! Try out these fun (and very scientific) experiments.

- Go to the zoo. There's a lot of science happening at the zoo. Plus, they have Dippin' Dots, the most scientific form of ice cream.
- Find the Higgs boson.* Win the Nobel Prize in physics. Go on a date, and wear the Nobel Prize on a chain around your neck so your date knows the caliber of person he's dealing with.
- Invent time travel. Go to the year 2437, and fling a cream pie in the face of the first person you see in a jet pack. Yell, "THAT'S FROM THE PAST!!!" and dash back to our time. The future just got so burned! Oh, and pick up the cures to all of our diseases, if you pass them on your escape dash.
- Crossbreed a horse and an eagle, duh. Why has this not been done yet?

*You *do* know what the Higgs boson is, right? What? You *don't?* Yo, Marty, get a load of this reader—doesn't know the Higgs boson! I know! I can't believe it, either. I gotta text my cousin, this is classic!

# The Writing Test

## What's One More Section Among Friends?

*The Writing Test always comes at the end, and it is made of chocolate.*

## How Optional Is Optional?

You know what we like to do after a three-plus hour exam? We like to yawn, stretch out our arms, fix the cricks in our backs, and settle down to a soothing 30-minute essay. After all, there's nothing to take the edge off a test like more test, right?

Both the SAT and the ACT added essays to their tests a few years ago. The SAT made the essay mandatory, while the ACT called its Writing Test "optional." Now, if you were given the option of more test or less test, what would you choose? If you said "more test," then you're just trying to impress us, which is silly because we can't hear you. No, the obvious answer is "less test, please."

But here's the thing: The Writing Test is not that optional at all. If you are applying to a liberal arts college, it is *very* likely that the college is going to require that you take the Writing Test. Even if the college *doesn't* ask for the test, you're going to be applying alongside a lot of students who certainly *did* take the extra section. In comparison, you're going to look lazy. So, for the sake of your sanity, just proceed as if the Writing Test is mandatory.

## How the Test Works

*I actually got a prompt about fast food.*

*—Jon*

In the 30 minutes of the Writing Test, you will be asked to respond to a prompt that the ACT-bot considers "relevant to high schoolers." This means you will be presented with an issue that concerns school or driving or the Internet or curfews or Facebook or tweeting or playing Skrillex too loud while your parents are trying to get a good night's sleep, dag-nab-it! Well, probably not those last three things.

You will be asked to take a position on the issue and defend your position using examples in an organized, clear, concise essay.

Once you've written your organized, clear, concise essay,

## Your Writing Score

For a refresher on how your Writing Test score works with your English Test score, see page 25.

it will be sent off to two readers. These readers will glance at your essay for 37 seconds. It will be the 258th essay they've read since lunch. While they read it, *The Real Housewives of Atlanta* will be playing in the background. (Well, at least metaphorically.) The readers each will give the essay a score between 1 and 6. The two readers' scores will be combined to give you a grade out of 12. If their scores differ by more than one point, the essay will be sent to a third reader, who will determine the final score while watching *I Didn't Know I Was Pregnant* on the Discovery Channel. (Again, metaphorically.)

The essays are graded "holistically." This means that the readers don't take off points every time you do something wrong, or add points every time you do something right. Rather, they read the entire essay and then give an overall score.

The readers will be "holistically" impressed by five very specific things. In order of importance, they are:

1. A clear thesis
2. Specific examples or arguments that prove your thesis
3. An organized essay, with an intro, three body paragraphs, and a conclusion
4. No digressions or lost focus
5. Proper style and diction

What this means is that it is far more important to have a clear thesis that you back up with cogent examples than it is to write gracefully, and an organized essay is going to score better than a beautifully written but disorganized essay. It's also important to note that the readers do **not** give you points for being brilliant or insightful or original. (It doesn't *hurt* to be brilliant, but searching for a brilliant idea is almost guaranteed to be a waste of precious time.)

The best way to write a well-organized essay with a clear thesis is to follow our patented Five-Step Guide to Writing a Powerhouse Essay.

# Patented Five-Step Guide*

This bears repeating. Answer the actual question.

—Zack

## Step 1: Read the prompt (1 to 2 minutes).

Duh, right? But here's the thing: It is very common for otherwise smart kids to misinterpret the prompt and write about something *close* to the subject. This can be disastrous, as writing about an even slightly different topic can chop off half your points!

Read the following:

> A computer scientist claimed that recent advances have brought us to the point where computer programs can "teach" subjects as effectively as, if not more effectively than, flesh-and-blood teachers. These programs, she argued, can give students the one-on-one attention and personalized instruction that they cannot receive in a traditional classroom. She has gone so far as to recommend that traditional schools be replaced by "Terminal Stations," where students will sit at individual computer terminals to receive instruction throughout the school day.
>
> Defenders of the traditional school model argue that this kind of instruction can never surpass that of a real teacher. Computers, the traditionalists hold, will never be capable of "reading" their students or discerning their particular academic, emotional, and social needs in the way that an experienced teacher can.
>
> Would you convert your school into a Terminal Station? Why or why not?

This prompt is asking for your position on computer-based, one-on-one instruction. But be careful! If you were to write an essay defending the use of computers in school, you would *sort of* be responding to the prompt, but not exactly. The prompt is specifically asking for your opinion on changing your school to a computer-*only* model.

*Okay, it's not patented. But stealing the idea would be rude.

*Once you've written your thesis, to make sure you've actually answered the prompt, reread the question (usually the last sentence of the prompt) and then read your thesis to confirm that it really makes sense as a response.*

*—Jon*

Before you start thinking about arguments and positions, in other words, you need to make sure you've pinpointed *exactly* what the prompt is asking you to consider.

## Step 2: Brainstorm examples or reasons and create a thesis (3 minutes).

What is a thesis? It is your *main idea,* your two-second response to the question. Let's say we give you the prompt, "Would you like extra melted cheese injected into your enchilada?" Your thesis would be: "I *would* like extra melted cheese injected into my enchilada." Your supporting reasons would be: "I like hot cheese in all my food," and "Enchiladas always need more cheese," and finally, "Me want cheese now for my mouth."

So that's what we should do here, right? Create a thesis, and then come up with three reasons or examples to support our thesis? *No, Cheese-Freak!*

*Before* you pick your thesis, you should brainstorm as many arguments as you can that are related to the prompt. Why? Because if you think of your arguments first, *then* create a thesis, you ensure that your thesis applies to all of your arguments. If you were to go the other way and create a thesis first, you would risk digressing from your main point as you create your arguments. So think about reasons and examples *first.*

The best way to brainstorm is to create a pro–con T-chart, like the one on the next page. On the pro side of the chart we list reasons or examples that support the "Terminal Station" model of school, and on the con side we list reasons or examples that oppose the model. The trick here is to go for quantity over quality. We want to quickly list as many things as we can. Why? Because if you tell your brain to think of only good ideas, it will get nervous under pressure. Tell your brain to relax and let it all out, and the outpouring of ideas will contain some gems among all the crap.

As you brainstorm, it is crucial to remember that this essay is not about intelligence or cleverness but about clarity. ✳ Your ideas do not need to be terribly original or exciting; they just have to make good sense to you. We like to put a "?" next to our flimsier ideas.

✳ You thought this exam tested intelligence? How silly . . .

—Ava

## TERMINAL STATION

| PRO | CON |
|---|---|
| 1. Personalized instruction | 1. Computer might not be as skilled at finding out *why* you are not learning |
| 2. Less distraction from other kids in class | 2. Teachers are easier to trick (?) |
| 3. Computers are fun (?) | 3. Some students learn best from working with other students |
| 4. Less social pressure/ academic anxiety | 4. Less risk of robot apocalypse (?) |
| 5. Help build computer literacy | 5. An important part of school is learning to socialize and work together |
| 6. All-day access to YouTube videos (?) | 6. Might be too expensive to install a Terminal Station |
| 7. Could be better suited to handicapped/ blind/learning disabled students | 7. Easier to insult a teacher than a computer (?) |

As you generate ideas, you will almost certainly find that you are leaning more to one side than the other. Pick the side you want to argue. Then, pick two of your juciest ideas from your side. Next—and here is the brilliant part of our strategy—pick one idea from the *opposing* side that you feel you can argue against. Why? Because defending your argument *against* the opposing side ultimately reinforces your argument. (We will talk more about this in a moment.)

So, here we've decided to argue in favor of the "Terminal Station." We'll write about "Personalized instruction" and "Less social pressure/academic anxiety" to support our side. Then, we're going to defend our point by arguing *against* the idea that "An important part of school is learning to socialize and work together."

Now that we've chosen our key points, we need to create our general thesis, or main idea. The thesis needs to do two things:

1. It needs to be broad enough to include all of our reasons. If our thesis was "The Terminal Station is better because it makes students more comfortable," this would cover *one* of our reasons but not all of them. It needs to cover everything we're saying.

2. The thesis needs to directly respond to the prompt. If our thesis is "It is important for students to feel comfortable in school," then this would not directly respond to the prompt, which is about the creation of Terminal Stations.

Here's our thesis:

> Building a Terminal Station will provide a more personalized and comfortable environment, so students will be able to achieve more than they would in a traditional school.

That's a pretty broad but also pretty clear thesis that definitely responds to the prompt and definitely includes both of our arguments in support of Terminal Stations. We know we will not deviate from that thesis in the course of this essay.

With some prompts, it might seem difficult or illogical to completely support one side and completely oppose the other, as both sides have merit, but it is _best_ to exclusively take one side for such a short essay. Attempting to qualify both risks making you sound wishy-washy or disorganized.

—Jon

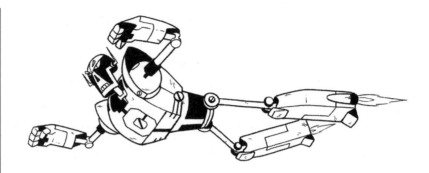

\* Creative organization is to be avoided. Remember, the ACT-bot hates creativity and originality and emotions and the human spirit and all kinds of baby animals.

—Jon

\*\* Oh, those hedonistic Roaring Twenties and their seven-paragraph essays.

—Zack

## Step 3: Sketch out a brief outline (2 to 3 minutes).

When the ACT-bot says that it is looking for an "organized essay," it is using robo-code to say that it wants a five-paragraph essay, with an introduction, three body paragraphs, and a conclusion.\* Now, perhaps you haven't read a classic five-paragraph essay since sixth grade, much less written one. They might seem a little simplistic to you. But you should know that the five-paragraph essay is an essential part of our history. When the U.S. forces stormed the beaches at Normandy, for example, they breached the German bunkers by huddling in hastily constructed trenches and writing five-paragraph essays. And remember when we landed on the moon, narrowly beating out the Soviet space program and ensuring our continued dominance during the Cold War? Do you know how we did that? That's right: by writing a five-paragraph essay. And have you heard of the Great Depression? Do you know the main cause of that catastrophic economic failure? The main cause was that we didn't write enough five-paragraph essays.\*\* So think twice before you scoff. In fact, think five times, once for each paragraph of the unbelievably important five-paragraph essay.

Moving on, there are a number of ways to write a successful five-paragraph essay, but we're going to stick to the *best* way, which involves writing a quick outline. It should be constructed like this:

1. Introduction: Just write your thesis statement here.
2. First body paragraph: This should be the first example arguing your point.
3. Second body paragraph: This should be the second example arguing your point.
4. Third body paragraph: Present an argument against your point, then *crush* it.
5. Conclusion: Just write the word "Conclusion," as this is going to be a simple restatement of your thesis.

Here's our brief outline:
1. *Thesis*: The creation of Terminal Station–style schools will create a more personalized and comfortable environment.
2. Computer terminals can respond to the particular weaknesses and strengths of a student, while a teacher has to "teach to the middle."
3. Being one-on-one with a computer will allow students to learn without the anxiety of having to speak in front of peers or a live teacher. This will create an environment with less social and academic pressure.
4. Some might argue that schools are also places for socializing. But there are plenty of other places where students can socialize, like in parks, on playing fields, etc.
5. Conclusion.

After you've sketched out an outline, run a check: Does it have one clear thesis? Does each paragraph help to prove the thesis? Is each paragraph making one *and only one* point? If your outline accomplishes all these things, then you're ready to write.

"Wait one second," you might be objecting. "That would take a whole six or seven minutes just to *plan* the essay. I only have 30 minutes total. That seems like too much planning!"

Excellent objection! But, here's the deal: Writing a 30-minute essay is a very different activity from writing a normal essay for school. When you're writing a normal essay, you are given much more time and are expected to write something *interesting* and *insightful.* That's an entirely different goal from the 30-minute essay, in which you are expected to write something *organized* and *clear.* This makes *planning* the 30-minute essay *the most important part* of writing the essay.

One of the biggest mistakes test takers make on the Writing Test is starting to write as soon as the proctor says "begin." We understand the impulse: Everyone around you is writing. By the five-minute mark your neighbors might have written a full page. But this almost always leads to the same result: The essay opens with a vague, open-ended thesis, then gets sharper and smarter as one example follows the next. This is because the writers are *thinking while they write.* By the time they get to the conclusion, they have a real thesis, but it is somewhat different from the vague thesis in their introduction. If you think while you write, in other words, your essay undergoes slight but noticeable changes that will end up costing you a lot of points. Instead, you need to *think first, then write.*

The other advantage of taking the time to plan is that you *get your thinking out of the way.* If you spend five or six minutes reading the prompt and brainstorming and planning, then you can spend the next 24 or 25 minutes focusing only on *clarity* and proper writing style. This is a huge benefit.

Think about it this way. Let's say you're walking down the street and you see Ryan Gosling. There are two ways this can play out:

> **Scenario 1:** You run up to the Gos. You say: "Oh my God. Oh my God. You're—I mean, you know who you are, obviously. But, oh my God. Okay. Sorry. So here's the—I mean—I just—You're really talented and handsome and— ANYWAY! I'm rambling, sorry. Here's the thing:

Will you marry me?" He smiles politely, shakes your hand, makes a jokey, charismatic refusal, and walks away.

**Scenario 2:** You take a moment and gather your thoughts. Ryan Gosling is a talented actor whose intelligence and maturity are evident in every role he plays. He is not yet married; you are not yet married. It would be pleasant to marry each other. You walk up to Ryan Gosling and calmly say, "Ryan Gosling, you are a talented actor whose intelligence and maturity are evident in every role you play. You are not yet married; neither am I. It would be pleasant to marry each other." He will consider this organized and persuasive argument and agree to marry you.

Get it? Planning is key.

## Step 4: Write the essay (22 minutes).

We know what we're going to say; all that's left to do is write it down. Let's take this paragraph by paragraph.

The **introduction** is a source of great confusion for a lot of test takers. In school, the introduction can be used for all sorts of purposes: to establish the tone, excite the reader, or pose a question, or all of the above. In the 30-minute essay, however, you are going to do only two things: 1.) Summarize the issue, and 2.) State your thesis. That's it! Here is ours:

Schools now face a choice between having computers teach students one-on-one, or sticking with a traditional teacher-and-classroom setup. While it might seem like a strange or even frightening idea, replacing classrooms and teachers

* This works for me every time I see him.
—Zack

You're not supposed to write a masterpiece. You're supposed to write a coherent, put-together essay.
—Ava

with computer-based Terminal Stations will create a more personalized and comfortable environment for learning.

And that's it! No fancy stuff here—just present the issue *in one sentence*, then state the thesis *in one sentence.*

"Hold the phone," you might be saying. "I can write only a two-sentence introduction? What happens if I write three sentences?"

The same thing that happens if you snitch on a Mexican drug cartel: You get buried up to your neck in the desert and your face gets covered in honey. The honey attracts fire ants, which slowly eat your face. Seriously, though, it is almost guaranteed that your third sentence is wasting precious time and space. If your thesis takes two sentences to explain, then it is too ambitious for a 30-minute essay.

In our first body paragraph, we have three jobs: Introduce a specific example or reason, explain the specific example or reason, then show how our specific example or reason proves our thesis. Why did we write "specific" three times? *Because your example or reason needs to be specific!* To the judges, specific examples or reasons are the second most important element of your essay, after a clear thesis. What do we mean by specific? Well, let's compare and contrast two different versions of our first body paragraph:

### [1]

A computer is better than a teacher at providing instruction to each individual student. When working with a computer, a student automatically has his or her work checked as soon as it is complete. Because spotting errors and reteaching is an essential element of teaching, we can say that a computer, which checks every problem as soon as it is completed, would be a better teacher than a live teacher in a classroom setting.

[2]

A computer is better than a teacher at providing instruction to each individual student. If a student is studying fractions, for example, and forgets to find a common denominator before adding or subtracting, a properly programmed computer would catch the error as soon as it is made and show the rule again. The computer could then give the student more fraction problems to make sure he or she has corrected the bad habit. A teacher, attending to all of the students in her class, could not be expected to catch that kind of error and provide new problems as quickly. All in all, a student in a traditional classroom is more likely to leave the class with a crucial gap in his math knowledge. Because spotting errors and reteaching is an essential element of teaching, we can say that a computer, which checks every problem as soon as it is completed, would be a better teacher than a live teacher in a classroom setting.

Both of the paragraphs have the same introduction, and they have the same concluding sentence. Their style and level of diction (word choice) is at the same level. But that second paragraph is clearer and more interesting because it has a specific example, so the reader can "see" what we are talking about. This is going to get us a higher score, and it's also just better writing.

We rinse and repeat for the second body paragraph, which we will skip here (because we know you have other homework, plus, you've got that horse and eagle gene-splicing project to work on). Let's take a look at our third body paragraph, in which we present an argument *against* our thesis, then smash it to pieces with our gigantic brain-hammers.

First off, why are we doing this? Well, have you ever watched adults argue at a dinner party? If not, sneak into a dinner party and check it out. You'll see that there are two types of arguers. The first, less impressive type, is the arguer who says, "Broccoli is for wimps!" If someone responds, "But broccoli is healthy," he will answer by slamming his fist on the table and shouting, "I don't care! Broccoli is for wimpy snotty wimps and I hate them and I hate broccoli!" (Most dinner parties are like this when you grow up.) ✳

But then there is the more impressive type of arguer. She will start the same way: "Broccoli is for wimps." Before anyone else can respond to this, she will continue: "Now, some of you might say that broccoli is healthy. And while this might be true, it is beside the point, because we all agree that being a healthy wimp is far worse than being an unhealthy but powerful, cool person." Everyone at the table will think that this second arguer is far more intelligent, perceptive, and thoughtful than the first arguer. And no one will eat broccoli at that dinner party.

In other words, it makes you sound wicked smart to anticipate a counterargument and defeat it. But be careful: You have to make it very clear at the beginning of the paragraph that you are presenting a counterargument. You don't want to confuse the reader! Let's try this out:

> Defenders of the traditional-school model might argue that a Terminal Station would not give students enough time to socialize. They might point out that schools are not just places where students learn academics, but also where they learn to work together, create friendships, and handle conflicts. Traditionalists may worry that a student who attends a Terminal Station school risks graduating at 18 without the social abilities necessary to handle job interviews or the workplace. While these folks are correct to say

✳ This is how dinner parties with my brother have been for the past twelve years. . . .

—Zack

Before you present the counterargument, make sure you know how to crush it. You don't want to find yourself halfway through the paragraph realizing that all you've written is a great example in support of the other side.

—Jon

that social skills are important, they forget that children can learn social skills in many other ways. Children can meet, play, and work together in the park; they can engage in after-school activities like team sports, chess clubs, and student newspapers, or do weekend community-service projects. Because the Terminal Station model does not take up all of their day, students will find plenty of time to socialize elsewhere.

Notice how we used phrases like "defenders . . . might argue," "they might point out," and "traditionalists may worry" to make sure that the reader knows we are presenting a counterargument and not our own point of view. We also tried to be as specific as possible, giving our example of the 18-year-old graduate. Finally, we made our devastating blow by allowing them some credit (they are correct to point to the necessity of a social education), but then showing why their point was essentially mistaken (there is plenty of time to socialize outside of school). Altogether, this kind of paragraph will make you look very, very clever indeed.

Finally, the conclusion should be as short and sweet as the introduction. Restate your thesis and "wrap it up" by answering the question: Why is this topic important? Here's ours:

> While it might seem shocking at first, it is clear that computerized one-on-one teaching provides greater educational benefits than traditional teacher-and-classroom models. Because education creates the next generation, we should always be looking for ways to improve it.

All we did was restate our thesis in different words, then say why it is important. Done and done.

### Step 5: Edit your essay (I to 2 minutes).
Take your last minute or so to review the essay, to make sure it

* "Misspellings" and "egregious": two words that you are allowed to misspell in your essay.

—Ava

reads clearly and succinctly. (Sometimes when we're rushing, we repeat ourselves.) Also look out for misspellings and grammatical errors. Bear in mind though, the readers will not deduct points for misspellings and errors unless they are so egregious * that they get between the reader and the meaning of the essay.

This is also a great time to check to make sure you aren't using the same word or phrase over and over. In our essay, for example, we used the phrase "teacher-and-classroom" more than once. We might want to switch to either "traditional classroom" or "teacher-led classes." Remember that it is fine to erase words and rewrite; just make sure that your essay is legible when you are done.

## But What If I Can't Write Five Paragraphs in 30 Minutes?

** Yes, you must use an egg timer. Other timers simply do not contain enough egg.

—Ava

Once you've practiced fully planning out your essay *before* you write, you should find that the actual writing moves a *lot* faster. After all, you don't have to pause to think! But the main way to get yourself up to five paragraphs in 30 minutes is to practice. Set yourself up at a desk with an egg timer ** and *The Real ACT Prep Guide*, which has actual ACT essay prompts. Cut this out and pin it up near your desk:

---

### Essay Schedule

1. Read the prompt (1 to 2 minutes).
2. Brainstorm and create thesis (3 minutes).
3. Sketch a brief outline (2 to 3 minutes).
4. Write the essay (22 minutes).
   A. Intro: 4 minutes
   B. Each body paragraph: 5 minutes
   C. Conclusion: 3 minutes
5. Edit (1 to 2 minutes).

---

Select a prompt and follow the above steps. When you're done with the essay, give it to someone to read. It doesn't matter if the person has no experience grading short essays; he or she just needs to be able to tell you whether your thesis is clear and the essay is organized.<sup>*</sup> You should start feeling comfortable with the process after you've written three to five practice essays.

But for some writers, 30 minutes is never going to be enough time.

You can stay safe by keeping your eye on the clock. Try to get through at least the introduction and two body paragraphs in 25 minutes. When you hit that 25-minute mark, leave some space and write a conclusion, then come back and finish whatever you were working on. You **absolutely need a conclusion,** as readers may take multiple points away if you don't have one. They will likely say that your essay is incomplete, improperly organized, and doesn't have a clear thesis, all because you didn't have a conclusion.

> ✳ That said, there's a good chance your English teacher would be willing to read it, if you ask nicely.
>
> —Zack

> Having a conclusion is worth more than having three body paragraphs. Get it done.
>
> —Ava

## Let's Get Fancy: Advanced Moves

**C**larity and organization will get you to the shores of Lake Success, but to dive in, you'll need to really impress the reader with some advanced writing techniques.

The first move is to **vary your sentences.**<sup>**</sup> Beginning-to-intermediate writers tend to develop sentence structures that feel familiar and "safe." But reading the same kind of sentence over and over puts the brain to sleep. Mix it up! If you've just written a longer sentence with a number of clauses and a semicolon, wake up the writer by following it up with a short, punchy declarative sentence. Read this paragraph:

> Legal reforms in the field of criminal justice are often slow and beset on all sides by critics, administrative disregard, and systematic lassitude. The lawyers of the Branfort Legal Aid Society,

> ✳✳ The way Miley Cyrus varies her hairstyles or Taylor Swift varies her boyfriends.
>
> —Jon

however, are seeking to change things with their vigor, their legal acuity, and their basic effectiveness.

The pattern of these two sentences, when reduced to its basic building blocks, is the same: "Nouns are adjective and adjective and adjective." That's why you fell asleep when you read it. But we can wake up the reader by throwing in a spicy little sentence:

Legal reforms in the field of criminal justice are often slow and beset on all sides by critics, administrative disregard, and systematic lassitude. But the lawyers of the Branfort Legal Aid Society want to change all this. Their vigor, legal acuity, and basic effectiveness are a challenge to the status quo.

In other words, turning that last sentence into two shorter sentences made the whole paragraph "punchier." This small change can lift your essay from a smart, clear, well-organized, and boring essay into one that is a lot more readable.

It is also helpful to impress the reader by throwing in some $10 or $15 words. In our paragraphs about legal reforms, for example, we used "lassitude" instead of "laziness," and we said "acuity" instead of "accuracy." Those two words alone made our paragraph sound "smarter" and "more adult," two qualities that tend to push the reader's score from a 5 to a 6. And how are you going to learn these $15 words? With your *weekly reading habit*, duh! (Don't remember your weekly reading habit? See page 243.) But be careful: Don't use a $10 word that you do not understand, or you will look pretentious and ill-informed. In other words, you'll sound like a real Falangist.*

Finally, a great essay has a clear voice. This means that the essay sounds like it is being spoken by a real person, albeit a grammatically advanced and very thoughtful person. Small flourishes of humor, unique turns of phrase, or even eccentric and engaging examples all communicate voice. Your voice, in other

* We have no idea what this means. Oh wait, we just looked it up and it means "fascist," so you REALLY don't want to sound like a Falangist.

A good voice is one that seems genuinely _interested_ in the topic being discussed. However, some topics are very difficult to immerse oneself in (like legal reforms), which means you'll have to use another Reading section strategy: Pretend. Just as you pretend to be interested in what you're reading, you should pretend to be interested in what you're writing.

—Jon

## How Do You Get to Carnegie Hall?

words, is your particular style. But we need to be careful with voice. Throwing in a bunch of "ain'ts" and contractions ("they're," "you've," etc.) and goofy zingers is more likely to lower your score than raise it.

The way we like to think about voice is by asking the question: Are you writing what you honestly think, or are you trying to please your readers? Don't make the mistake of writing what you think they want to hear. If so, it is more likely that you are using words that you think they approve of and writing ideas that you think are acceptable, which is all going to make you sound like a machine. And because this section is read by humans, you do not necessarily want to sound like a machine. But if you are writing honestly and trying to communicate something that you find interesting and valid, then your voice will shine through. Now, this might be too much to ask in a 30-minute essay, but if you practice enough to get comfortable with this format, then the next step is to work on writing with a confident, honest voice. Here's an example:

**LESS INTERESTING:** The increasingly competitive environment of college admissions requires that students achieve higher scores on standardized tests.

**MORE INTERESTING:** While my dad likes to tell stories of waking up, rubbing the sleep out of his eyes, and taking the ACT, that is simply no longer possible. Today, students are logging many hours each week studying for standardized tests. Using the "dad method" these days is like committing academic suicide.

By now you know what we're going to suggest as a next step— _and_ the answer to this question: Practice, practice, practice. We've already recommended that you take a look at _The Real ACT Prep Guide_, which has actual prompts from old tests. But here are some ACT-like prompts that you can also use to write practice essays. **Read these only when you're ready to time yourself and write for 30 minutes.**

1. Some high schools have recently experimented with paying their students for achieving high grades. Proponents of this model argue that the incentive, though not necessarily noble, effectively encourages students who otherwise see little reason to perform academically. Others argue that the model fails to teach students the values of hard work, dedication, and taking pride in their intellect. Should schools pay students for high grades?

2. A New York State Supreme Court judge recently ruled against a proposal to limit the size of soft drinks that city residents could purchase. Supporters of scaling down sodas argued that large soft drinks are contributing to an escalating obesity epidemic. Nobody needs 32 ounces of soda, they said, and removing the option would make it easier for people to regulate their sugar intake. Opponents of the proposal claimed that people could make their own choices. Soda, they argued, is not like alcohol or cigarettes. People do not get addicted to soda, nor does soda consumption pose any risk to anyone other than the consumer. What do you think? Should states or cities limit the size of sodas and other high-sugar beverages?

3. Recent military-style video games—games in which the player assumes the role of a soldier in a battlefield situation—have included advertisements for the U.S. Army. Critics argue that this practice tricks impressionable young people into joining the army by capitalizing on the thrill of simulated violence. Others claim that placing advertisements in video games is no better or worse than placing them on television. Should the Army be allowed to place ads in military-style video games?

Even though the ACT graders aren't supposed to consider handwriting, if you have atrocious handwriting, it <u>will</u> distract and frustrate them. Good handwriting will subconsciously improve the reader's opinion of your essay before he or she even starts to read it.

—Jon

4. Many school districts place police officers with the power to arrest and charge students in high schools. Los Angeles, for instance, has more school safety officers than many cities have regular police officers. While some argue that these officers make schools safer and reduce the rates of truancy, vandalism, and violence, others say that these officers escalate disciplinary events into criminal events, and can engender resentment among the students against the police force. Do you think that police officers should be placed in high schools?

5. A high school teacher in Missouri was criticized by the PTA last year for showing four films in a literature class entitled "The 19th-Century Novel." Parents argued that the point of a literature class is to expose students to written works. The teacher argued that showing and discussing the movie versions was a great way to analyze contemporary attitudes toward older works. Do you think that it is appropriate to show movies in a literature class?

Once you've written out a response to some of these prompts, show them to an adult (or a super-smart friend). Ask your reader to respond to the essays by looking for clarity, a consistent and well-argued thesis, and relevant examples.

Congratulations, you've finished the Writing chapter and—if you've read the book in order—*every single test-section chapter*! Amazing! You're a champ. Gold medal and trophy to come, we promise.

So . . . are we done here?

Friend, we are *so close* to done. But here's the thing: Sometimes the actual day of the test can present its own curveballs. So in order to be totally and completely prepared, let's talk about the final 24 hours.

# Countdown to Test Day

## The Final 24 Hours

*"Just one REM cycle. One itty-bitty REM cycle. Please, sleep gods!"*

## The 18th Hole

Tomorrow is test day.

You've done all the work you can do. You've read this entire book. You've ingested all of the rules, the explanations, the practice questions, and the many references to Mountain Dew Code Red and Double Stuf Oreos. You've taken to heart Jon's pearls of wisdom, Ava's thoughtful insights, and Zack's trenchant musings. And that's not all: You've logged so many hours reading *Harper's* and *Scientific American* that you wake yourself up thinking about education reform. You've upped your mental math game and you can now calculate sales tax in nine states as soon as you see a price tag. You've honed your grammar skills to the point where you can chide William Faulkner for his run-on sentences (gently, of course, and using a Ouija board), and you're so good at reading the stories in data charts that you're starting to find nutrition labels thrillingly dramatic. You've done countless practice tests with all of our advice rattling around your brain till it's become second nature. You have a PhD in skipping and coming back. Your score has improved, on some tests, by a whopping six points.

Wow!

That's a life-altering improvement. If you can get that high of a score on your ACT, you might get in to IU or NYU or BU or U of T or UCSB or UCLA or MIT—or some other equally impressive combination of letters! And after four years at that college, you could be well on your way to . . . *greatness*. The kind of greatness that means a separate mansion to visit when you're bored of your regular mansion. The kind of fame that will require hiring a ghostwriter to manage your Twitter account.

But wait a minute. That's a lot of pressure. You've got a lot— *a lot*—riding on this outcome. What if you choke?

Well, if you've worked as hard and effectively as the student we just described, you have little to fear. Your nervous energy will transform into a laserlike focus on test day.

But what if you *haven't* worked that hard or effectively?

We know you're human. You may not have busted 100 percent of your tush and despite our best efforts to lay out the process as clearly as possible, experience tells us that, even if you've worked  very, very hard, you still may not have absorbed *all* the advice contained in this book. So you might be feeling a touch of *fear*, a flutter of *anxiety*, as you prepare to go human-toe-to-metal-toe against the ACT-bot.

What if you fail?

## I ♥ Failure

We mentioned this earlier, but it's worth repeating one of the greatest advantages the ACT enjoys over the SAT: *You can take the ACT many, many times.*

Many colleges still insist on seeing every SAT score you ever get. Not so with the ACT. You can take the ACT a dozen times and the colleges you apply to will only see the score or scores you want to show them. Okay, twelve times is exhausting. But you could comfortably take it four or five or even six times in a period of a year or more.

So go ahead and fail. We mean it.

Because here's the thing: America loves its success stories. The founding fathers succeeded in founding and fathering the nation. Abraham Lincoln led the way in reuniting a war-torn country. But in truth, America is one long story of people *failing*, over and over, and still being hardheaded enough to keep trying until things worked out. Do you know what the founding fathers did at the *First* Continental Congress? NOTHING! They sent a letter to the king saying, "Dear King, Could you, like, *not* coerce us?" And the king wrote back, "Dear Colonies, No. xoxo, The King."

And Abraham *Lincoln*? Here's Abe's biography:

+ Born in a log cabin in Kentucky made out of American flags and bald eagle beaks.

+ Got a job, lost it.
+ Ran for state legislature, lost.
+ Started a business, which failed.
+ Got a girlfriend, who died of fever.
+ Had a nervous breakdown. His doctor said, "Why don't you just stop tryin' stuff?" Abe said, "Why don't *you* give me some smelling salts or whatnot, so I can get back out there and fail some more?"
+ Elected to state legislature. Things were looking up!
+ Nominated to become Speaker of the House. Came in last.
+ Sought nomination for U.S. Congress. Didn't get it.
+ Picked himself up by his bootstraps and ran again for U.S. Congress. Won. Wow!
+ Ran for U.S. Senate. Lost big time.
+ Nominated to run for vice president. Won. Just kidding— of course he lost.
+ Grabbed ahold of those same bootstraps, lifted himself up again, and ran again for U.S. Senate. "Bootstraps, don't fail me now!" he said. His bootstraps failed him and he lost.
+ Got elected president! Hooray!
+ Endured the most grueling presidency in the history of the country.
+ Emancipation Proclamation! Country reunited!
+ Took a night off to relax and take in a popular new play; instead got assassinated.

In Lincoln's life, as in most storied lives, his success was the product of *many, many failures.* Indeed, it could be said (and has been said) that success is nothing more than the ability to fail intelligently; to try, fail, learn from your failure, and try again.

So tap into your American birthright: *Fail! Fail! Fail!*\*

Take the test, mess it up big time. Look at your score breakdown, which will tell you exactly what you need to

\*If you are not an American citizen, you can purchase American Failure at a slightly increased price, due to international tariffs.

study before your next sitting. Take it again and—heck, this is America!—*fail again*. Why not? The point is that as long as you are able to pick yourself up, study harder, take another whirl through this book, and steel yourself for another round with the ACT-bot, you will succeed.

## Okay, nice pep talk, but it's the night before the test. Now what?

The key for Test Day's Eve is to relax. But how? For some folks a candlelit bubble bath with Norah Jones's *Come Away with Me* playing in the background is peace on earth; for others it's a soggy soak in jazz-pop fusion hell. You've got to find what works for you. There are a number of different theories about the best way to unwind on Test Day's Eve. Here are some of the most popular methods:

### THE BUDDHA

Allow all concerns and worries to melt away. If you are finding this difficult, then set up 10 or 11 lava lamps around your room. Light some incense. Download a relaxing playlist (we recommend the classic "Sounds of the Babbling Brook 2: Even More Babbling"), and lounge on your most comfortable pillows. Clear your mind of all thoughts, and picture a family of deer nibbling on some grass. Those deer aren't going to take an ACT. They're just going to nibble away, nibble away, forever. Become the deer. And sleep. (Caution: Be careful not to nibble on the lava lamps, which get extremely hot.)

The Buddha approach worked for me.

—Jon

I didn't listen to "Sounds of the Babbling Brook," but I did chill out the day before the test, and it really paid off.

—Zack

### THE ANTI-BUDDHA

Turn that "Babbling Brook" junk off and crank up some *Rammstein!* Don't *play* the music, *crank* it! Hear that solid wrath flowing out of your speakers? That's 2,000 decibels of Righteous Rage, and if you aren't smashing stuff right now, well, you'd better get with the program, because your room ain't gonna wreck itself! And if you need to take a break from all of the smashing, drop down and do

I'm more of an Anti-Buddha type. I like being busy—doing anything but worrying about the test.

—Ava

a hundred push-ups. Tired? Didn't think so. Give yourself a tattoo of a snake wrestling a lion. Add some flames to it. Add some more flames to it. Ready to get a good night's rest? Didn't think so. If we see a good night's rest, we're gonna smash it! When the sun comes up, lace up your combat boots, *stomp* to the test center (don't forget your admission ticket, though, or your number-2 pencils and calculator, or your official photo ID), and fling open the doors with an almighty wolf-howl. Better yet, ride to the test center on the back of a real wolf. Let the wolf do the howling, because you're busy laying down a sick solo on an electric guitar that's plugged into the sun. Now you're ready to take the test.

## THE GROUPIE

Meet up with some friends to talk out your stress about the ACT. It is an enormous relief to realize that you are not the only person feeling pressure. If your group wants to do some final reviews, or look at some particularly tough math questions, that's fine. But you can also just go down to the river and throw rocks, or you can log on to the website GoDownToTheRiverAndThrowRocks .com to watch videos of other kids throwing rocks. Or, if you feel particularly inspired and angry, you can compose a mean comment to post on the ACT's Facebook page. Better yet, head to *Up Your Score*'s Facebook page (facebook.com/upyourscore) and post stories about your anxiety and frustration, and read the stories of other kids who are in the exact same boat.

**I didn't sleep last night and I feel like garbage.**

Getting little-to-zero sleep, fitful sleep, or even nightmare-filled sleep are all very common experiences on the night before the ACT. You might lay your head on your pillow as you would any other night (or perhaps you went to bed early, to ensure a full night of rest), but after five minutes, you'll start to wonder why you're not falling asleep. You'll tell yourself that sleep

If you're worried about not being able to fall asleep, go to bed early each night the week before the test; that way, when you hit the hay earlier than usual, you won't be wide-awake.

—Jon

\* Yeah, this is important. The anxiety can keep you alert and focused, but you need to direct it.

—Zack

\*\* Discouraged surfaces include busy freeways and airport tarmacs.

—Jon

is *very* important, because you need to be rested for your gigantic, terrifying test the next day. You'll beg and plead with the gods of sleep, asking for just five hours. Then you'll pray for *four* solid hours, or even just one REM cycle. One itty-bitty REM cycle. *Please*, sleep gods!

When you wake up, or when your alarm snaps you out of your anxiety coma, you might not feel so fresh. Don't worry! This is a totally natural way to feel before a test. If you're worried that you are *actually* sick, take your temperature. If it's normal, then you are most likely just suffering from nerves.

The nice thing about test-day anxiety is that, even if it keeps you up the night before the test, it will also keep you wide-eyed and alert *during* the test. \* Test-day anxiety is like a Red Bull that itself just drank a Red Bull. It gives you tonz-o-energy. All you need to do to control your test-day anxiety is to remember to skip and come back, and not to burrow too deeply into a tough problem and lose time. Do this, and you will be fine.

But don't be surprised if, after the test, you collapse on the nearest flat surface and wake up only after a two-day power nap. \*\*

## I'm too nervous to eat.

It is statistically proven that 97 percent of ACT takers who do not eat a hearty breakfast end up consuming more than a third of their test pages. But seriously, you should eat before the test. We recommend food that you can slowly digest throughout the day, providing you with little bursts of energy. Cook up some steel-cut oats. Throw some cinnamon in there, some crushed walnuts. If you've got 'em, toss in some dried cranberries. Dried cranberries never hurt a bowl of oatmeal. Even better, if you are

Even if snacking is forbidden, you can probably slip a hard candy into your mouth.
—Ava

I chew gum constantly during tests. I recommend 5 Cobalt.
—Zack

used to eating breakfast, is to get some protein in your system: meat, eggs, etc. If you're not accustomed to a hearty breakfast, however, don't eat your first on test morning. Your unaccustomed stomach might distract you with complaints about how full it is.

Now, official ACT policy on in-center snacking is a bit of a mystery, but most test centers will allow you to bring a snack to eat outside the testing room during the break (or two breaks, if you are taking the Writing Test). Take advantage of this!

You're definitely going to want a burst of energy between the first and second halves of the test. There are lots of ways to rev yourself up (stapling your thumb will get you going, as will ruminating on the coming global water shortage that will in all likelihood reduce the planet to an apocalyptic desert of roving motorcycle gangs, trading water as cash and killing without scruple). But the quickest and most reliable way is to eat a handful of the following snack.

### GameFace Quintuple-36 Granola-Blast SnakMix

*3 cups granola*
*3 tbsp craisins*
*½ cup chocolate chips*
*½ cup coarsely chopped dried pineapples*
*½ cup coarsely chopped dried apple slices*
*1 York Peppermint Pattie*

**Preparation:**
In large bowl, mix together all the ingredients, except the Peppermint Pattie. The pattie is for you to eat now, because who doesn't enjoy a nice Peppermint Pattie while they're mixing up a tasty bag of granola? Nobody, that's who.

Put the mixture in a Ziploc bag and put it in your backpack to bring to the test center. If the proctor is enforcing a strict no-eating policy, call him a "Rule-Following Rodney" under your sadly granola-free breath.

**I gotta be honest: Despite all the encouragement, I'm still feeling pretty stressed.**

To reduce unnecessary stress, plan to arrive at the test center <u>at least</u> 10 minutes early. You're stressed enough already. No need to pile on by worrying about whether or not you're going to make it on time.

—Jon

Totally natural. Remember that *some* stress is a good thing; it will bring you energy, help you refocus, and light the fire under your derriere. Many test takers get their *best* score on the real test because the heightened stakes make them serious, attentive, and driven.

But there *is* such a thing as too much stress. If you allow your stress to take over, you can land yourself in the panic zone. Here, the stress becomes distracting—even overwhelming—and interferes with your performance.

There are three things you can do if you're worried about panicking. First, try controlling your breathing. Close your mouth, and breathe in through your nose for four seconds. Do this by either counting to four (obvi) or by saying in your mind, "I am in a field with many kind ponies." Then breathe out through your nose for six seconds, or while saying, "And every pony is having a cup of chamomile tea with me." Repeat this until you feel your heart returning to a normal rate. You can also do this during the test, if you feel like stress is starting to distract you. This technique has the added bonus of putting in your head the image of a tea party with ponies, which is scientifically proven to be the most relaxing image in the world.*

Second, you can use positive visualization. Imagine yourself arriving at the test center (which may or may not be your school), presenting your identification, waiting, then being taken to your room. Imagine sitting in the room; hear the distracting hum of the air conditioner; see the kid fidgeting in front of you. Imagine moving through the test question by question, and skipping and coming back on any question that gives you grief. Imagine finishing the test and being able to enjoy the rest of your weekend with the test behind you. It will all be just fine.

Third, remember that in truth the ACT is of minor importance, once you get outside your own head. Sure, you want to do the best you can so you can go to a good college, but there are also oppressed peoples trying to throw off the yoke of tyranny and governments struggling to cleanse themselves of corruption

*Unless you're afraid of ponies and tea, in which case this is probably terrifying.

When I took the ACT, I was worried about a lot of homework that was due the Monday after the test. Try to finish as much schoolwork as you can ahead of time so that the Friday before—and the Sunday after—you can focus on relaxing.

—Jon

and graft and election fraud. There are planets in orbit around the sun. And beyond all this, there are countless other stars, each with their own planets, circling in their own orbits. Somewhere, as you read this, a star is exploding, destroying every planet unfortunate enough to lie in its path. And you're worried about a *test?!?*

Seen from another angle, the ACT is not a big deal even in your *own* life. Honestly, there is nobody, *nobody* who looks back on his or her life and says, "All of my riches, all of my many golden nuggets and delicious pies, I owe to that rockin' ACT score," or the opposite: "That darned ACT is the reason I'm living in this cardboard box suspended by yarn over a pit of spikes and vipers." Nobody has *ever* said either of those things.

Finally, remember what we said at the beginning of this chapter: You can take the ACT as many times as you please. If you mess this up, you can mark it off as a practice test.

## But, but, but . . . what am I going to *wear*?!?

⁎ This is pretty much what you should wear for everything in life. Except weddings. And funerals, maybe.

—Zack

This is a crucial question. The test centers might be air-conditioned to approximate a North Dakota winter, or they might be heated to mimic a sweltering Miami summer. Be prepared for all weather types by wearing a short-sleeved T-shirt under a light long-sleeved shirt and *bringing a sweatshirt.* ⁎ The key here is to bring clothing that is easy on, easy off. Having to struggle out of your full-length Snuggie will cost you valuable time. Plus, you will look like a butterfly hatching from its cocoon and will no doubt attract a swarm of lusty fellow butterflies whose pheromonal mist will only distract you further.

Also, socks are key for an air-conditioned room. Have you ever heard the phrase "I got cold feet"? You know what that refers to? Being distracted during a standardized test by your chilly toes and then shortsightedly chopping them off. We swear that's the origin of the saying.

Finally, wear an easy-to-read watch, to help you keep time. (If

*Find a watch with a timer or chronometer. You won't want to waste valuable seconds trying to figure out how much time you have left.

—Zack

## What about personal grooming?

I also like to take a quick, five-minute jog before I go to the test center just to get my blood flowing.

—Zack

A few sun salutations can be a good thing, too.

—Ava

## My proctor is a bit of a spaz, and I'm worried he's going to mess this up.

you're not generally a watch wearer, place it on your desk.) There is no guarantee that the room will have a clock on the wall, so this is your responsibility. If your watch beeps on the hour or ever, turn that function off, unless you want to get scorched by hate vibes from everyone else in the room. And while we're talking about wrist wear, avoid bangly, jangly bracelets. They will interfere with your bubbling (not to mention irritate your fellow test takers).

Start your day with a shower. It will wake you up, and being clean will make you feel like a competent, put-together person—a good way to feel. We recommend washing and conditioning your hair. Your squeaky-clean, well-conditioned hair will flow and shine so effortlessly that other kids in the room might get distracted and perform poorly, thus improving the curve and, consequently, your score.

And brush your teeth, because c'mon, you're in high school and you should be brushing your teeth. Do whatever it takes to get yourself feeling pulled together. If that means a little makeup or aftershave, do it.

If you like to wear nail polish, try to choose a calming, nondistracting color. We recommend pastels or light colors. Like a pale coral? Or lilac! That'd be nice, right?

Alternatively, a bold, happy color—tangerine? Sunflower?—can be a pick-me-up.

It's a sad fact of the standardized testing world that proctors are sometimes terrible at their jobs. They are given instructions on what constitutes proper identification, how far apart to space seats, and rules for section timing and breaks, but sometimes they do not rigorously follow these instructions.

I had one proctor who told us we would get a five-minute warning, but forgot. I freaked out.

—Zack

We've heard all sorts of stories about proctors mistiming sections, forgetting to grant breaks, rereading rules, giving their opinions ("No, you should never guess," "The answer is almost never C," "A perfect 0 gets you into Super Harvard!"), etc. If you get a terrible proctor, try not to stress over it. It is highly unlikely that the proctor will muddle things so badly that it jeopardizes your test score. The only person who can really screw things up is you. So take the bungling in stride, and move on.

## What about these bubbles? What do I do with them?

Fill them in. Check your sheet *frequently* to make sure you aren't misgridding. Don't be too sloppy. But also don't be obsessive. The scoring machines are good at detecting marks inside the bubble. After all, it is their *only* job and the reason they exist. If they mess it up, they will be destroyed. So just fill in the bubble with three quick back-and-forths of the pencil and move on.

## I think the two kids behind me are cheating; is that . . . can *I* do that?

The best way to avoid the temptation to cheat is just to be so phenomenally well prepared and awesome that you don't need to cheat.

—Jon

Here comes a sad fact: Cheating is becoming more and more rampant every year. In 2011, one high schooler in Long Island, New York, was discovered to have earned thousands of dollars taking SATs for more than 15 students. Interviews with local parents revealed that cheating on the SAT was widely known, and sometimes tacitly encouraged. It would be silly to think that the same thing is not happening on the ACT.

Cheating comes in all shapes and sizes. A student might glance at a partner's answer sheet, or two students might whisper to each other during a test. At particularly lax test centers, it is common to hear students comparing answers during the break, and then going back to old sections to make corrections. Students can also "pull a Long Island" and hire someone to take the test for them.

This is a gigantically lame thing to do. When people cheat on the

Why cheat? You're the most prepared person in the room.

—Ava

ACT, they are creating a fiction that gets them into college (which is bad) and taking the place of someone who deserves to be there (which is terrible). Oh, and that kid from Long Island? He's been charged with several felonies, so while his college dreams might be ruined, his going-to-prison dreams are about to come true!

## I've heard that these tests can be biased; is that true?

There have been far more accusations of unfairness leveled against the SAT than the ACT. But there are people who say that timed, multiple-choice tests are always biased. The argument here is that these types of tests favor men, who have been shown by some researchers to be more comfortable with guessing than women. This is an interesting argument, and if you find it compelling, we recommend that you check out the national organization FairTest (fairtest.org) and get involved—*after you take the test*. Before the test, there's really nothing you can do.

## Alright, I finished the test; now how should I feel?

Exhausted. Your goal during this test is to apply all of your focus, all of your energy, and all of your drive. You want to press on the gas until the tank is empty. If at any point you feel like you are coasting over the problems, tell yourself to get that nose back to the grindstone. By the end of the test, you should have no nose left.

## I'm freaking out. I feel like I messed up. Should I cancel my score?

No! Remember: **You get to choose which scores are sent to colleges.** The ACT allows you to cancel your score (they tell you how on their website), but there is no reason to do this. Wait for your score, and see how you did. If you messed up, you will simply take it again, but in the meantime, use your score report to direct your studying between now and the next test date. In other words, you can mess up without consequence, so don't sweat it!

## So . . . I'm done; I can have fun until college?

To avoid any post-ACT question stress, don't discuss the answers with your friends afterward. It's a waste of time that will probably stress you out in some way. Once you leave the test room, your answer sheet is final, so let it go and move on with your life.

—Jon

After taking a standardized test, you are allowed two days of wild, out-of-control fun. We're talking break-into-the-zoo-type fun; we're talking police-helicopters-filling-the-sky, your-face-on-the-cover-of-every-newspaper-type fun. Okay, not *that* much fun, but you can definitely chill with an eleven-hour *Lord of the Rings* Trilogy: Director's Cut marathon.

But after that, it's time to get back to work.

Unfortunately, there is a *lot* to do to make yourself an attractive candidate for your dream schools. There are a bunch of great books out there that detail the college application process and you've probably heard many opinions from your parents and guidance counselor, but here are the basics:

### GRADES AND CURRICULUM

Consider your grades the foundation of your application. You can have fancy extracurriculars, a couple glowing recommendations, and even a fairly sparkly ACT score, but if your grades are spotty, then all of these things will lose some of their value. Think about your grades as a quick indicator of your commitment to academics. If colleges see enough slippage in your grades, they might doubt your commitment to learning, which, for a college, is a major turnoff. Like the ACT score, you should see this less as a stress than as an opportunity. Even if you've royally messed up your grades in your past, you still have the upcoming semesters to demonstrate improvement. And colleges *love* improvement. If you're a senior and you've already bumbled your junior-year grades, you can still increase your odds by improving your grades now.

## EXTRACURRICULARS

These days, everybody knows that extracurriculars are essential to getting into college. After all, your extracurricular activities are what set you apart from all of the other applicants who have the same grades and ACT score as you. If you are not involved in some extracurricular activity, you need to get involved. Like, now.

But here's what everybody *doesn't* know: Finding *one* activity that you truly care about, and exploring that activity in a number of ways is far more impressive than doing a wide variety of activities. This secret can give you a substantial edge. Think about it from the admissions officer's perspective: More and more students are applying with six to nine extracurriculars on their résumés. While this certainly makes the kid look *busy*, all of those activities kind of blend into one another. In the admissions officer's mind, the kid becomes just another busy kid. But if an application has *one* activity that the kid obviously is invested in and takes seriously, that activity will define the kid and allow him or her to stick out in the admissions officer's mind. A student who not only created a recycling club but also started an awareness campaign that increased recycling in her town by 20 percent, then brought this model to two neighboring towns, is going to leave an impression! So will the student who not only joined the film club but also started a neighborhood film festival, and taught a screenwriting class at a local middle school on Friday afternoons, and applied for a grant to rent film equipment for these students to make their own movies. Get the picture?

## ESSAYS

The other way to make your application stand out is your college essay. Like the ACT, you can choose to look at the essay as a pain-in-the-rump or as an opportunity. This is the one place in your application where you get to speak your mind. Our big recommendation here is to *start early*. The summer before your senior year, you should brainstorm a few ideas and try writing at

---

*Just don't overdo it. Leave time to sleep.*

—Ava

Even your school's Justin Bieber fan club will look impressive if you started it yourself, serve as its president-for-life, and planned a service project that brought His Royal Biebness to your school to play a benefit concert.

—Jon

Get lots of people to read your essays once you're happy with them. Don't work on them obsessively, but revisit them periodically so that you have a fresh perspective every time.

—Zack

least three different essays (now that you're an old hand at writing the five-paragraph essay, this should be no problem). Don't worry about whether they are smart, engaging, or impressive. Just write. The best essays, the ones that really stick out, are the ones in which your honest voice can be heard. Take time to scrape away the baloney and reveal the truth that is in your mind. Don't be afraid of sounding irreverent, strange, or goofy. If anything, these are three qualities that will give your essay *personality*, and that's a great thing. That said, don't *try* to stand out by sounding irreverent or strange or goofy. Admissions officers read thousands of essays, including plenty that are off-kilter or offbeat. What they're looking for is your genuine voice.

## RECOMMENDATIONS

Colleges are going to ask that you provide some recommendations from teachers. There is one right way to do this, and *many wrong ways*. Let's take a look at two popular unsuccessful strategies. Pretend that you are Ms. Bakerfeldt, a Latin teacher.

**Wrong Way 1:** For the past six months, Jen Dwyer has sat at the back of the class with headphones in her ears. When you ask her to remove her headphones, she says, "I'll remove my headphones when you get the (expletive deleted) out of my (expletive deleted) face and go (expletive deleted) (expletive deleted) until the sun comes up." One day, Jen shows up in your office, holding a single carnation. Her headphones are still in her ears. "Hey, Ms. Baker-whatever. Here's a flower. Can you write me a college recommendation?"

**Wrong Way 2:** For the past six months, Chuck Nwenyi has sat in the front row with a big smile on his face. At the end of each class, he says, "Another excellent teaching job, Ms. Bakerfeldt!" Once a month, he shows up at your office with a large cupcake, on which he's written, in icing, "#1 Teacher." Meanwhile, he has never once raised his hand in class, and his homework seems rushed. You've asked him on multiple occasions if he would like any help,

I started thinking about which teachers to ask to write me recommendations early in junior year, and I made sure I got to know them and they got to know me.

—Zack

but he always says, "Who needs extra help when you have the most informative teacher in the world?" One day, he shows up in your office and asks for a college recommendation.

Teachers can see right through brownnosing, because they see it every day of their lives, and they notice when you are zoning out or putting in the bare minimum of effort. But let me (Chris), a former teacher, tell you a little secret: Teachers love to see students genuinely engaged and interested in the material of the class. It's the *reason* they became teachers. So if you are worried about getting a great recommendation, there is only one real piece of advice you will ever need: Take an actual interest in the class, explore the material, and ask questions whenever you are confused. Listen to the teacher, certainly, but also to other students. If you are doing all of this just to impress the teacher, the teacher will know. But if you are active in the classroom because you are really feeling the material, the teacher will be truly impressed.

## So, are we done here?

Almost. We have one last thing to say: Congratulations. By getting through this book, you've done more than most of the students who are going to be taking the test with you on test day.

We hope that you enjoyed this as much as someone can enjoy a book about studying for a gigantic test. We know that you're now an authority on the ACT, but we also hope you've learned some strategies that you can use even after the test. Skipping and coming back, regulating your stress, and becoming a good reader can all make your life more productive and more enjoyable. (Also, becoming an excellent bubble-filler-inner can land you a long career in filling in bubbles.)

And remember that all of us here at *Up Your Score* went through the same thing you're going through now. We understand the pressure, the pain, and the toil involved in preparing for this test. But we want you to know that there is life after the test, and it is *so* much better than life before the test. It is filled with soft green grass, babbling brooks, and all the Internet videos of startled llamas you could ever hope to see. You are almost there.

So, as a parting gift, we now present the last list of suggested activities. Without further ado:

## THREE IDEAS FOR CELEBRATING AFTER THE TEST

1. Hire 3,000 singers who have perfect pitch and impeccable dance skills. Have them practice for months. When you walk out of the test, the singers, who will be playing the part of citizens of your town, will burst into "spontaneous" song and dance. While they cartwheel and twirl around, you should stroll down the street as if this sort of thing happens every day.
2. Build a piñata in the shape of the ACT-bot. Fill it with fake college acceptance letters. (Joking, joking.) Fill it with scrumptious treats, of course. Invite all of your fellow test takers to vent their rage in this safe, delicious way.
3. Take a well-earned nap.

Good luck,

## Who are these people, anyway?

**CHRIS ARP** grew up in Brooklyn, New York, then attended Princeton University, where he wrote stories and plays, edited a newspaper, and became a head writer for the Triangle Club, a musical-comedy troupe. He also wrote a play that was produced for one night in New York City. His aunt attended the performance, and whispered at the top of her lungs: "My nephew wrote this. Also, he's handsome."

After college, Chris enrolled in the New York City Teaching Fellows program, hoping to teach high school English. Instead, he was placed in a second-grade classroom, where he taught Elementary Running Around and Pretending You Are a Pirate. During these years, he earned a Masters in Education from Brooklyn College. He also wrote long and short-form journalism for various news websites and was briefly a reporter for GothamSchools, which covers the New York City public school system.

In 2011, Chris joined Veritas Tutors and Test Prep. He has taught test-taking, reading, and writing classes in public and private schools and colleges across the tri-state area. He has also written one award-winning short film, and is currently pursuing an MFA at the NYU Creative Writing Program. At present, he is working on a novel about a test-prep book author who is also an international diamond thief with a heart of gold.

**AVA CHEN** was born and raised in Louisville, Kentucky, where she attended DuPont Manual High School. In her free time she dreams up designs for prosthetic arms. Her research focus is designing prostheses with local and inexpensive materials in order to encourage industry in developing countries. She enjoys making a mess with soap sculptures and climbing trees (but not at the same time—sculpting soap is slippery), and she's a sucker for all sorts of teas, coffees, and sodas. Many people have also successfully bribed her with Redberry Sour Patch Kids and other tasty candies. She is currently studying at MIT.

**JON FISH** was born in the small hamlet of Finchville, Kentucky, which, he assures himself, is just the kind of small hamlet in which every adventurer begins his quest to save a princess while amassing killer test scores. So far, said quest hasn't involved any magic swords or enchanted musical instruments, but it has led Jon to achieve a 36 on the ACT and a good number of 5s on his AP exams, all thanks to study sessions backed by a New Order Pandora station. He enjoys ~~wasting~~ passing his free time by blogging, watching TV, and playing video games with his friends. Since he doesn't currently know of any career that incorporates those three activities (if you know of one, please email him immediately), his future plans are still under debate, but for now he's studying Political Science at the University of Kentucky.

**ZACK SWAFFORD** was born in Bellevue, Washington, but moved to Kansas City, Missouri, when he was a few months old. From there he made his way to Portland, Oregon, where he eventually went to Woodrow Wilson High School. His most recent domicile is Palo Alto, California, where he attends Stanford University. Zack enjoys playing guitar while walking along the beach, sipping piña coladas, and staring deeply into the sunset. His more practical (and less likely to cause retinal scarring) interests include math and computer science, and he intends to study engineering in college. Zack can bench-press 350 pounds—just not all at once. He spends a good deal of time each summer making stained-glass art. After graduating from college, Zack plans to work for several years, then return to school to study business. If that doesn't pan out, he will move to Peru with his friend Alan and put his hard-earned Spanish skills to good use while living off the land.